Stories from the Bible

ADDITIONAL SERIES IN THE
**FORGOTTEN CLASSICS
FAMILY LIBRARY**

Great Lives Series

Freedom Series

Rediscovered Treasures Series

World History Series

Nature, Art, and Music Series

Stories from
the Bible

W.H. Bennett
Helen Brown Hoyt

FORGOTTEN CLASSICS FAMILY LIBRARY
Libraries of Hope

Stories from the Bible

Compiled From:

The Old Testament Story, Retold for Young People, by W.H. Bennett, New York: The MacMillan Company, (1898).

A Child's Story of the Life of Christ, by Helen Brown Hoyt, Boston and Chicago: W.A. Wilde Company, (1902).

Libraries of Hope, Inc.
Appomattox, Virginia 24522

Website www.librariesofhope.com
Email support@librariesofhope.com

Printed in the United States of America

Table of Contents

Table of Contents Continued

Table of Contents Continued

Table of Contents Continued

The Old Testament Story

Retold for Young People

By W. H. Bennett

The Patriarchs

Chapter 1

Israel in the Wilderness

The Bible tells us the story of the Jews and of Jesus Christ. All the Old Testament and almost all the New were written by Jews, and Jesus Christ was born a Jew. The history of the Jews is part of the story of Jesus Christ, because it explains how God prepared the way for Christ; how the teaching of the prophets helped men to understand the words of Christ; and how wealth and poverty, victory and defeat, imperial power and shameful slavery, alike fashioned the Jews to be kinsfolk of the Savior of the world.

The Jews, as we call them, called themselves Israel, or the children of Israel, or, as we should say, the Israelites; and so, in speaking of Old Testament times, we too will call them Israel or the Israelites.

In this chapter we go back to the first beginnings of the Bible and of Israel. Today there are millions of Jews scattered all over the world, and there are very many times more Christians. But in the beginning the Israelites, who were the ancestors of the Jews, and whose faith in God was the first step to Christianity, were a few handfuls of people in a corner of Western Asia. The records of their laws and customs, and the stories they told of the events of their history, became, under God's guidance, the beginning of the Bible. Very soon I will tell you some of these stories, but first let us try to picture the people by whom and about whom the stories were told.

In these early days so early that there are no dates for you to learn about them–the people was not at first called Israel; but the ancestors of the Israelites were nomad tribes wandering like the Bedouin through many lands. They were closely related to the Arabs in race and language, and very similar in manner of life, so that we might almost call them Arabs. They lived in tents, not little white cones of canvas, such as we see in soldiers' camps, but large black tents of goats' hair, often divided into two or three rooms. Their property was camels, cattle, sheep and goats, and slaves. With these the Israelite chiefs, or sheikhs, Abraham, Isaac, and Jacob, and their clans, wandered to and fro, seeking water and pasture for their flocks. Now they would encamp at some oasis in the desert, now in the pasture lands of Palestine. There they were neighbors of the Canaanites and Philistines in their towns. Often difficulties arose between the Israelites and their neighbors as to the use of the land and the wells. Sometimes such quarrels were settled by friendly agreement, sometimes by fighting. And all the men of a tribe counted each other brethren, and stood by one another in their quarrels; and if one was killed, all the rest held it a most sacred duty to punish his murderer. So that, though the Israelites and their neighbors were brave and warlike, they did not fight without due cause, lest they should be pursued by the untiring vengeance of the kinsfolk of the slain. We have hardly any stories of battles fought by the patriarchs.

Sometimes in their early wanderings the patriarchs and their followers encamped in the neighborhood of the great cities of Egypt cities that were as great and wonderful in their day as London and Paris are now. These Arab sheikhs and their clansmen mingled in the motley crowd of many nations that thronged the streets of Thebes or Memphis, and admired the magnificence of palaces and temples, and the grandeur of great kings and princes. Yet they thought it nobler and better to wander at will through the wide desert than to live cooped up in houses and shut in by city walls. They told how, in days gone by, their fathers had lived among the Chaldeans, who had cities as wonderful as Thebes and Memphis, and who were as great and wise as the Egyptians; and how God, whom the Israelites called Jehovah, had sent them away from Chaldea to live a nomad life in the pastures of Syria, that they might the better worship and serve Him. And though in later times the Israelites had cities and palaces and temples of their own, they always looked back to their life in tents as a holy and happy time, when their fathers lived very near to God.

So long after, in the time of the kings of Israel and Judah, men still loved to tell the ancient stories of the patriarchs, as the Israelite herdsmen round the camp fire and the maidens at the well told them in days of old. Some of these stories are written for you here.

Chapter 2

Abraham

Abraham and his wife Sarah lived amongst the Chaldees, by the Euphrates and Tigris, two great rivers north of the Persian Gulf, at a place called Ur. And Jehovah said to Abraham, "Leave your own country and your home and your friends, and go to another country, to which I will show you the way. And I will make you a great nation, and I will bless you, and I will bless those who bless you, and curse those who curse you; and the best that a man can wish for his friend will be that he may be as happy as Abraham."

Abraham did as Jehovah told him. Abraham and Sarah had no children, but their nephew Lot went with them. They left their own country, and journeyed for many weeks with their camels and flocks and herds, their slaves and followers, till they came to Shechem in the land of Canaan. There Jehovah appeared to Abraham, and promised to give that land to his children. And Abraham built an altar to Jehovah at Shechem; and he kept on journeying southward, and built another altar at Bethel. And after journeying into Egypt, Abraham and Lot came back to the altar at Bethel; and each of them had a great many sheep and cattle and tents and followers; and there was not room for them together in the pastures and at the wells. Then Abraham's herdsmen and Lot's herdsmen began to quarrel with each other. And Abraham said to Lot, "We are kinsfolk, we cannot quarrel, and we must not let our servants quarrel. We must separate, that each of us may have room for his flocks and herds. Do you choose a place for yourself: if you take the left hand, I will go to the right; or, if you take the right hand, I will go to the left."

Lot looked and saw that the land by the Jordan was well watered, and he chose all that land for himself, and moved there with all his tents and cattle and followers. Then he went to live in Sodom, a city of that land; though the people of Sodom were very wicked.

But after Lot had gone, Jehovah said to Abraham, "Lift up your eyes and look every way, north, south, east, and west: for all that land will I give to you and your children. Your children shall be like the dust of the earth; if anyone can count the dust, he will be able to count your descendants." And Abraham journeyed to Hebron, and built another altar.

But while Lot was living in Sodom, four kings from the East invaded Canaan. The kings of the Canaanite cities had been subject to one of these kings, Chedorlaomer, king of Elam, and had paid tribute to him for twelve years. But in the thirteenth year they rebelled, and Chedorlaomer came with three other Eastern kings to punish the Canaanites and make them pay their tribute. These four kings ravaged the country far and wide till they came towards Sodom, and the king of Sodom and four neighboring kings got together an army and fought against Chedorlaomer. But the four Eastern kings beat the five Canaanite kings, and the kings of Sodom and Gomorrah were killed. Then Chedorlaomer and his allies plundered Sodom and Gomorrah; they took all the food they could find, and everything else that was worth carrying away, and a number of prisoners, men, women, and children, and set off on their homeward march. Amongst these prisoners, of whom they intended to make slaves, were Lot and his wife and daughters.

But one of Lot's servants escaped, and went and told Abraham that his nephew was being carried off as a slave. Then Abraham started with his tribe of more than three hundred men to rescue Lot.

The invaders were marching northwards, by way of Damascus, and Abraham followed on their track for some days. At last he overtook them, far away in the north; he surprised their camp at night, and they fled panic-stricken by the sudden attack, so that Abraham rescued Lot and the other prisoners, and recovered the plunder, and took them back to Sodom and Gomorrah. On the way there came out to meet Abraham, Melchizedek, king of Salem, or Jerusalem. Melchizedek was also, like many ancient kings, the priest of his city the priest of El Elyon, or God Most High, the name under which God was then worshipped at Jerusalem. He brought bread and wine for Abraham and his followers, and blessed Abraham, who gave him a tenth of the spoil. The new king of Sodom, too, came to meet Abraham; he offered to let Abraham keep all the other plunder if he would release the prisoners whom he had rescued. "Give me the men and women," said the king of Sodom, "and take the goods for yourself."

"I have sworn," answered Abraham, "by Jehovah, El Elyon, Lord of heaven and earth, that I will not take even a thread or a shoe-latchet, lest you should say, I have made Abraham rich." So Lot and his wife and daughters went back to Sodom, and lived there till Jehovah rained fire and brimstone upon Sodom and Gomorrah, and destroyed them, and all the people in them, because of their wickedness. God told Abraham of His purpose, and Abraham entreated God to spare Sodom, and God promised to spare it if there were ten righteous men in it. But Lot and his family were the only righteous people, and God sent angels to bring them out of the city.

Chapter 3

Isaac

God often promised Abraham that his descendants should be a great nation, and yet Abraham and Sarah had no child through whom these promises could be fulfilled. The years went on, and they grew very old. Abraham had a son Ishmael by another wife, a slave of Sarah's; but though Ishmael, too, became the father of a nation, the great promises made to Abraham did not refer to him. God promised that Abraham and Sarah should have a son, and at last the son was born. Sarah called his name Isaac, "Laughter," because it seemed so ridiculous that two old people should have a son. Now that Sarah had a boy of her own, she persuaded Abraham to send Ishmael and his mother away, in order that Ishmael might not prevent Isaac from succeeding his father as head of the tribe.

"After these things," the story goes on, perhaps when Isaac was twelve or fourteen, God tried Abraham, to see if he would obey Him when obedience was very hard. In ancient times men chiefly worshipped God by sacrifices, by offering Him gifts, and especially by killing animals and burning part or all of them on an altar. Oxen and sheep were precious possessions, and men showed their love and gratitude and loyalty by giving God their best. But a man had possessions even more precious than sheep and oxen, he had his children; and when an Eastern people was specially anxious to show its devotion to God, men killed and burnt their own children on the altar as sacrifices.

Such sacrifices were common among the Canaanites, and were sometimes offered by the Israelites themselves.

"After these things," then, to go back to the Bible story, after Isaac was born and Ishmael sent away, and other things had happened, and when Abraham was encamped at Beersheba, in the south of Palestine, God tried Abraham, and said to him, "Abraham."

And he said, "Here am I."

God said, "Take now thy son, thine only son Isaac, whom thou lovest, and offer him up as a burnt-offering on one of the mountains which I will tell thee of." So Abraham got up early in the morning, and saddled an ass, and took with him two servants and his son Isaac; and he cleft wood for the burnt-offering, and set out for the place of which God had told him. And on the third day of their journey, Abraham looked and saw the place afar off; and he said to his servants, "Stay here with the ass; and I and the boy will go yonder, and will worship, and come back to you."

Then he took the wood for the burnt-offering and laid it on Isaac his son; and took the fire and the knife in his hand. So they two went together.

And Isaac said to his father, "My father."

He said, "Here am I, my son."

"Here are fire and wood," said Isaac, "but where is the sheep for the burnt-offering?"

Abraham said, "God will provide Himself a sheep for the burnt-offering, my son." So they went both of them together, until they came to the place of which God had told Abraham. Then he built an altar and laid the wood in order on it, and took

Isaac and bound him, and placed him on the altar over the wood. And Abraham stretched forth his hand, and took the knife to kill his son.

But the angel of God called to him out of heaven, "Abraham! Abraham!"

And he said, "Here am I."

The angel of God said, "Do not lay your hand upon the boy to harm him; for now I know that you fear God, because you were ready to give me your son, your only son."

Then Abraham lifted up his eyes and looked, and saw behind him a ram caught in a thicket by its horns; and he took the ram and offered it up for a burnt-offering instead of Isaac; and Abraham and Isaac went back to the servants, and they all went together to Abraham's camp at Beersheba.

When the Israelites read this story they understood that God had never intended Abraham to kill Isaac, and that He did not wish them to sacrifice children to Him. The neighboring peoples believed that God was cruel and selfish, and wished men to worship Him by making themselves uncomfortable and sad, and by torturing themselves; but the revelation which God gave to Israel taught them that God was a Father to His people.

When Isaac was old enough to marry, Abraham, after the custom of those times, found a wife for him. He would not let Isaac marry any of their Canaanite neighbors, but sent Eliezer, his chief slave, the overseer of his household, to his own relations in the East for a wife for Isaac. Eliezer took ten camels loaded with provisions for the journey and presents for Isaac's future wife and her family, and journeyed till he came to the home of Nahor, Abraham's brother, in Mesopotamia. And in the evening, at the time when women go to draw water, he made his camels kneel down outside the town by the well. And he prayed to God and said:

"Jehovah, God of my master Abraham, send me good speed today, and show kindness to my master Abraham. May the maiden to whom I shall say, 'Let down your pitcher, I pray you, that I may drink,' and who shall say to me, 'Drink, and I will give your camels drink too' may she be the maiden whom Thou hast chosen for Isaac's wife."

Before he had done speaking, a beautiful girl, named Rebekah, Isaac's cousin, the daughter of Bethuel, the son of Nahor, Abraham's brother, came to the well with her pitcher on her shoulder, and went down to the fountain and filled her pitcher, and came up again. Then Eliezer ran to meet her and said, "I pray you, give me a little water out of your pitcher."

And she said, "Drink, my lord."

And she let down her pitcher quickly on her hand and gave him to drink. And when he had finished, she said, "I will draw water for your camels too, till they have had enough to drink."

The man gazed at her in silence, wondering whether Jehovah was really showing him that she was to be Isaac's wife; but when the camels had done drinking, he took a nose-ring and bracelets of gold, and said, "Whose daughter are you? Tell me, I pray you. Is there room for us to spend the night in your father's house?"

She answered, "I am the daughter of Bethuel, the son of Nahor and his wife Milcah; we have straw and fodder for the camels, and room for you to spend the night."

Then Eliezer bowed down and worshipped Jehovah, and said, "Blessed be Jehovah, the God of my master Abraham, who has not failed to be kind and true to my master, and has led me to the home of his kinsfolk."

While he was thanking God, Rebekah ran to the harem, the women's rooms, and told them what had happened. Afterwards her brother Laban saw the nose-ring and bracelets of gold, and his sister told him about Eliezer. Then Laban ran out and found Eliezer standing by the camels at the fountain, and said, "Come in, thou blessed of Jehovah; why do you stand without? I have made ready for you and your camels."

So Eliezer went to the house, and Laban took off the camels' harness and gave them straw and fodder, and brought water that Eliezer and his men might wash their feet. Then Laban set food before him, but he said, "I will not eat till I have told my errand."

And Laban said, "Speak on."

Then Eliezer told him the whole story from the beginning, almost in the same words as I have told it: how he was Abraham's slave, how Abraham was very great and rich, and wished his son Isaac to marry one of his own kinsfolk, and how God had shown Eliezer that Rebekah was to be Isaac's wife. "And now," he said, "if you will be kind and true to my master, tell me, and if not, tell me, that I may turn right or left."

Then Laban answered, "Jehovah has decided, we can say nothing. Here is Rebekah; take her and go, and let her marry your master's son, according to the word of Jehovah."

So Eliezer thanked God, and brought out jewels of silver and gold, and garments, and gave them to Rebekah, and gave also rich presents to her brother and mother. Then they all feasted, and Eliezer and his men spent the night there, and early next morning he said, "Send me away to my master."

But her brother and mother said, "Let Rebekah stay with us a few days."

And he said, "Do not hinder me, since Jehovah has prospered me, let me go to my master."

Then they said, "Rebekah shall decide for herself." Rebekah was eager to start at once, so they let her go, and wished her all happiness, and said, "O our sister, mayest thou become thousands of myriads, may thy descendants possess the gate of them that hate them."

So Rebekah and her foster-mother and her maidens rode away on the camels with Eliezer and his men, and they journeyed many days.

Meanwhile, Isaac had gone to live at a place called Beerlahairoi, south of Judah; and one day as he was walking in the fields in the evening, he saw camels coming. And Rebekah, for these were Eliezer's camels, looked and saw a man coming towards them; and she said to Eliezer, "Who is that man in the fields walking to meet us?"

And he answered, "It is my master Isaac."

Then she took her veil and covered herself. And Eliezer told Isaac everything, and Isaac married Rebekah and took her to his tent.

Chapter 4

Jacob and Esau

For a long time after Isaac and Rebekah were married they had no children; but Isaac prayed to God, and He gave them two sons, Esau the elder, and Jacob the younger. When they grew up Esau spent his time chasing deer and buffalo, because he was a clever hunter; but Jacob was a quiet man, and stayed at home amongst the tents, and looked after the flocks and herds. Esau was his father's favorite, for Isaac was fond of game, and Jacob was his mother's darling. One day Jacob was making lentil soup, and Esau came home from his hunting, tired and hungry. "Make haste," said he to Jacob, "and give me some of that red stuff, that red stuff there."

But Jacob said to Esau, "First sell me your birthright."

Now, because Esau was the elder son he would have had the birthright – that is, he would have been the head of the tribe after Isaac's death, and the heir to his property. Yet Esau said, "I must die sooner or later, and then what will be the use of my birthright?"

So he consented to sell the chieftainship and the inheritance for a basin of soup. Jacob made him swear to keep the bargain, and then gave him soup and bread, and Esau ate and drank, and got up and went his way: so Esau made light of his birthright.

Years afterwards Isaac lay dying, old and almost blind, and he called Esau and said, "I am so old that I may die any day; take your bow and arrows, and go out hunting and get me game; and make me savory meat such as I love, and bring it me that I may eat of it and bless you before I die."

Now Rebekah was listening while Isaac talked to Esau, and when Esau had gone out to shoot the game, she said to Jacob, "I have just heard your father tell Esau to get him game and make him savory meat that he may eat, and that before he die he may bless Esau in the name of Jehovah. Now, my son, you must do exactly as I bid you: get me two goodly kids from the flock, and I will make them into savory meat for your father, such as he loves. Then you must take it to your father, that he may eat it and give his last blessing to you instead of to Esau."

"But," said Jacob, "Esau is a hairy man and I am smooth. Perhaps my father will feel me and think that I am a buffoon or playing the fool, and I shall bring on myself a curse and not a blessing."

But Rebekah said, "On me be the curse; do as I tell you, and get me the kids."

So he fetched them, and his mother made savory meat, such as his father loved. Then she took Esau's best clothes, which she was taking care of for him, and put them on Jacob; and she covered the smooth skin of Jacob's hands and neck with the hairy skin of the kids; and she gave him the savory meat and bread, and he went to his father.

And he said, "My father."

Isaac answered, "Here am I; who are you, my son?"

Jacob said to his father, "I am Esau, your first-born. I have done what you told me; rise now, sit and eat of my game, that you may bless me."

"How, then," said Isaac, "have you found it so quickly?"

"Because," said he, "Jehovah thy God put it in my way."

But Isaac said, "Come closer, my son, that I may feel you, and find out whether or not you are my son Esau."

So Jacob went close to Isaac, and he felt him, and did not recognize him, because the skins made his hands hairy like Esau's; and Isaac said, "The voice is the voice of Jacob, but the hands are the hands of Esau. Are you really my son Esau?"

Jacob said, "I am."

Then Isaac said, "Put the savory meat before me, that I may eat of my son's game, and may bless you."

Then Jacob put the meat before him; when he had eaten it, he brought his father wine, and Isaac drank it, and said, "Come close to me and kiss me, my son."

Jacob went to his father and kissed him, and Isaac smelt the smell of his clothes and blessed him, and said:

"The smell of my son is as the smell of a field which Jehovah has blessed.

"God give thee of the dew of heaven,
And of the fatness of the earth,
And plenty of corn and wine.

Let peoples serve thee,
Let nations bow down to thee.

Be thou a lord over thy brethren,
Let thy mother's sons bow down to thee;

Cursed be every one that curseth thee,
Blessed be every one that blesseth thee."

Jacob and Esau

As soon as Isaac had finished the blessing, and Jacob had left him, Esau came in from his hunting. He, too, made savory meat, and brought it to his father, and said to him, "Rise, my father, and eat of your son's venison, that you may bless me."

"Who are you?" said Isaac.

"I am your son," said he, "your first-born, Esau."

Then Isaac shook and trembled in every limb, and said, "Who was it, then, who brought me game, so that I ate of all before you came, and blessed him? Yea, and he shall be blessed."

At his father's words Esau uttered a cry, exceeding loud and bitter, and said, "Bless me, me also, my father."

But Isaac said, "Your brother has cheated you of your blessing."

Esau said, "Is it because he is named Supplanter that he has twice supplanted me? First he took my birthright, and now he has taken my blessing. Have you not kept back a blessing for me?"

"I have made him your master," answered Isaac; "I have made all his kinsfolk his slaves, and I have given him the corn and wine for his portion. What, then, can I do for you, my son?"

Esau lifted up his voice and wept.

Then said Isaac,

"Yea, far from the fatness of the earth be thy dwelling,
And far from the dew of the heavens.
Thou shalt live by thy sword, and be thy brother's slave,
But, when thou strivest, thou shalt break his yoke from
Off thy neck."

Chapter 5

Jacob and Laban

Esau longed to be revenged on Jacob, and only waited till Isaac was dead and buried. But Rebekah sent Jacob away to her brother Laban at Haran. So Jacob started from Beersheba to go to Haran, just as Eliezer did when he went to find a wife for Isaac. And at the end of his first day's journey, he lay down to sleep with a stone for his pillow. And he dreamt, and in his dream he saw a ladder set on the earth, with its top in the skies, and the angels of God went up and down it. Then Jehovah stood beside Jacob, and said, "I am Jehovah, the God of Abraham, and the God of Isaac," and Jehovah promised that Jacob's children should be a great and mighty nation.

When he awoke he was afraid, and said, "Certainly Jehovah is in this place, and I knew it not. How dreadful is this place! This is none other than the house of God and the gate of heaven." Then Jacob set up his stone pillow for a sacred pillar, and poured oil on the top of it as an offering to Jehovah. And Jacob vowed a vow, saying, "If God will be with me, and will keep me on my journey, and give me bread to eat and clothes to wear, and bring me safely home again, then this pillar shall be a temple of God, and I will give Thee a tenth of all that Thou givest me."

And he called the place Bethel, which means House of God or Temple; and after the Israelites conquered Canaan they worshipped God at the temple at Bethel, and paid tithes to the priests there.

And Jacob went on his journey, and after many days he came to a well, with three flocks of sheep lying by it; and the shepherds told him they belonged to Haran. Then Jacob knew that he had reached the end of his journey, and he said to them, "Do you know Laban the son of Nahor?"

They said, "We do."

"Is he well?" said Jacob.

They said, "Yes, and here comes his daughter Rachel with the sheep."

When Jacob saw his cousin Rachel with her sheep, he went to the well and rolled back the great stone that covered it, and drew water for the sheep. Then he kissed Rachel, and wept aloud for joy that he had come safely to his kinsfolk; and he told Rachel that he was her cousin, and she ran and told her father Laban. When Laban heard that his sister Rebekah's son had come, he ran to meet him, and embraced him and kissed him, and took him to his house; and Jacob told him all that had happened. So Jacob lived with Laban, and helped him with his flocks and herds. Laban offered to pay him wages, but Jacob had fallen in love with Rachel, who was very beautiful; and he said to Laban, "I will be your servant for seven years, if you will let me marry your younger daughter Rachel."

Laban agreed, and Jacob worked seven years to get Rachel, and they seemed to him only a few days because of his great love to her. At the end of the seven years, Laban pretended that he was going to give Rachel to Jacob. He invited all the neighbors to the wedding, and made a great feast for them. The bride was brought in veiled, and Jacob supposed it was Rachel; but when the wedding was over, he found out that he had married her elder sister Leah, and he was very angry. But Laban explained that in Haran the elder sister was always married first, and he offered to let Jacob marry Rachel too next week, if he would work for him another seven years; and Jacob consented, and married Rachel as well as Leah. And Rachel and Leah were jealous of each other, and made Jacob's life a burden to him by their quarrelling. Later on, he married also two slave-girls, Bilhah, Rachel's maid, and Zilpah, Leah's maid; and he had twelve sons and a daughter. When the second seven years were ended, he agreed to work for Laban for a certain portion of the lambs of his flocks; and Laban and Jacob were always trying to get the better of each other in the matter of wages, but Jacob was cleverer than Laban, and Jacob got rich and Laban got poor. Then Laban and his sons hated Jacob, and Jacob was afraid they would rob him, or perhaps even kill him; so he fled away by night with his flocks and herds and slaves, and his wives and children, to go back to Canaan. When Laban heard that they had gone, he gathered his kinsfolk together and pursued them, and in three days he overtook them. But God would not let Laban harm Jacob. So when Jacob had promised that he would be kind to Laban's daughters, Laban left him and went home again.

And now Jacob bethought him of Esau, and he sent to tell Esau that he was on his way home; and the messengers returned to Jacob and said, "We found your brother Esau, and he is coming to meet you with four hundred men."

Then Jacob was terribly frightened. He got ready a present for Esau two hundred and twenty goats, two hundred and twenty sheep, thirty camels, fifty oxen, and thirty asses. He arranged them in separate droves, each with a servant to drive it; and Jacob said to each of the servants, "When my brother Esau meets you, and asks who you are and to whom the cattle belong, you must say, 'They belong to your slave Jacob; it is a present sent to my lord Esau.'"

So the present for Esau was sent on in front, one drove after the other, and behind came the other slaves and flocks and herds, and then the wives and children. Jacob put Bilhah and Zilpah and their children first, Leah and her children next, and last of all his beloved Rachel and his darling Joseph, her son, that they might have the best chance of escaping if Esau was still vindictive. When Jacob saw Esau and the four hundred men coming, he went on in front to meet them, and prostrated himself on the ground seven times before Esau. But Esau ran to meet him, and embraced him, and fell on his neck and kissed him, and they both wept. And Esau proposed that he and Jacob should live together, but Jacob made excuses, and they separated.

Chapter 5

Joseph the Spoiled Darling

After Jacob left Esau, Rachel had a son Benjamin, and died when he was born; but for a long time before, she had only one son, Joseph, and he was Jacob's youngest child; and Rachel was his favorite wife. Jacob loved Joseph more than all his other sons, because he was the son of his old age; and he made him a long robe with sleeves, such as princes wore. So his brothers hated him, and could scarcely bring themselves to speak a civil word to him.

Once Joseph had a dream, and told it to his brothers. "I dreamed," said he, "that we were binding sheaves in the harvest field, and my sheaf arose and stood upright; and your sheaves came round about and bowed to my sheaf."

His brothers answered, "Do you really think you are going to be king over us?" and they hated him more than ever.

Soon after he had another dream, and told it to his brothers. "I dreamed," said he, "that the sun and moon and eleven stars bowed down to me."

Then his father rebuked him, and said, "What an absurd dream! Am I, and your brothers, and your mother to bow down before you?"

And his brothers were jealous of him, but his father kept the dreams in mind.

Now, sometimes Joseph went with his brothers to help them keep the sheep, and he used to come home to his father and tell tales about his brothers. Once they went to feed their father's flock in Shechem. Afterwards Jacob sent Joseph to go and see his brothers, and bring back word about them. But when Joseph got to Shechem, his brothers were gone, and as he was wandering about looking for them, he met a man who told him that they had gone to Dothan; and he went after his brethren, and found them in Dothan. And they saw him coming, and said to each other, "Here is this dreamer. Let us kill him, and throw his body into one of the cisterns, and say that a wild beast has devoured him; and we will see what will come of his dreams."

But the eldest brother Reuben said, "Do not shed blood, throw him into this cistern, do not hurt him." Now Reuben intended, some time when the rest were not there, to take Joseph out of the cistern, and send him safely home to his father.

So when Joseph came to them, they stripped off his princely robe, and threw him into a cistern without any water in it, and went away and left him there.

And when they were gone, there passed by some Midianite merchants, and they drew Joseph out of the cistern, and took him away to sell him for a slave.

Later on, Reuben came back to the cistern to take Joseph out and send him home, but he was nowhere to be found. Reuben tore his clothes in his grief, and went back to his brothers, and said, "The boy is gone; and I, whither shall I go?"

Then they took the robe, and killed a goat, and dipped the robe in its blood, and brought it to Jacob, and said, "We have found this; is it Joseph's robe?"

And Jacob recognized it, and said, "It is my son's robe; a wild beast has devoured him: Joseph is without doubt torn in pieces."

And he tore his clothes, and put on sackcloth, and mourned for his son many days. And all his sons and daughters rose up to comfort him, but he refused to be comforted, and said, "Mourning will I go down to my son in the land of the spirits of the dead."

Meanwhile the Midianites took Joseph down into Egypt, and sold him to Potiphar, the captain of Pharaoh's bodyguard.

Chapter 7

Joseph in Prison

God helped Joseph when he was a slave in Egypt, so that he was able to do his work well. His master saw that he was clever, and industrious, and faithful; and set him over all his fellow-servants, and over his house and fields and cattle, and all that he had. Then God blessed Potiphar's house for Joseph's sake, and the blessing of Jehovah, the God of Israel, was upon all that he had in the house and in the field. Potiphar trusted everything to Joseph, and asked for no account of anything, so that he knew nothing about his house and his estate, except that he had a good dinner every day.

But Potiphar's wife was a wicked woman, and brought false charges against Joseph, so that Potiphar was angry, and had him put in prison. And still Jehovah was with Joseph, and showed him kindness, so that the governor of the prison was pleased with him, and trusted him just as Potiphar had done. The governor put Joseph in authority over all his fellow-prisoners, and did not ask for any account of what he did, and Joseph managed everything well, because Jehovah was with him.

When Joseph had been in prison a long time, there were brought in two new prisoners, two great nobles from the court of Pharaoh, King of Egypt, the Chief Baker and the Chief Cupbearer. They had offended the King, and he had sent them to prison; and the governor put Joseph in charge of them. One morning he found them looking very sad, and asked them why they were so downcast, and in such low spirits; and they said, "We have each of us dreamed a dream, and there is no one to interpret."

And Joseph said, "Do not interpretations belong to God? Tell me the dreams."

Then the Chief Cupbearer said, "In my dream I saw a vine with three branches; and while I looked at it, it seemed to bud, and the buds grew into blossoms, and there grew clusters of ripe grapes. And I had Pharaoh's cup in my hand, and I took the grapes and pressed them into Pharaoh's cup, and gave it into Pharaoh's hand."

Joseph said, "This is the interpretation: the three branches are three days; in three days Pharaoh will take you out of prison, and make you Chief Cupbearer again. Then, I pray you, remember me, and tell Pharaoh about me, that I, too, may be taken out of prison; for I was stolen away from my own country, and I have been put into prison on a false charge."

When the Chief Baker saw that the interpretation was good, he said, "In my dream I had three baskets of white bread on my head, and in the top basket there were all manner of dainties for Pharaoh, and the birds ate them out of the basket on my head."

Joseph said, "This is the interpretation: the three baskets are three days; in three days Pharaoh will cut your head off, and hang you on a tree; and the birds shall eat your flesh off your bones."

And the third day was Pharaoh's birthday, and he made a feast for all his courtiers, and he had the Chief Baker and Chief Cupbearer brought before him, and restored the Chief

Cupbearer to his office, and hanged the Chief Baker, just as Joseph had said. Yet the Chief Cupbearer forgot all about Joseph.

But, two years after, Pharaoh had a bad dream one night; and he awoke in the morning anxious and frightened, and sent for all his magicians and wise men, and asked them to interpret his dream; but none of them could tell him what it meant. Then said the Chief Cupbearer, "One night, when the Chief Baker and I were in prison, we each of us had a dream. And we told our dreams to a young Hebrew, and he interpreted them; and the interpretation came true; the Chief Baker was hanged, and I was restored to my office."

Then Pharaoh sent to the prison to fetch Joseph.

Chapter 8

Joseph the Ruler of Egypt

So the messengers came to fetch Joseph to the court. They hurried him out of the prison, and he changed his prison clothes for others, and shaved himself, and went with them to Pharaoh.

And Pharaoh said, "I have dreamed a dream, and there is no one that can interpret it; and I have been told that, if you hear a dream, you can interpret it."

Joseph answered, "It is not in me: God shall give Pharaoh an answer of peace."

Then Pharaoh said, "In my dream I stood upon the brink of the Nile, and seven fat, sleek cows came up out of the Nile and fed amongst the reeds; and there came up after them seven poor, lean, ugly cows, the worst I ever saw in all Egypt; and the lean, ugly cows ate up the seven fat cows; and when they had eaten them up, no one could have known that they had had anything to eat, they were as ugly as they were before.

"Afterwards I dreamed another dream. There came up on one stalk seven full and good ears, and there sprung up after them seven other ears, withered, thin, and blasted with the east wind; and the thin ears swallowed up the good ears."

Joseph said, "The two dreams are one. The seven good cows and the seven good ears both mean the same seven years of plenty; and the seven lean cows and the seven blasted ears both mean the same seven years of famine. God sent this dream to tell Pharaoh that there shall be seven good harvests in Egypt, and then seven bad harvests, and the famine shall consume the land so that the good harvests shall be forgotten; and the dream was doubled because God's purpose is fixed, and shall soon be accomplished. Now, therefore, let Pharaoh find a sensible, capable man, and let him store up corn in the good years against the years of famine."

And Joseph's advice pleased Pharaoh and all his court, and the king said, "Since God has showed you all this, there is no one as sensible and capable as you are. You shall be over my house and rule my people; without you no one shall stir hand or foot in all Egypt. Only I myself, the king, will be greater than you."

Then Pharaoh took off his signet-ring and put it on Joseph's finger, and arrayed him in princely robes, and made him ride in the second-best royal chariot. So Joseph rode in state through the city, and heralds went before him and cried out, "Bow the knee."

And Pharaoh gave Joseph a wife Asenath, the daughter of an Egyptian priest. Now, in Egypt, the priests were great nobles and very rich.

So Joseph was Pharaoh's Grand Vizier or prime minister, and ruled all Egypt. When the seven good harvests came, he stored up thousands and thousands of sacks of corn, and at last he had more sacks than he could count, and the corn in the granaries was like the sand on the seashore. Then came the years of famine, and Joseph sold corn out of his granaries to all the Egyptians.

And the famine was in the countries round about, so that many foreigners came into Egypt to buy corn, and Joseph sat in state and received them, and gave them permission to buy. One day there came amongst the other foreigners Joseph's ten brethren all except Benjamin. And they bowed humbly to the great Egyptian prince, and did not know that it was Joseph, the lad whom they threw into the cistern. Joseph knew them, and remembered how he had dreamed that they should bow down before him. But he behaved as if he were a stranger to them, and accused them of being spies from some enemies' country.

And they said, "We are no spies, we are true men. Thy servants are twelve brothers from Canaan, but one of our brothers is dead, and our youngest brother is at home with his father."

But Joseph put them in prison for three days, and then he said to them, "I will give you a chance of proving that you are honest men: one of you must stay here in prison, but the rest may go home, and take food to feed your families. But you must come back again, and bring me your youngest brother, that I may know that you told me the truth when you said you had another brother."

And they said to one another in Joseph's presence, "We are being punished for our cruelty to Joseph, because we would not listen to his entreaties when he was in trouble."

They thought that this Egyptian prince could not understand their Canaanite language, because Joseph had talked with them by means of an interpreter. But Joseph understood it all, and he turned from them and wept.

Then Simeon one of the brothers was left behind in prison, and the rest started for Canaan with their sacks full of corn; and when they halted on the first night, one of them opened his sack to get some corn to give to his ass, and he found the money he had paid for his corn put back at the top of his sack; and so it was in all the other sacks. And they were puzzled and frightened, but Joseph had had it put there, because he would not take money from his brothers for the food he gave them.

And the brothers came home to Jacob and Benjamin, and told the whole story; and, when the corn was finished, they wished to take Benjamin and go to Egypt to buy more corn, and bring Simeon home. But at first Jacob would not let Benjamin go. He said, "Me have you bereaved of my children; Joseph is not, and Simeon is not, and you will take Benjamin away; all these things are against me."

But, at last, when they seemed likely to starve for want of corn, they persuaded Jacob to let Benjamin go with them. So the eleven brothers went down to Egypt, and stood before Joseph as he sat in state to sell corn to the foreigners. And when Joseph saw that Benjamin was with them, he said to the steward of his house, "Take the men into my house, and prepare a feast, for they must dine with me at noon." And the steward did as Joseph said; and, when Joseph came home to dinner, his brothers were there to meet him, and still they did not know him.

And he said to them, "Is your father well, the old man of whom you spoke?"

And they said, "Thy servant our father is well; he is still alive."

And he looked and saw his brother Benjamin, mother's son, and said, "God be gracious unto thee, my son."

Then he altogether broke down. He was greatly moved at the sight of Benjamin, and he hurried out and went to his own room to weep alone. And when he was himself again, he washed his face, and came back to the banquet-hall, and bade them serve the dinner. And they laid three tables, one for Joseph, one for the Egyptians, and one for the Hebrew strangers, for the Egyptians thought it wicked to eat with foreigners. Joseph placed his brothers according to their age, the oldest first, and the youngest last, and they wondered how he knew their ages. And he sent portions to them from his own table, but Benjamin's portion was five times as much as anyone else's.

Next day the eleven brothers started home again, with their sacks filled with corn. But Joseph had had a silver cup hidden in Benjamin's sack, and sent his steward after them. The steward caught them up, and accused them of stealing the cup; and, when he had searched in all the sacks, he found the cup in Benjamin's. Then he took them all back to Joseph's house; and Joseph said that Benjamin must be a slave, but the rest might go home.

Then Judah reminded Joseph that Benjamin had only come to Egypt because Joseph asked for him. "Now, therefore," said he, "when I come to thy servant my father, and the lad is not with us; since his life is bound up in the lad's life, when he sees that the lad is not with us, he will die, and thy servants shall bring down the grey hairs of thy servant our father with sorrow to the grave. I pray thee, let me stay to be thy slave instead of the lad, and let him go with his brothers. How can I go home without him, and see my father's grief?"

Then Joseph could not contain himself any longer, and he made all the Egyptians go out, so that he was left alone with his brothers. And he wept aloud, so that the Egyptians heard him outside. And he said to his brothers, "I am Joseph. Is my father still alive?"

And his brothers were troubled, and could not answer him; but he bade them not be grieved or angry with themselves because they had wronged him, for God had brought good out of their evil, and made him a savior of Egypt and of his own people from the famine. And he fell upon his brother Benjamin's neck and wept, and Benjamin wept upon his neck. And he kissed all his brothers, and they all talked together.

And they heard about it in Pharaoh's court. They said, "Joseph's brothers are come," and Pharaoh and his courtiers were glad. Pharaoh bade Joseph send wagons to fetch his father and his brothers' wives and children down into Egypt. And Joseph sent the wagons with his brothers, and sent presents for his father, and food for the journey.

They came to Jacob and said, "Joseph is still alive, and he is ruler over all the land of Egypt."

His heart fainted, because he could not believe them. But when they told him the whole story, and showed him the wagons, his spirit revived, and he said, "It is enough; Joseph my son is still alive; I will go and see him before I die."

So they all journeyed to Egypt; and Joseph came in his chariot to meet Jacob, and fell on his neck and wept a good while. And Joseph brought Jacob into the presence of King Pharaoh, and Pharaoh asked Jacob how old he was.

Jacob said, "I am a hundred and thirty years old. Few and evil have been the years of my life; they have not been so many as the years of my fathers in the days of their sojournings."

Then Jacob blessed Pharaoh, and went out from his presence. And Pharaoh gave the Israelites (that is, Jacob and his sons and their tribe, for Jacob was also called Israel) the land of Goshen for their flocks and herds, and they dwelt there.

Moses and Joshua

Chapter 1

The Son of Pharaoh's Daughter

When the Israelites came to Egypt, they lived very much as they did before. Their wealth was still their flocks and herds; they lived in tents, and roamed about from one pasture to another. Only they did not wander through many different lands, but kept in Goshen, on the borders of Egypt. The years went on; first Jacob died, and then Joseph; and the king who had made Joseph his prime minister died. After a while there was a king of Egypt who forgot how Joseph had saved the country in the time of the famine; but he saw that the Israelites were growing into a great people. And he said to his captains and chief men, "These Israelites are too many and too mighty for us; and perhaps, when we are at war, they will join our enemies and fight against us."

So, to break the spirit of the Israelites, the Egyptians took them from their flocks and herds, and made them work hard in the broiling sun to build great cities. They had poor food and little of it, and were often cruelly beaten. Their lives were made bitter with hard work. But the worse they were treated the more they multiplied and increased in number, and the more frightened the Egyptians became.

Then the king of Egypt tried another way of preventing the Israelites from getting too numerous. He ordered that every baby boy should be thrown into the Nile as soon as it was born. Now, after the king had issued this order, two Israelites,

Amram and his wife Jochebed, had a little baby boy; and his mother thought him the most beautiful baby that ever was, and she hid him away to prevent his being thrown into the Nile. She kept him hidden for three months, till he got so big and noisy that she was sure the Egyptians would hear him. Then she took an "ark," or basket of bulrushes, and daubed it with mud and pitch so that it would float like a little ship. She put the boy in it, and laid it in the reeds by the river's bank. When it was left there, his sister stood some way off to see what would become of him. And Pharaoh's daughter came down to bathe in the river, and walked along the bank with her maids, or ladies-in-waiting, and she saw the "ark" amongst the reeds, and sent her maid to fetch it. When she opened it, she saw the child; and, sure enough, he was crying. Then she felt very sorry for him, because she saw he was one of the Israelite babies whom her father had ordered to be drowned. When the boy's sister saw the princess open the ark, she came to see what would be done with the baby; and she saw that the princess would like to keep him and take care of him. So she said, "Shall I find a Hebrew woman to nurse the child for you?"

And the princess said "Yes."

So his sister went and fetched his mother, and she had her son home again safely, and took care of him and enjoyed him in peace and comfort, without having to hide him away; and she was paid for nursing her own baby, because he was the adopted son of the princess. But when he grew to be a big boy, she had to take him to Pharaoh's daughter, and he was treated as if he were her son, and she called his name Moses.

Chapter 2

The Reproach of Christ

While the other Israelites were being ill-treated and overworked, Moses grew up in a palace, and lived like a prince. But somehow he came to know that these wretched and despised people were his kinsfolk and fellow-countrymen; and one day he went out to see them at their hard work, and he saw one of them being beaten by an Egyptian. And he looked this way and that, and there was no one else to be seen; and then he struck the Egyptian and killed him, and hid his body in the sand.

The next day he went out again, and saw one of his own people beating another Israelite. And he said, "Why do you beat him?"

But the man answered, "Who made you a prince and a judge over us? Do you mean to kill me as you did the Egyptian?"

Then Moses knew that someone had seen him kill the Egyptian; and soon Pharaoh heard of it, and tried to kill Moses. But Moses ran away and escaped, and after a time he came to a well in the land of Midian, and sat down there. And the seven daughters of Reuel or Jethro, the priest of Midian, came to the well, and drew water into the drinking troughs for their father's flock. But the shepherds came and wanted to drive them away. Then Moses stood up and helped them, and watered their sheep. And when they came back to their father, he said, "How is it that you have come back so soon today?"

They said, "An Egyptian helped us against the shepherds, and gave water to our sheep."

Jethro said, "Where is he? Why did you not bring him with you?"

So they went and fetched Moses, and in the end he agreed to stay with Jethro, and keep his sheep. Afterwards he married Zipporah, one of the seven daughters. And so instead of being a prince in Egypt, he was a shepherd in Midian, in exile from his countrymen and all his old friends.

The New Testament tells us that Moses bore "the reproach of Christ," which teaches us that those who make sacrifices for their country and their kinsfolk are serving and pleasing Christ, even when, like Moses, they have never heard of Him.

Chapter 3

The Burning Bush

While Moses was keeping sheep in Midian, he was called by God in a vision to be the deliverer of Israel. The Angel of Jehovah appeared to him. He saw what seemed like flames of fire in a bush, but the bush was not burnt up by the fire.

And Moses said, "I will turn aside now, and see this great sight, why the bush is not burnt."

Then God called to him, "Moses! Moses!"

He said, "Here am I."

God said, "Do not come near; take off your shoes, for you are standing on holy ground."

For in the East, when men went into a temple, they took off their shoes as we take off our hats; and the place where God appeared by His angel was holy, as if it had been a temple.

God said, "I am the God of thy fathers, the God of Abraham, the God of Isaac and the God of Jacob."

Then Moses hid his face, because he was afraid to look at God.

And God said, "I have seen how my people suffer in Egypt, and how the Egyptians ill-treat them; and I have heard their prayers, and have come to deliver them, and to take them to Canaan, a land flowing with milk and honey. Come now, therefore, and I will send you to Pharaoh, and you shall bring my people the Israelites out of Egypt."

But Moses said that he was not able to do so great a work, and especially that he was not clever enough at speaking to persuade Pharaoh to let the Israelites go. Even when God promised to tell him what to say, he still shrank from the task. But God said that his brother Aaron should go with him to be the spokesman.

Then Moses went home and said good-bye to Jethro, and put his wife and his two sons on an ass, and started for Egypt. And on the way Aaron met him, and Moses told Aaron all that God had said to him. When Moses and Aaron came to Egypt, they gathered together all the elders or leaders of the Israelites, and Aaron told them that God was about to deliver them, and the Israelites believed them, and thanked God.

Then Moses and Aaron went to Pharaoh and said, "Thus saith Jehovah, the God of Israel, 'Let my people go, that they may hold a feast unto Me in the wilderness.'"

But Pharaoh said, "Who is Jehovah, that I should obey Him, and let Israel go?"

That very day Pharaoh ordered the taskmasters to make the Israelites work harder than ever. Before Moses and Aaron went to Pharaoh, the people had to make so many bricks a day, and had straw given them for the bricks; but now they had to find straw for themselves, and yet to make just the same number of bricks. And they went and complained to Pharaoh, and said, "Why are we so badly treated? The taskmasters give us no straw, and yet they tell us to make bricks, and we thy servants are beaten, and it is not our fault that we cannot make bricks."

And Pharaoh said, "You are idle! You are idle! So you pretend to wish to go and sacrifice to Jehovah. Go and do your work, and make your full number of bricks, and get straw for yourselves."

As the Israelites came away from Pharaoh, they met Moses and Aaron, and they abused them, and said, "Jehovah look upon you and judge; you have made Pharaoh and his officers hate us, and have given them an excuse for killing us."

And the Israelites no longer believed that Jehovah was going to deliver them.

Chapter 4

The Ten Plagues

God did not desert His people, although they so easily lost faith in the deliverer He had sent to them. He made Egypt suffer terrible plagues, to frighten Pharaoh into letting the Israelites go. These are called the "Ten Plagues." They were:

1. The Plague of Blood. The water of the Nile was turned into blood.

2. The Plague of Frogs.

3. The Plague of Vermin.

4. The Plague of Flies.

The Egyptians were pestered first with frogs, then with vermin, and then with flies.

5. The Plague of Murrain. Their cattle all died of murrain, or cattle disease.

6. The Plague of Boils and Blains. The Egyptians were afflicted with boils.

7. The Plague of Hail. There was a thunderstorm with great hailstones, which destroyed the crops.

8. The Plague of Locusts. There came multitudes of locusts, and ate up what had not been spoilt by the hail.

9. The Plague of Darkness. For three days Egypt was covered with thick darkness, "which could be felt," as the story puts it.

10. The Plague of the Firstborn. All the firstborn children in Egypt died in one night.

Now, the Israelites were not afflicted with any of these plagues; they did not lose their cattle or their children, and, when it was dark in all the rest of Egypt, it was light in Goshen, where the Israelites were. Before each plague Moses warned Pharaoh; and, when the plague came, Pharaoh always begged that it might be taken away, and promised that, if it was, he would let the Israelites go. But each time when the plague was over Pharaoh broke his promise, and did not let them go. Only when all the firstborn died, and his own firstborn son amongst them, he allowed the Israelites to go; and they went away at once, before he had time to change his mind. But you shall hear more about this in the next chapter.

Chapter 5

The Exodus

I must tell you more of the story of how the Israelites came to leave Egypt at last. After the darkness had been taken away, and Pharaoh had again broken his promise, Moses told him that, unless he let the Israelites go, all the firstborn would die. But Pharaoh would not listen.

And Moses told the Israelites that after this plague Pharaoh would at last let them go; and he bade them get ready for their journey.

That night they kept a great feast. Every family killed a lamb and roasted it, and ate it together in their house, with unleavened bread and bitter herbs. And, because they were so soon to set out on their journey, they ate it in travelling dress, with their long robes girded round their waist, and their shoes on, and their staves in their hands. And they ate it in haste. But before their meal, they put some of the blood of the lamb at the top and sides of the doors of their houses, as a sign that God would not kill their firstborn. This feast, which the Jews still observe, is called the Passover, because God passed over the Israelites when he punished the Egyptians. The New Testament speaks of Christ as "our Passover," and as "a lamb slain from the foundation of the world," because Christ suffered when the Jews were keeping the Passover, and because by His death we have assurance that God will be merciful to those who believe in Him, as He was to the Israelites.

But to come back to the story. It goes on at midnight, while the Israelites were feasting, Jehovah smote all the firstborn in the land of Egypt, from the firstborn of Pharaoh on his throne to the firstborn of the prisoner in the dungeon. Pharaoh rose up in the night, and all his servants, and all the Egyptians; and there was a great cry in Egypt, for there was not a house where there was not one dead. Pharaoh called for Moses and Aaron by night, and bade them and the Israelites leave Egypt at once; and all the Egyptians were eager for the Israelites to go, for they said, "We are all dead men." The Israelites asked them for gold and silver and clothes; and the Egyptians were willing to give them anything, if they would only go.

So they started on their journey, a very great host of men, women, and children, with many flocks and herds.

Chapter 6

The Red Sea

After the Israelites were gone, Pharaoh and the Egyptians began to get over their fright, and they were sorry that they had let them go. And Pharaoh got together a great army, with chariots and horses, and pursued the Israelites. Now the Israelites in their journey had come to the sea, and were encamped upon the shore, so that the water was in front of them, and the great army of Pharaoh behind them; they were shut in, and could not escape. When they saw the Egyptians, they were very frightened, and their faith failed them again.

They said to Moses, "Were there no graves in Egypt, that you have brought us out to die in the wilderness? Let us alone, that we may serve the Egyptians. We had better be their slaves than die in the wilderness."

But Moses said, "Do not be afraid; stand still, and see the great victory which Jehovah will win for you today. You have seen Pharaoh's army, but you will never see it again. Jehovah will fight for you, while you stand still and look on."

And Jehovah said to Moses, "Speak to the Israelites, that they go forward; lift up your rod, and stretch out your hand over the sea, and it shall divide, and the Israelites shall go into the midst of the sea on dry ground."

Moses stretched out his hand over the sea, and Jehovah drove back the sea all the night by a strong east wind, and made the sea dry land, and the waters were divided. The Israelites went into the midst of the sea upon the dry ground, and the waters protected them like a wall on their right hand and on their left. And the Egyptians pursued, and went in after them into the midst of the sea, with all Pharaoh's chariots and horsemen.

And Jehovah said unto Moses, "Stretch out your hand over the sea, that the waters may flow back upon the Egyptians."

Moses stretched out his hand over the sea, and when the day dawned the waters returned to their usual place. Then the Egyptians tried to flee back again to the shore. But the waters covered the chariots and the horsemen and all Pharaoh's army that went in after them into the sea; they were all drowned, not one escaped. But the Israelites walked on dry land in the midst of the sea; and, before the waters returned, they were all safe on the other side. In the morning they saw the dead bodies of the Egyptians strewn along the seashore. Then the Israelites feared Jehovah, and believed in Him, and in His servant Moses.

And Miriam the prophetess, the sister of Moses and Aaron, took a timbrel in her hand, and all the women went out after her, and they danced and played upon their timbrels, and sang:

Sing to Jehovah, for He hath triumphed gloriously: The horse and his rider hath he thrown into the sea.

Chapter 7

The Wanderings in the Wilderness

When the Israelites had crossed the sea, they found themselves in the wilderness through which their forefathers had often journeyed on the way to Canaan, where the patriarchs had pitched their tents. But, before they reached Canaan, they wandered many years in the old nomad fashion from one desert pasture to another, very much as they had done before they went down to Egypt. And they met with God in the wilderness, like Abraham, Isaac, and Jacob in the days of old, and Elijah long afterwards. Through all their history the Israelites looked back to this wandering in the wilderness, as to the days of the patriarchs, as a time when God was very near to His people. They felt that the deliverance from Pharaoh was a token of God's love for Israel, an assurance of His care and protection.

They loved to tell how the presence of God was with Israel then, as a pillar of cloud by day and a pillar of fire by night, and how with His own voice He gave them from Mount Sinai the laws which we call the Ten Commandments. But the story of the wandering is chiefly the story of Moses; how, through that great leader and chieftain, Jehovah taught Israel to know Himself and His will. Through long years Moses led and governed the people, and the magic of his authority taught the wild tribes to keep the peace together, and to fight loyally side by side. And the bond of union was their common faith in

Jehovah, the God of Israel. For the secret of the strength of great nations is their faith in God.

But in these days Israel was only beginning to be a nation, and to know Jehovah. The same stories which tell us of God's great goodness to them, tell us also of their ingratitude; how God gave them food straight from heaven, just as He gives us fresh air and warmth and sunshine, just as parents provide food for their children; and how they grumbled and were disobedient, just as children sometimes do, and just as men nowadays grumble against God and disobey Him, though they have far more delightful and wonderful things to enjoy than food rained down from heaven.

And so it was a long time before Israel reached Canaan; nearly all the Israelites who left Egypt died, and still their children wandered in the wilderness. But all the while, in spite of their grumbling and disobedience, Moses was still their master, and God still helped him to train them to be His people. And at last they came to the lands east of the Jordan, and conquered the kings of that country, and settled there for a time. But when they were just about to cross the Jordan into Canaan, Moses died. He only lived to look across the river, and see the Promised Land, and then God took him to Himself.

Chapter 8

The Conquest of Jericho

After the death of Moses, the Israelites began to conquer the country west of Jordan, which was divided between a number of cities, each with its own king. Their new leader was Joshua, and as the stories you have been reading are taken out of the Books of Moses, which tell us about Moses, so the stories about the conquest of Canaan are from the Book of Joshua, which tells about Joshua.

It tells us that, after Moses was dead, God commanded Joshua to lead the Israelites into Canaan. They were encamped in the plain east of the Jordan, not far from the river; and just opposite, on the plain to the west of the river, stood the great Canaanite city of Jericho, which was the first city they would have to attack when they had crossed the river. So Joshua sent two spies secretly across the Jordan to find out about Jericho. They disguised themselves and got into Jericho, and lodged at the house of a woman named Rahab. But someone had seen them, and recognized that they were Israelites; and the king of Jericho heard of them, and sent to Rahab's house to fetch them. But Rahab hid them upon the roof, under a heap of flax-stalks; and when the king's messengers came, she said that the Israelites had left her house, and gone out of the city. And the messengers hurried away to try and catch the spies before they could get across the Jordan again. Rahab made the spies promise that, when the Israelites took Jericho, they would spare her and her family; and they told her to tie a scarlet cord in her window, that they might know her house.

Rahab's house was on the wall of the city, so she let the spies down by a rope out of her window, and they went and hid themselves amongst the hills till the men of Jericho had given up looking for them; and then they crossed the river, and told Joshua that they were sure that Israel could conquer Canaan, because all the people were very much afraid of them, or, as the story puts it, "did melt away before us."

The next day the Israelites crossed the Jordan. The Ark – the sacred chest, which was the symbol of God's presence went first, and the waters of Jordan divided before it, and left a dry passage for the Israelites. So they crossed the river and encamped before Jericho. And, at the command of God, the Israelites marched round and round Jericho, and the Ark was carried at the head of the army. For six days they marched round once every day; and the seventh day they marched round seven times, and at the end of the seventh time the priests blew with their trumpets, and the people shouted, and the walls fell down all of a heap. Then the Israelites took the city and burnt it, and killed all the people of Jericho. But first the spies went to Rahab's house, and brought her and her family away safely, and they lived amongst the Israelites.

Chapter 9

The Gibeonites

If the Canaanites were afraid of Israel before, their fear was much greater when they heard that Jericho had been taken and destroyed.

Some of them submitted to Israel. The people of Gibeon played the Israelites a trick, in order to make peace with them. They feared that, if the Israelites knew that they were Canaanites, they would kill them all, as they had killed the men of Jericho. So they sent ambassadors to Joshua, with old sacks upon their asses, and worn-out wine-skins patched and mended. And the ambassadors wore old clothes and worn-out clouted shoes, and they brought dry, moldy bread with them. And they came to Joshua and said, "We are come from a far country to make a treaty of friendship and alliance with you, because we have heard what great things your God, Jehovah, has done for you. You can see what a long way we have come, for this dry and moldy bread was hot from the oven, and these mended wine-skins and shabby, travel-stained clothes and patched shoes were all new when we started, and they have worn out because our journey has been very long."

Then the Israelites ate a very little of the moldy bread as a sign of friendship, and made a treaty with the Gibeonites.

But, the next day but one, the Israelites came to Gibeon, and found that the city of these shabby ambassadors was really a Canaanite city close by. Then they were very angry because the Gibeonites had told lies and deceived them, and they wished to put them all to death. But Joshua would not let the Israelites break their promise, and the Gibeonites became tributary to them, and had to be their hewers of wood and drawers of water, without being paid for it.

Chapter 10

The Battle of Beth-Horon

The Gibeonites only escaped one danger to fall into another. When the Canaanite kings heard that Gibeon had made peace with Israel, they were very angry. Adoni-zedek, king of Jerusalem, sent to the kings of four other cities, and the five of them got together a great army, and laid siege to Gibeon. Then the Gibeonites sent to Joshua to help them. Joshua and his army marched as fast as they could all through the night, and came suddenly upon the Canaanites, and defeated them, and put them to flight. They chased them up the pass of Beth-horon, and killed a great many of them; and they went on chasing them down the pass, and Jehovah sent a terrible storm of hail, and more Canaanites were killed by the hailstones than by the swords of the Israelites. The Book of Joshua quotes some lines from an old book of Hebrew poetry, the Book of Jashar. Joshua said:

"Sun, stand thou still upon Gibeon;
And thou, moon, in the valley of Aijalon.
And the sun stood still, and the moon stayed
Until the nation had avenged themselves of their enemies."

The Israelites kept on chasing and killing the Canaanites until those who were still left escaped to their cities. Then the Israelites went back to their camp. Meanwhile the five kings had been taken prisoners, and Joshua put them to death.

After the glorious victory of Beth-horon, Joshua took a great many of the Canaanite cities. He won another victory far away in the north of Canaan, at the Waters of Merom, over the kings of the northern cities. Before Joshua died, the tribes of Israel were firmly established east of Jordan, and were masters of much of the country. But a great deal of the land still belonged to the Canaanites, and Israel had to fight many battles, winning some and losing some, before they conquered all Canaan. The settlement in Canaan made a great change in the life of the Israelites. Most of them gave up living in tents, and wandering about with their flocks and herds. They built houses, and lived in villages and towns; and had cornfields and vineyards; and made wine and oil.

The Judges, Ruth, and Samuel

Chapter 1

Deborah and Barak

For a long while after the death of Joshua there was no Israelite chief who was obeyed by all the tribes. They were not united as they were in the time of Moses. Sometimes one tribe would have a little war of its own against its Canaanite neighbors; sometimes three or four tribes united against the enemy; and sometimes the tribes of Israel had civil wars, and fought against each other. They were disobedient to Jehovah, as they had been in the wilderness, and often worshipped other gods. As the Book of Judges, which tells us most of the stories about this time, says: "There was no king in Israel in those days; every man did that which was right in his own eyes."

The leaders of Israel in these days were called "Judges," but the stories in the book which tells us about them are all about fighting. The first you shall hear is that of Deborah and Barak.

The Israelites disobeyed God, and He allowed Jabin, king of Hazor, to the north of Palestine, to oppress them for twenty years. Then they prayed to God, and He raised up Deborah and Barak to deliver them.

Deborah was the wife of a man named Lappidoth. She was a prophetess, and could teach people the will of God, and what was right for them to do; and disputes were brought to her to be settled: as the Book of Judges says, "She judged Israel at that time." But, when it came to be a question of fighting, she wanted a man to help her; so she sent for Barak, and told him that it was the will of Jehovah, God of Israel, that he should gather together an army, and conquer Jabin, and deliver Israel.

Barak said, "If you will go with me, I will go; but, if you will not go with me, I will not go."

And she said, "To be sure I will go with you; but then you will get little honor from this war, for people will say that God gave victory to Israel by means of a woman."

So Deborah and Barak went together, and gathered an army.

The Book of Judges gives us a very ancient Hebrew poem about the war with Jabin. This poem is often called the Song of Deborah. The Song tells us which of the tribes united to follow Deborah and Barak. Ephraim came and Benjamin and Machir, which was a part of Manasseh, and Zebulun and Issachar and Naphtali, Barak's own tribe. These were the tribes in the center and the north. But the Song says that Dan and Asher on the seacoast, and Reuben and Gilead, that is Gad, beyond Jordan, stayed at home. Reuben

Sat among the sheepfolds

To hear the shepherds pipe to their flocks.

While Deborah and Barak were mustering their soldiers, Jabin sent against them a great army with nine hundred chariots of iron, under his general, Sisera. They met near Mount Tabor, and Jehovah gave the victory to Israel. The Song says:

The stars in their courses fought against Sisera;

The river Kishon swept them away.

Barak pursued the chariots and all the army of the Canaanites, and they were all killed; not a man was left alive.

But the general Sisera got out of his chariot, and ran away alone on foot, and came to the tent of Jael, the wife of Heber the Kenite. Now the Kenites were friends both with the Canaanites and the Israelites. Jael went out to meet Sisera, and said to him,

"Come into my tent, my lord; you will be safe there."

He was tired and thirsty, and he came in and lay down; and Jael covered him with a rug, and gave him milk to drink. And he said, "Stand in the door of the tent, and if anyone asks if there is a man here, say 'No.'"

Then he went to sleep, feeling quite safe, because these ancient tribes counted it a shameful and wicked thing to betray the stranger whom they sheltered and fed. But Jael waited till he was fast asleep, then she took a tent-peg and a mallet, and crept softly behind Sisera, and drove the peg through his temples and killed him.

Now Barak was pursuing Sisera, and he came to the tent, and Jael went out to meet him, and said,

"Come, and I will show you the man you are looking for."

And she brought him in, and there was Sisera lying dead, with the tent-peg through his temples.

After this victory, the Israelites gained other victories over Jabin, king of Hazor, until they were quite delivered from him.

Chapter 2

Gideon

At another time, the Midianites from the east of Jordan oppressed Israel, so that the people left their fields and villages, and went to live in the mountains, in dens and caves and strong places amongst the rocks. The Israelites sowed their corn; but, when it was ripe and ready to be cut, the Midianites came in countless swarms, with tents and cattle and camels, and took all the harvest and all the sheep and oxen and asses. There was no food left for the Israelites. And the Israelites prayed to Jehovah, and He sent them a deliverer.

Gideon, the son of Joash, of Abiezer in Manasseh, was beating out wheat in the wine-press, instead of the threshing-floor, to hide it from the Midianites. And the Angel of Jehovah appeared to him, and said, "Jehovah is with thee, thou mighty man of valor. Go and save Israel from the Midianites. Have not I sent thee?"

But Gideon said, "O Lord, how shall I save Israel? My clan is the poorest in Manasseh, and I am the least in my father's house."

But Jehovah promised to be with him, and give him victory; and Gideon asked for a sign, and the angel gave him a sign. Gideon brought meat and cakes of unleavened bread and broth; and he laid the bread and meat, and poured out the broth, on a rock before the angel. And the angel touched the food with the end of the staff he had in his hand; and fire came out of the rock, and burnt up the meat and cakes, and the angel vanished.

The same night Jehovah said to Gideon, "Take one of your father's bullocks, and pull down the altar of Baal, the false god of the Canaanites, which belongs to your father; and build an altar to Jehovah, and sacrifice the bullock upon it."

Gideon did as God told him; and when the neighbors got up in the morning, they saw Baal's altar had been pulled down, and there was a new altar built, and a bullock lying upon it. When they found out that Gideon had done this, they wanted to kill him. But his father Joash said, "If Baal is really a god, he himself can punish Gideon." So the people of Abiezer did not harm Gideon; and, when they saw that Baal did not punish him, they most likely left off believing in Baal.

About this time the Midianites, with a great many other eastern tribes, crossed the Jordan to plunder Israel, and they encamped in Jezreel. But the spirit of Jehovah came upon Gideon, and he blew a trumpet in Abiezer, and the people came to fight under his leadership; and he gathered an army from the northern tribes, Manasseh, Asher, Zebulun, and Naphtali.

And Gideon asked God for another sign, and said, "I will put a fleece of wool on the threshing-floor. If there be dew on the fleece only, while all the ground round about is dry, it will be a sign that I shall lead Israel to victory."

When Gideon got up next morning, the ground was dry, but the fleece was so wet with dew that he wrung a bowlful of water out of it. Still he was not satisfied, but asked for yet another sign, and said to God, "Do not be angry with me, if I ask for just one more sign. This time let the fleece be dry, and all the ground round about wet with dew."

And next morning the fleece was dry, and the ground was wet.

Then Gideon took courage, and marched against the Midianites with a large army. But Jehovah told Gideon that the army was too large. If they got the victory, they would think it was by their own strength, and not by Jehovah's. He bade Gideon tell his men that all who were afraid might go home; and twenty-two thousand went home.

But there were still ten thousand left, and Jehovah said that these were too many; and He bade Gideon bring them down to the water, and to send home all who knelt to drink, and to keep those who stooped and raised the water to their mouth with their hands. They all knelt except three hundred, so Gideon kept the three hundred, and sent the rest home.

He and his men were on the hills, and the camp of the Midianites was in the valley beneath; and at night he and his servant went down, and got close to some of the enemy without being found out. And they heard a man telling his companion a dream.

"I dreamed," said he, "that a cake of barley-bread tumbled into the camp of Midian, and rolled along till it came to a tent and struck it, and turned it upside down, and laid it flat on the ground."

"This," said his companion, "is nothing else than the sword of Gideon, the son of Joash, a man of Israel. God has delivered Midian and all the army into his hand."

Gideon was much encouraged when he heard the dream and its interpretation, and he went back to his men, and said, "Arise, for Jehovah has delivered the army of Midian into your hands."

And he gave each of them a trumpet and an empty pitcher with a torch inside it, and said to them, "Watch me, and do what you see me do. When I blow my trumpet, all of you blow your trumpets, and shout, 'For Jehovah and for Gideon.'"

He divided his men into three companies of a hundred each, and the three companies marched down in the night, and came close to three different sides of the camp, just when the Midianites had posted fresh sentinels. And the Israelites blew the trumpets; they broke the pitchers, and waved the torches with their left hands, while they held their trumpets in their right hands; and they shouted, "The sword of Jehovah and of Gideon." They did not attack the enemy, but just stood, and shouted, and waved the torches and blew the trumpets. When the Midianites were awakened by such a din of shouting and trumpet-blowing, and saw lights on every side, they thought they were surrounded by a great army of enemies; and in their fright and confusion they began to fight with each other in the dark, and then they all ran away. And Gideon sent messengers, and the Israelites came from far and wide, and pursued them, and killed a great many, and gained more victories over them, and captured and slew four of their princes, one of whom was called the Wolf, and another the Raven.

So Gideon delivered the northern tribes of Israel from the Midianites, and was judge over Israel all his life.

Chapter 3

Jephthah

At another time the Ammonites came to fight against the Israelites who lived in Gilead, east of Jordan, and the Israelites wanted a brave captain to lead them against the enemy. Now there was a man named Jephthah, whose half-brothers had driven him away from home that they might have all their father's property for themselves. And Jephthah gathered a robber band and did many daring deeds, so that all Gilead spoke of him as "a mighty man of valor," just as men in later days spoke of Hereward the Saxon or Rob Roy. So, in their trouble, the elders of Gilead asked Jephthah to be their leader, and the people and their elders swore a solemn oath before Jehovah at His temple at Mizpah, that, if Jephthah would lead them against the Ammonites, he should be head and chief of Gilead. So Jephthah consented. And the spirit of Jehovah came upon Jephthah, and he gathered an army from Gilead and Manasseh, and marched against the enemy.

But first he vowed a vow to Jehovah, and said, "If thou wilt indeed give me the victory over Ammon, and I return home in peace, the first living thing that comes out to meet me shall be Jehovah's, and I will offer it up for a burnt-offering."

Then Jephthah fought against the Ammonites, and Jehovah gave him the victory; and he pursued them, and took twenty of their cities, and killed a great many of them. So Gilead was delivered from the Ammonites.

Then Jephthah went home to Mizpah, and his daughter came out to meet him, dancing and playing on the timbrel. She was his only child; he had no other son or daughter. When he saw her, he tore his clothes, and said, "Alas, my daughter! You have brought me very low, and into sore distress; for I have made a promise to Jehovah, and I cannot go back."

And she said, "My father, keep your promise to Jehovah, since He has given you vengeance over your enemies; but let me go with my companions to the mountains for two months, and lament."

He let her go, and after two months she came back; and the story says, "He did with her according to his vow which he vowed."

And there was other trouble in store for Jephthah. The men of Ephraim were jealous and angry because they had not been asked to fight against Ammon; and they threatened to burn Jephthah's house; and they insulted and abused the men of Gilead, though Ephraim and Gilead were both tribes of Israel. The Ephraimites crossed the Jordan to fight against Jephthah, but they were defeated by him and his Gileadite followers. After the battle, the Gileadites guarded the fords of the Jordan, by which the Ephraimites would have to get back to their homes on the west of the river. When an Ephraimite came to one of the fords, and said, "Let me go over," the men of Gilead would say to him, "Are you an Ephraimite?" And if he said "No," then they said, "Say now Shibboleth," and he would say "Sibboleth," because the Ephraimites could not pronounce "sh" properly, but said "s" instead. Then they knew he was an Ephraimite, and laid hold of him, and killed him. Altogether forty-two thousand Ephraimites were killed. So Jephthah delivered Gilead from Ammon and from Ephraim, and was judge over the Gileadites.

Chapter 4

Ruth

The story of Ruth has a whole book of the Bible to itself, but I have put it with the stories about the Judges, because it begins, "In the days when the judges judged." It goes on: there was a famine in the land of Israel, and there were living at Bethlehem, in Judah, Elimelech and his wife Naomi, and their two sons Mahlon and Chilion. And because of the famine, they went across the Jordan into Moab, where there was more food to be had. They lived in Moab a long time, and Elimelech died, and Mahlon and Chilion married two Moabite wives, Orpah and Ruth. When they had been ten years in Moab, Mahlon and Chilion died, and Naomi heard that through the goodness of Jehovah there was now plenty of food in Judah, and she decided to go back to her friends and her old home. So she set out for Bethlehem, and Orpah and Ruth started to go with her.

But Naomi said to them, "Do you each of you go back to your mother's house; may Jehovah deal kindly with you, as you have dealt with the dead, and with me. Jehovah grant that each of you may find a home with a second husband."

And she kissed them, and they wept aloud, and said to Naomi, "Nay, but we will go back with you to your people."

But still Naomi tried to persuade them to go back to their old homes; and at last Orpah kissed her, and bade her good-bye, and went away home to her mother.

But Ruth would not leave Naomi; she said, "Where you go I will go, and where you stay I will stay; your people shall be my

people, and your God my God; where you die I will die, and
there will I be buried."

So they both went on together till they came to Bethlehem.
And the whole town was greatly excited about them, and the
women came round them, and said, "Is this Naomi?"

Now Naomi means "pleasant," and she replied, "Don't call
me Naomi, call me Mara which means bitter for the Almighty
has dealt very bitterly with me; I went out full, and Jehovah has
brought me home again empty."

So the two widows, Naomi and Ruth, settled down at
Bethlehem, but they were very poor and lonely.

They had come just when the farmers were beginning to
cut their barley; and at harvest time the poor people were
allowed to go into the fields and gather up the loose ears that
were dropped by the reapers; and Ruth went to glean to get a
little food for Naomi and herself. And by chance she went into
the field of a very rich man named Boaz, who was a relation of
Elimelech, Naomi's dead husband. And Boaz came to see how
the work was getting on.

He said to the reapers, "Jehovah be with you."

They answered him, "Jehovah bless you," just as we should
say, "Good morning."

He saw Ruth gleaning, and asked who she was; and they
told him that she was Naomi's Moabite daughter-in-law. Then
Boaz called her to him, and said she might glean in his fields all
through the harvest, and must not go anywhere else.

"For," said he, "I have heard all about your goodness to
your mother-in-law Naomi. May Jehovah recompense you,

and may you be fully rewarded by Jehovah, the God of Israel, under whose wings you have come to take refuge."

At meal-time, Boaz made her sit down with the reapers, and gave her food and drink, and she ate all she could, and still she had some left. And he bade the reapers leave whole handfuls of ears on purpose for Ruth, so that in the evening she had a great bundle; and she beat out the corn, and took it to Naomi, with what she had left of the food Boaz had given her. And she told Naomi that she had been gleaning in the fields of a man named Boaz, and that he had been very kind to her, and had said, "You must keep with my young men till my harvest is quite finished."

Naomi said, "Yes, my daughter, you had better keep with his maidens, and not let them see you in anybody else's fields."

So Ruth kept fast by the maidens of Boaz, and gleaned with them, all through the barley harvest and the wheat harvest; and every evening she took her gleanings home to Naomi.

Now there was a custom in Israel that, when a man died, his widow had a right to ask his nearest relation to marry her, and he had her dead husband's land; but if they had a son, then the land went to him. So, after the harvest, Naomi said to Ruth, "It is time for me to find you another husband. Go and tell Boaz that he is your near relation."

Ruth did as Naomi told her, and Boaz was delighted that she had chosen him for her husband instead of some young man. But he told her that there was a man more closely related to her husband than he was, and that this nearer relation must first be consulted.

Ruth

In Eastern towns people gather to talk and do business in the open space of the gate. Next morning Boaz went and sat down by the gate, and the other near relation came by, and Boaz made him sit down too. Then he got elders, or chief men, to sit with them, and they were ready to do business in a proper legal way. Boaz told the near relation that there was a field of Elimelech's that he had a right to buy back from a stranger who held it, and the near relation said he would buy the field.

"But," said Boaz, "if you take the field, you must marry Ruth."

But the near relation replied that it would be very inconvenient for him to marry Ruth. Perhaps he had wives who would have objected. "Do you," said he to Boaz, "do you take the field and marry Ruth."

And, according to ancient custom, he took off his shoe and passed it to Boaz as a sign that he gave up his rights to him. Then it was formally settled before the ten elders and all the people that Boaz was to marry Ruth. And in due time they were married, and had a little son, and Naomi nursed it. This little son was Obed, the grandfather of David, from whom our Lord Jesus Christ was descended.

Chapter 5

Hannah and Samuel

This story, too, is not out of the Book of Judges, but out of the Book of Samuel, which tells us how the Israelites left off having judges and began to have kings. The first two stories about Samuel are also about a judge named Eli, who was priest of the "house" or temple of Jehovah at Shiloh.

There was a man named Elkanah, living not very far from Shiloh, amongst the hills of Ephraim, in the middle of Palestine. He had two wives, Hannah and Peninnah. Peninnah had children, but Hannah had none. Once every year they all went up to the temple at Shiloh to worship and offer a sacrifice to Jehovah. Now, when a sheep or an ox was killed for an ordinary sacrifice, part was burnt on the altar, part was given to the priest, but the greater part was eaten by the man who offered the sacrifice, and his friends. Such a sacrifice meant a feast, or, as we should say, a great dinner party. These yearly sacrifices were very special occasions for Elkanah's family, something like our Christmas dinners. Elkanah always helped Peninnah and her children very freely, but he gave Hannah twice as much as any one of them, because he loved her dearly. But Peninnah was jealous of Hannah, and kept on making very disagreeable remarks about her having no children, till Hannah cried, and could not eat her dinner. So every year the great sacrifice was spoiled for all the family by Peninnah's evil temper.

Hannah and Samuel

One year Peninnah was as nasty as usual, and Hannah cried, and Elkanah tried in vain to comfort her. But, after they had finished, she went to the temple and prayed and wept bitterly. In her prayer she promised that, if God would give her a son, she would give him to Jehovah all his life.

While Hannah prayed, the priest Eli was watching her; he saw her lips move, but he could not hear anything, and he thought she was drunk, and reproved her sharply for coming to the temple in such a state. But she told him she was not drunk, but only in great trouble.

And he said, "Go in peace; may the God of Israel give you what you have asked for."

Then she was greatly comforted, and went and took food, and left off looking sad. In time God gave her a son, and she named him Samuel; and when he was old enough, but still quite a little boy, Elkanah and Hannah went to Shiloh, and took Samuel to Eli. Then Hannah told Eli that she was the woman he had seen praying, and the little boy was the son for whom she had prayed. And because he was God's gift to her, she wished to give him to God, to be a servant in the temple.

So Elkanah and Hannah went home, and Samuel stayed behind to help Eli. But his father and mother came to see him every year when they came up for the sacrifice, and Hannah always brought him a new cloak. And God gave Hannah three sons and two daughters besides Samuel.

Chapter 4

Eli and Samuel

As the years went on, and Samuel grew to be a man, Eli got very old and feeble, and had to leave the care of the temple to his sons, Hophni and Phinehas. They were bad men, and took more than their proper share of the sheep and oxen which men sacrificed to Jehovah, and did many other wicked things, so that the temple got a bad name, and the people did not care to come to worship Jehovah. Eli scolded his sons, but they did not heed him.

Now Samuel used to sleep where the Ark of the Covenant was, in the temple, to watch over the Ark. One night Eli had gone to bed, and Samuel lain down to sleep; but the temple lamp had not yet gone out, and Samuel heard a voice say "Samuel!" And he thought it was Eli calling him, and he answered, "Here am I."

And he ran to Eli, and said, "Here am I; you called me."

But Eli said, "No, I did not call; lie down again."

But, when he had lain down, he heard the voice again, "Samuel!" And again he ran to Eli, and Eli said he had not called, and sent him to lie down again.

And the voice came for the third time, "Samuel!" and again he ran to Eli; but now Eli understood that Jehovah was calling the lad.

And he said to him, "Go and lie down, and if He calls you, say, "Speak, O Jehovah, for Thy servant is listening."

So Samuel went and lay down, and Jehovah came and called, "Samuel! Samuel!"

And Samuel said, "Speak, for Thy servant is listening."

Then God told Samuel to tell Eli that he would punish Eli and his family because of the wickedness of Hophni and Phinehas.

And Samuel lay till morning, and opened the doors of the temple; but he did not go to Eli, because he was afraid to tell him the words of God. But Eli called Samuel, and made him tell everything; and, when he had heard it all, he said, "It is Jehovah; let Him do what seems right to Him."

Not long after, the Israelites were at war with the Philistines, and they wished to have the Ark with them, because they thought that if the Ark, the sign of God's presence, was with the army, God would give them victory. And Hophni and Phinehas took the Ark to the army; but in the next battle the Israelites were defeated, Hophni and Phinehas were killed, and the Philistines captured the Ark; for sacred chests and books and vessels used in temples and churches do not protect wicked men. When the news came to Eli, he fell from a high seat, where he was sitting, and broke his neck; and the wife of Phinehas died when she heard the news.

But Samuel grew to be a great prophet, and all Israel knew that he could teach them what was right, and what was the will of God. And when the Philistines came again to fight against Israel, Samuel prayed, and God gave Israel the victory. So Samuel judged Israel.

Saul, David, and Solomon

Chapter 1

Saul, the First King of Israel

When Samuel got too old to judge Israel himself, he made his sons judges. But they turned out badly, like Eli's sons. If they were asked to settle a dispute, they decided in favor of the man who gave them the most money. The people were very angry, and grew tired of having such wicked judges. They thought that if they had a king, he would govern justly, and they would be better off. Just then, too, they were very much troubled by the Philistines, the Ammonites and other enemies; they hoped that a king over all the tribes of Israel would unite them, and give them victory.

Now, there was a tall, handsome young man of the tribe of Benjamin. There was not a finer man than he in all Israel; he stood shoulder high above everyone else. His name was Saul, the son of Kish. One day Kish lost some asses; and he sent Saul with one of the servants to look for them. They went a long way without finding them; till at last Saul said, "Let us go home, lest my father leave off caring for the asses, and get anxious about us."

But the servant said, "There is a man of God in the town close by, who has a great reputation for telling people anything they want to know. Let us go to him. Perhaps he can tell us about the asses."

Saul said, "But we have no present to give him."

The servant answered, "I have a quarter shekel; we will give him that."

So they went towards the town, and on their way they met some girls going to draw water, and they asked if the man of God was at home.

The girls said, "Yes; he has come to the town today to be present at a great sacrifice and feast at the high place the temple. If you make haste, you will catch him before he goes to the high place. They don't begin the feast till he comes to bless the food."

So Saul and the servant hurried on, and met the man of God on his way to the high place.

The man of God was Samuel, and God had told him that He would send him a man of Benjamin, whom he should anoint to be prince over Israel, to save the people from the Philistines. And, when Samuel saw the two strangers coming, he knew that Saul was the man whom God had chosen to be king over Israel.

But Saul did not know Samuel, and he went up to him, and asked the way to the house of the man of God.

Samuel said, "I am the man of God; come and feast with us today at the high place. Tomorrow I will let you go, and I will tell you all you want to know. Don't trouble about the asses; they have been found; and soon you will be master of all the wealth of Israel."

And Saul wondered what he meant. Then Samuel took Saul and his servant, and brought them into the guest-chamber. There were about thirty guests, the chief men of the town; but Samuel put Saul and his servant in the chief places;

and he made the cook bring Saul a special portion that had been kept back for him. So Saul feasted with Samuel, and went to his house with him, and stayed there that night. Next morning, they got up at daybreak, and Saul started to go home. Samuel went with him to see him on his way. When they were out of the city, he made Saul send the servant on in front.

Then Samuel took a vial of oil, and poured it on his head, and told him that this was a sign that Jehovah had anointed him to be king over Israel. When they parted, Saul went home; but he said nothing to his friends about his being king. Afterwards God made the Israelites choose Saul to be king; but some evil men hated Saul, and did not wish to obey him.

Chapter 2

Saul's Victories

About this time the Ammonites, under their king Nahash, invaded the lands of Israel east of the Jordan, and besieged the city of Jabesh-gilead. Soon he brought the city into such straits that they sent ambassadors to Nahash, offering to surrender if he would spare their lives.

But Nahash said, "I will only spare you on condition that you all have your right eyes put out, that I may mock at Israel."

The elders of Jabesh said, "Make a truce with us for a week, that we may send messengers through all Israel for help. If no help comes, we will surrender to you on your own terms."

The messengers came to Gibeah, where Saul lived. Saul was away ploughing in the fields, but they told their story to the people, and the people broke out into loud cries of grief and anger. As Saul came home from the fields with his oxen, he heard their outcry, and asked what the noise was about. They told him. And the spirit of God came mightily upon Saul when he heard of the shameful cruelty of Nahash, and he burned with fierce anger. He took a yoke of oxen and cut them in pieces, and sent messengers with the pieces to all parts of Israel, saying, "If any man does not come to help Saul rescue Jabesh-gilead, his oxen shall be cut to pieces."

So Saul gathered a great army, and sent back the messengers from Jabesh-gilead to tell their friends that help would come before the sun was hot next day. The men of Jabesh rejoiced greatly over the good news; and, to put Nahash off his guard, they sent out a message to him that next day they would surrender, and he should do with them as he pleased.

But next day Saul came with his army very early in the morning, and took the Ammonites by surprise, and defeated them with great slaughter. They were so scattered that there were not two left together. So Jabesh-gilead was delivered; and now Saul was most popular, and the people wished to kill those who objected to his being king.

But Saul said, "No one shall be put to death today, for today Jehovah has given victory to Israel."

Then they celebrated their victory and the accession of their new king by great sacrifices and feasts at Gilgal.

Chapter 3

David, Saul's Minstrel and Armor Bearer

The Book of Samuel tells us two quite different stories about the way in which David and Saul first met. I cannot explain to you how these stories fit into one another, but I will tell you them separately, one in this chapter, and one in the next.

After Saul became king, he and his brave son Jonathan gained many victories over the Philistines and their other enemies, and did very much to make the separate Israelite tribes into a strong, united people. But sometimes Saul did evil, and sinned against God.

Now comes our first story. The spirit of Jehovah had left Saul, and Jehovah allowed an evil spirit to trouble him. He was gloomy, irritable, almost mad. His servants begged that they might find him a clever minstrel, who might play upon the harp, and soothe and cheer him, and put him in good spirits. And Saul said they might.

One of them said, "I have seen the son of Jesse of Bethlehem. He is a clever minstrel and a brave warrior; he can talk well, and is very handsome, and Jehovah is with him."

So Saul sent messengers to Jesse, and said, "Send me your son David."

Then Jesse loaded an ass with bread and a bottle of wine and a kid, and sent them with David as a present to Saul. When David came, he was presented to Saul; and Saul was greatly taken with him, and made him his armor-bearer. The king sent and asked Jesse that David might stay with him always, because he was very fond of him. So David stayed with Saul; and, when the king became gloomy and irritable, David played upon the harp, and Saul was refreshed, and got bright and cheerful again, and the evil spirit left him.

Chapter 4

David and Goliath

Once, when the Israelites were at war with the Philistines, King Saul and his army were encamped on a hill on one side of a valley, and the Philistines on the hill opposite. Amongst the Philistines was a giant from Gath named Goliath, about ten feet high. He was clad in bronze armor, helmet, coat of mail, and greaves, and a small shield slung behind his back. His coat of mail weighed about a hundred-weight and a half. His shield-bearer went before him, carrying a large shield. This giant came down every day into the valley between the two armies, and challenged any Israelite to meet him in single combat, and decide the war.

"Choose a man," said he, "and let him come down and fight with me. If he kills me, we Philistines will be your servants; but if I kill him, you shall serve us. I defy the armies of Israel this day; find a man to fight with me."

When Saul and all Israel heard this challenge of the Philistine giant, they were terribly frightened. Goliath came down into the valley morning and evening for forty days, and repeated his challenge, but no one had courage enough to accept it.

Now comes our second story of the meeting of Saul and David. There lived at Bethlehem an old man named Jesse, who had eight sons. The three eldest Eliab, Abinadab and Shammah were in Saul's camp; and the youngest, David, stayed at home and looked after the sheep. One day Jesse said to David, "Get

ten loaves and some corn, and take them quickly to the camp
to your brothers; and take these ten cheeses to the captain of
their thousand (or, as we should say, the colonel of their
regiment), and find out how they are, and bring me word."

Next morning David left the sheep with a shepherd, and
went to the camp with the food for his brothers and the present
for the captain; and he came to the wagons belonging to the
army, just as the Israelites and the Philistines were setting
themselves in array of battle against each other. David was
eager to see the fighting, so he left his loaves and cheeses with
the officer in charge of the wagons, and ran to the army, and
found his brothers and greeted them. Just then Goliath came
forward from the ranks of the Philistines, and uttered his usual
challenge; and when the Israelites saw him, they were
frightened and ran away. But David asked the men near him
what reward would be given to the man who killed Goliath.

They answered him, "The king will make him a rich man,
and he shall marry the king's daughter."

But when David's eldest brother, Eliab, heard him talking
about fighting Goliath, he was very angry.

"What did you come for?" said Eliab. "With whom did you
leave those few sheep in the wilderness? I know your pride and
the naughtiness of your heart. You came out of idle curiosity to
see the battle."

But David took no notice; he went about asking people
what reward would be given for killing Goliath, and they all
gave him the same answer. By-and-by Saul heard that there was
a lad in the camp who talked about fighting the Philistine giant,
and Saul sent for David.

And David said to Saul, "Let no one be distressed because of Goliath. I, your servant, will go and fight with this Philistine."

But Saul said, "You! Fight with the Philistine! You are only a stripling, and he has been fighting ever since he was a boy."

Then David told Saul that he had fought with lions and bears that came to carry off the lambs of his flock, and had killed them. And he was sure that Jehovah, who saved him from the lion and the bear, would help him to kill the heathen Philistine, who defied the armies of the living God.

And Saul said to David, "Go, and Jehovah shall be with you."

He clothed David with his own armor, and gave him his sword; but David had to take it all off again, because he was not used to such armor.

And he went to meet the Philistine with nothing but his staff and a sling, and five smooth stones from the brook in his shepherd's bag. And the Philistine came on, with his shield-bearer before him, and he looked about for the enemy he was to fight with, and saw no one but a handsome, rosy-faced lad with a staff and a sling.

"What!" said he, "am I a dog, that you take a stick to me?"

And he cursed David by his gods, and said, "Come to me, and I will give your flesh to the birds of prey and the wild beasts."

But David said, "You come to me with sword and spear and shield, but I come to you in the name of Jehovah Sabaoth, the God of the armies of Israel."

And as Goliath came towards David, David ran to meet him, and put his hand in his bag, and drew out a stone, and slang it, and hit the Philistine in the forehead; and the stone sank into his forehead, and he fell forward upon his face. Then David ran, and stood over him, and, because he had no sword of his own, he took Goliath's sword, and drew it out of its sheath, and cut off his head with it. When the Philistines saw that the champion was dead, they ran away; and the Israelites arose and shouted, and pursued them a long distance; and when they came back from the pursuit, they plundered the Philistine camp.

Meanwhile Saul had been asking his general Abner whose son the stripling was. And Abner could not tell him; but when David came back again, Abner took him in to Saul with the head of Goliath in his hand. And Saul said to him, "Whose son are you, my lad?"

David answered, "I am the son of your servant Jesse of Bethlehem."

Chapter 5

David and Jonathan

When David was brought to Saul with Goliath's head in his hand, Saul's son Jonathan was standing beside his father. And Jonathan was greatly drawn to David, so that, before David had finished speaking to Saul, "the soul of Jonathan," as the story says, "was knit with the soul of David, and Jonathan loved him as his own soul." From that moment they were fast friends, and even now we call two very great friends "David and Jonathan." And, because of Jonathan's great love for David, they made between them a covenant, a solemn promise that they would always be friends and brothers. And in token of this, Jonathan took off his robes, with his sword and bow and girdle, and gave them to David.

Soon Jonathan had an opportunity of showing his friendship to David. Saul made David one of his generals, and David was very successful, and became popular, so that the women sang:

"Saul hath slain his thousands,
But David his ten thousands."

Then Saul became jealous of David, and the evil, gloomy spirit came upon him, and now, when David played to Saul, the music did not soothe the king but he threw his spear at him twice. Afterwards he tried in other ways to get David killed. All this while David was fighting bravely for Saul and for Israel, and became more popular than ever. And Saul was even obliged to let him marry his daughter Michal, as he had promised, although he tried to break his promise.

At last Saul told Jonathan and all his servants to kill David. But Jonathan warned David, and tried to reconcile Saul to him. But after a while David had to run away from Saul's court. He went to his own house, but Saul sent messengers after him to kill him. And his wife Michal let him down out of the window, and he escaped. Then Michal put an image in David's bed, with the clothes over it to look like David. When Saul's messengers came, she told them David was ill in bed, and let them just look in. Then they went back and told the king, but Saul told them to go back and bring David, bed and all; and when they came to carry him away, they found there was nothing in the bed but the image and a pillow. Then Saul was very angry, and sent out men in all directions to hunt for David.

But David found Jonathan, and begged him to try and pacify the king, and to find out whether Saul still wished to kill David. For Saul was often generous, although he was hot-headed and passionate; and when the evil, jealous spirit left him, he loved David as in the old times. Jonathan and David fixed upon a place where they would meet, and arranged a signal by which David might know whether it was safe for him to come back to Saul. Then David went back to his hiding-place.

Soon after, the king was keeping the feast of the new moon, and he asked why David's seat was empty; and Jonathan made an excuse for him, and said he had gone to a family gathering at Bethlehem. Whereupon Saul broke out into fierce abuse of

David, and of Jonathan because Jonathan was his friend, and he threw his spear at Jonathan.

Then Jonathan knew that it would not be safe for David to come back. And he went to the place where he had arranged to meet David, and took with him a little lad to carry his bow and arrows, as if he were going to practice shooting. They came to the place; and David was hiding, so that he could see and hear them, but they could not see him. Jonathan told the lad to watch where each arrow went, and bring it back. Then he shot an arrow beyond him, and, when the lad was looking for it, he shouted to him, "Is not the arrow beyond you?"

These words were the signal to David that Saul was still trying to kill him. Jonathan sent the boy away, and David came out of his hiding-place; and they kissed each other, and wept together, and they promised with a solemn oath to God, that David and his children would always be faithful friends to Jonathan and his children. Then they parted; David went away to hide himself, and Jonathan went back to Saul; and we do not read that David and Jonathan ever saw each other again.

Chapter 4

David Spares Saul's Life

Saul kept on hunting for David, and David had many hair-breadth escapes. He gathered a band of brave men, and made raids upon the neighboring tribes. Once when Saul, at the head of three thousand men, was hunting for David, David heard of it, and came with his men to the neighborhood of Saul's camp. Saul was sleeping within a barricade of wagons – a laager, as they say in South Africa with his general Abner by his side, and his warriors all round about him, and his spear stuck in the ground at his head. And David took one of his followers, named Abishai, and came to Saul's camp in the night. They passed through the sleeping warriors till they came to where Saul and Abner lay, and no one awoke. Abishai wanted to kill Saul, but David would not let him. Only they took the spear and pitcher of water that were at Saul's head, and got away before anyone awaked.

When David had got to the top of a hill a good way off, he shouted to Abner, and to the people. He said to Abner, "You call yourself a brave man, and you pretend to guard the king, and last night he might have been killed, and you none the wiser. See, here is the king's spear and his pitcher of water!"

Saul knew David's voice, and said, "Is this thy voice, my son David?"

David answered, "It is my voice, my lord, O king. Why do you try to hunt me down? What evil have I done?"

David Spares Saul's Life

Then said Saul, "I have sinned. Return to me, my son David; for I will not try any more to harm you, because you have spared my life. I have certainly played the fool, and made terrible mistakes."

But David knew that the evil spirit might come upon Saul again. So he did not go to Saul, but sent back the spear. And Saul blessed David, and they parted.

Not long afterwards Saul and Jonathan were killed in a great battle against the Philistines. And David made a poem, like Lycidas or In Memoriam, in which he lamented for Saul and Jonathan, and said:

Saul and Jonathan were lovely and pleasant in their lives,
And in their death they were not divided;
They were swifter than eagles,
They were stronger than lions.

I am distressed for thee, my brother Jonathan:
Very pleasant hast thou been unto me:
Thy love to me was wonderful,
Passing the love of women.

Chapter 7

David and the Ark on Zion

After Saul's death, the men of Judah chose David to be
their king; but Abner, Saul's general, made Ishbaal, Saul's son,
king of the rest of Israel. There was civil war in Israel between
the followers of the two kings, until Ishbaal was murdered by
two of his own officers. Then all the tribes agreed to make
David king of the whole country, as God had promised him
long ago.

David gained great victories over the Philistines, so that
there was no longer any danger of their conquering Israel; and
he besieged and took the ancient city of Jerusalem, which had
been held up till his time by the Jebusites, a tribe belonging to
the old inhabitants of Canaan. After these victories David felt
that he was really king, and he made Jerusalem his capital, and
built himself a palace there, and married more wives.

Moreover he wished to have a temple of Jehovah in his new
capital, and he bethought himself of the Ark of Jehovah. For the
Israelites had no other sign of the presence of Jehovah so
sacred as the Ark; and the temple which had the Ark was sure
to be held in high honor. We have no one thing now that we
hold more sacred than anything else as the Israelites did the
Ark.

I must now return to the stories about the Ark. The last we
heard of it was that it was captured by the Philistines; but the
Ark brought many misfortunes upon them, so that they were
afraid to keep it, and were glad to send it back again to its own

country. Since that time the Ark had been kept in the house of a man named Abinadab. But now David went with thirty thousand men to bring the Ark in solemn procession to Jerusalem. They brought it out of the house of Abinadab, and put it on a new cart drawn by oxen, and Uzzah and Ahio, the sons of Abinadab, drove the cart. David and the Israelites walked before it, playing upon harps and timbrels, and castanets and cymbals.

But as they went, the oxen stumbled, and Uzzah took hold of the Ark to prevent its being thrown out of the cart. Because Uzzah handled so sacred a thing too familiarly, Jehovah was angry with him, and he died suddenly. Then David was afraid to take the Ark into his new city, and it was put for a time into the house of a Philistine from Gath, named Obed-edom. When it had been there three months, David heard that Jehovah had blessed Obed-edom, and given him three prosperous months. Then David knew it would be safe to bring the Ark into Jerusalem. He set out again with a great company to fetch the Ark in solemn procession, with music and dancing, with shouting, and blowing of trumpets. So they brought the Ark to Jerusalem, and put it into a tent which David had set up for it. And they offered great sacrifices to Jehovah; and David feasted all the people.

But after a time David felt that it was not right that he should live in a palace of cedar while the Ark of Jehovah had nothing but a tent to shelter it; and he wished to build a magnificent temple for the Ark. He asked the prophet Nathan whether Jehovah would be pleased with such a temple, and Nathan said that He would. But Nathan had made a mistake, for Jehovah bade him tell David that he should not build the temple, but that David's family should always reign in Jerusalem, and that his son should build the temple.

So David reigned in Jerusalem in great glory and prosperity. He did not forget his promise to Jonathan, but he found a lame son of Jonathan's, Meribbaal, and gave him the lands that had belonged to Saul; and Meribbaal lived at the court, and ate at the king's table.

Chapter 8

David and Absalom

In spite of all his glory and prosperity, David had many terrible troubles in the latter years of his reign. He fell into grievous sin, for he used the royal power to inflict shameful wrong upon one of his brave and faithful soldiers, and to bring about his death. The rebukes of Nathan the prophet soon made David feel that he had acted meanly and wickedly, and he repented bitterly of his sin. Nevertheless he suffered severe punishment.

David had a favorite son named Absalom, and another son Amnon. The two brothers quarreled, and Absalom killed Amnon, and fled to his grandfather – his mother's father – the king of Geshur, in the north of Palestine. When he had been there three years, Joab, the commander-in-chief of the army, persuaded David to let Absalom return. But David did not wholly forgive him – he would not see him. So for two years more Absalom was not allowed to come to the court or to see his father, but at last Joab persuaded David to send for his son. Absalom came to the king, and bowed himself to the ground before him, and the king kissed Absalom, and wholly forgave him.

But Absalom was not content – he wished to be king instead of David. He was popular because he was handsome; in all Israel there was none so much to be praised as Absalom for his beauty; and he had long, beautiful hair. He set to work to make himself more popular, and to make David unpopular.

He got a chariot and horses, and fifty men to run before him. He would get up early, and post himself by the gate – like the Cadi, or magistrate, at Jerusalem to meet the people coming to the king to make complaints and get justice done them. When anyone came, Absalom would greet him, and ask his name and city, and what his business was, and would say to him, "It is quite clear that you are in the right, and judgment ought to be given in your favor; but the king is getting too old for business, and he has appointed no one else to see to it. If only I were judge, I should be ready to hear everybody's case, and to do him justice."

And when the man wished to bow down to him, Absalom went to him, and raised him up, and kissed him. So Absalom stole the hearts of all the men of Israel.

After a time Absalom asked the king's leave to go to Hebron to offer a sacrifice at the temple there, and David let him go. Now Absalom has sent messengers through all the land, saying, "As soon as you hear the sound of the trumpet, say, 'Absalom is king in Hebron.'" So Absalom went to Hebron, and took with him two hundred nobles from Jerusalem, whom he had invited to his sacrifice. They knew nothing about the conspiracy, but when they came to Hebron, and found people flocking in from all sides to make Absalom king, they could scarcely help joining with him. When David heard of it, he fled from Jerusalem with his friends and his body-guard of foreign mercenaries, and after many adventures he reached Mahanaim on the east of Jordan, and gathered a great army round him; and Absalom and his army crossed the Jordan to fight with David. David mustered his army, and divided it into three parts under Joab and his two brothers; and he wished himself to lead the army to battle. But his followers would not let him, lest he should be killed; they persuaded him to stop at Mahanaim while they went out to fight. And the king stood by the gate, and watched the army march out, one regiment after another. He commanded Joab and the other two generals, "Deal gently for my sake with the young man, even with Absalom." And all the people heard him give this charge to the generals. In the battle that followed, David's army won a great victory; and Absalom was riding away upon a mule, when the mule went under the thick boughs of a great oak, and his head caught in the oak, and he hung between earth and heaven, while the mule went away from under him. One of David's soldiers saw him, and told Joab. And Joab rebuked the man for not killing Absalom; but the man said that they had all heard the king's command to spare his son, and he said that after that he would not have harmed him for a thousand pieces of silver. But Joab said he could not stop to argue with him. Joab took three darts and went to the oak tree, and thrust them through Absalom, and Joab's body-guard helped him to kill the young prince; and they cast him into a great pit in the forest, and raised over him a very great heap of stones. Then Joab blew a trumpet to call back his army from pursuing the rebels.

Meanwhile, David sat between the two gates of the city waiting for news; and the watchman went up to the roof of the gate, and looked, and when he saw a man running alone, he called out and told the king.

The king said, "If he is alone he brings news."

Soon the watchman saw another man running alone, and told the king; and the king said, "He also will bring news."

And the watchman said, "I think the running of the foremost is like the running of Ahimaaz, the son of Zadok."

"He is a good man," said the king, "and comes with good news."

Ahimaaz came and bowed down before the king, and said, "Blessed be Jehovah thy God, who has given you victory over the rebels."

But the king said, "Is Absalom safe?"

Ahimaaz answered, "When Joab sent me, your servant, I saw a great tumult, but I did not know what it was."

The king bade him stand aside. And the second messenger came and said, "Tidings for my lord the king; Jehovah has revenged you this day upon all who rebelled against you."

But the king said, "Is Absalom safe?"

And the messenger answered, "May the enemies of my lord the king, and all that rise up against you to do you hurt, be as that young man is."

Then the king was much moved, and went up to the chamber over the gate, and wept, and as he went he said, "O my son Absalom, my son, my son Absalom! Would God I had died for you, O Absalom, my son, my son!"

So the victory that day was turned into mourning for all the people, for they heard how the king grieved over his son; and they crept quietly back into the town, as if they were fugitives instead of conquerors. But Joab persuaded David to show himself to the people, lest they should be too discouraged.

Chapter 9

Solomon

When David died, he was succeeded by another favorite son, Solomon, whom he had crowned king before his own death. David's victories had made Israel powerful and prosperous, so that Solomon ruled over a wide territory, and possessed great riches. At the beginning of his reign he went to worship God at the great high place or temple at Gibeon, and offered a thousand burnt offerings. And at night Jehovah appeared to Solomon in a dream, and said, "Ask what I shall give you."

Solomon said, "Thou hast made Thy servant king, instead of David my father; and I am but as a little child, not skilled in governing. And Thy servant is in the midst of Thy chosen people, a great people, too many to be counted. Give Thy servant, therefore, an understanding heart to judge Thy people, that I may discern between good and evil."

Jehovah was pleased that Solomon had asked for wisdom, and said unto him, "Because you have not asked for yourself long life or riches or the life of your enemies, but have asked for understanding, that you may be a wise and just judge, I have done as you have asked. I have given you a wise and understanding heart, and I have also given you the riches and honor you did not ask for."

And Solomon awoke, and, behold! it was a dream. And he came to Jerusalem and offered sacrifices before the Ark of Jehovah, and made a feast for all his servants.

Solomon was famous for his wisdom and for his many great buildings. He built magnificent palaces for himself and for his queens, especially one for himself that took thirteen years to build, and one for Pharaoh's daughter, whom he had married. And, above all else, he spent seven years in building the palace or temple of Jehovah at Jerusalem, which came to be the greatest and, at last, the only temple of Jehovah.

And as Solomon's temple was above all other temples, so he was said to be wiser than all men, wiser even than those who were most celebrated for their wisdom--the Men of the East and the Egyptians. He was famous amongst all the nations round about for his three thousand proverbs and his thousand and five songs. He spoke of trees, from the cedar in Lebanon to the herbs, like hyssop, that grew on the wall; and of birds and creeping things and fishes. And the kings of all peoples round about heard so much of his wisdom that they sent their servants to hear his wise sayings. And one queen, the Queen of Sheba, in Arabia, came herself to ask Solomon difficult questions, and find out if he was as wise as reports said. She came to Jerusalem with a great retinue, with camels loaded with spices and jewels and gold. She came to Solomon, and asked him her difficult questions, and he was able to answer them all. When she saw how wise he was, and his splendid palace and luxurious banquets and crowds of finely dressed courtiers and servants, and especially the flight of steps by which he went up to the temple, there was no more spirit in her.

She said to the king, "I did not believe what I heard about your wise sayings, your wealth and your splendor; but now I have seen it all with my own eyes, and, behold, the half was not told me. Your wisdom and prosperity are greater than the reports of them."

And she gave the king gold and spices and jewels. Such an abundance of spices was never again seen in Jerusalem. And Solomon gave the Queen of Sheba all that she asked for, and many presents besides; and she and her servants went back to their own land.

But, in spite of his wisdom and prosperity, Solomon fell into many grievous sins. In order to build his palaces, he oppressed the people by making them work for nothing, so that they became discontented; and when he died, and his son Rehoboam refused to promise to reign better, almost all Israel, ten tribes, revolted from Rehoboam, and chose another king, Jeroboam. From that time there were kings of Israel ruling over the ten northern tribes; but the descendants of David still ruled in Jerusalem, over Judah and Benjamin.

Elijah and Elisha

Chapter 1

The Famine

Sometime after this, there arose a great king in Israel, named Omri; and, like David and Solomon, he was friendly with the Phœnecians of Tyre and Sidon; and his son Ahab, who succeeded him, married Jezebela, the daughter of the king of Sidon. Omri and Ahab waged long wars with the Syrians of Damascus, and gained victories over them and other enemies, so that they made Israel strong. But Ahab oppressed his own people, and encouraged the worship of false gods, especially of Baal, the god of the Phœnecians.

The stories about Elijah and Elisha tell us how Ahab and his family were punished. The prophet Elijah, from Gilead, came to Ahab and said, "As Jehovah, the God of Israel, liveth, before whom I stand, there shall be neither dew nor rain but according to my word." Then he fled, lest Ahab should kill him, and hid himself by a brook in the land east of Jordan; ravens brought him bread and meat, and he drank of the brook. But the brook dried up, and he went to Zarephath, a city belonging to Sidon; and, when he came to the gate of the city, he saw a widow gathering sticks, and he called to her, and said, "Fetch me, I pray you, a little water to drink."

As she was going to fetch it, he called to her again, and said, "Bring me, I pray you, a morsel of bread."

But she said, "As Jehovah your God liveth, I have no bread, only a handful of meal in the barrel and a little oil in the jar; and I am gathering two sticks, that I may go in and bake a cake for me and my son, that we may eat it and die."

Nevertheless Elijah said, "Do not be afraid that you will starve; go and do as you have said; but make me a little cake first, and bring it out to me, and then make for yourself and your son. For thus saith Jehovah, the God of Israel, the barrel of meal shall not waste, neither shall the jar of oil fail, until Jehovah sends rain upon the earth."

She went and did as Elijah bade her, and she and he and her household lived many days on the meal and the oil. But one day her son fell ill, and got worse till there was no breath left in him; but Elijah prayed to God, and the boy recovered; and his mother believed that Elijah was a prophet, and could teach her the will of God.

Chapter 2

The Rain

For three years there was no rain in Israel, so that there was a terrible famine. Then God told Elijah to go to Ahab, and tell the king that there would be rain.

When Ahab saw Elijah, he said, "Is it you, you troubler of Israel?"

Elijah answered, "It is not I, but you and your father's house that have troubled Israel, for you have disobeyed the commands of Jehovah, and worshipped the Baals. Send and gather all Israel to Mount Carmel, with the four hundred and fifty prophets of Baal that eat at Jezebel's table."

So Ahab sent and gathered all Israel and the prophets of Baal to Mount Carmel; and Elijah came and said to them, "How long will you halt between two opinions? If Jehovah be God, follow Him; but if Baal be God, follow him."

For the people thought that Jehovah would not object to their worshipping other gods, if they worshipped him as well. And when Elijah spoke to the people, they answered him not a word.

Then Elijah proposed that the prophets of Baal should sacrifice a bullock to Baal, and he should sacrifice a bullock to Jehovah; and whichever of the two, Jehovah or Baal, sent fire to burn up the sacrifice offered to him, should be the God of Israel. And the people agreed.

Then the prophets of Baal offered their bullock, and called on the name of Baal from morning till noon; but there was no voice nor any that answered. And they leaped about their altar.

And Elijah mocked them, and said, "Shout louder; he is a god; perhaps he is in a brown study, or on a journey, or perhaps he is asleep, and must be awaked."

Then they shouted louder than ever, and cut themselves with knives and lancets, as men were wont to do in worshipping Baal, till the blood gushed out upon them. But there was no voice and no answer, and no god took any notice of them.

Then Elijah offered his sacrifice, and prayed that Jehovah would let the people know that He was the God of Israel, and that Elijah was His prophet. At his prayer the fire of Jehovah fell and burnt up the bullock and the wood and the stones of the altar. When all the people saw it they fell on their faces, and said, "Jehovah is God! Jehovah is God!"

Then Elijah had all the prophets of Baal killed. Afterwards he told Ahab that there was the sound of abundance of rain. And Elijah went up to the top of Carmel, and bowed himself to the earth in prayer. After a while, he told his servant to go and look out over the sea, but the servant came back and said he could see nothing. Seven times Elijah sent him to look, and the seventh time the servant came back and said, "There is a little cloud no bigger than a man's hand coming up out of the sea."

Then Elijah sent him to tell Ahab to have his chariot got ready, and to make haste home, lest he should be stopped by the rain. Soon the sky grew black with clouds and wind, and the rain came down in torrents. And Ahab drove home to his palace at Jezreel as fast as he could. And the hand of Jehovah was on Elijah, and he girded up his robe, and ran before Ahab's chariot to the gate of Jezreel.

Chapter 3

The Still Small Voice

When Ahab got home, he told Jezebel all that Elijah had done, and how he had killed all her prophets. Then Jezebel sent a messenger to Elijah, saying, "So let the gods do to me, and more also, if I make not your life as the life of one of them by tomorrow about this time."

Then Elijah was afraid, and fled for his life, and came to the southernmost part of Judah, to Beersheba, and left his servant there. But he himself went on further south, a day's journey into the wilderness, and found a juniper tree, and sat down to rest in its shade. And he prayed that he might die, and said, "I have borne enough; now, O Jehovah, take away my life, for I am not better than my fathers."

Then he lay down and went to sleep under the juniper tree, and while he was asleep an angel touched him, and said, "Arise and eat."

Elijah got up and looked about, and saw beside him a cake of bread and a pitcher of water; and he ate and drank, and lay him down again. But the angel of Jehovah came again the second time, and touched him, and said, "Arise and eat, because the journey is too long for you."

Then Elijah got up again, and ate and drank, and went in the strength of that food to the sacred mountain of Horeb; and there he found a cave, and lodged in it.

Then Jehovah passed by. Before Him, a great and strong wind rent the mountains and broke the rocks in pieces, but

Jehovah was not in the wind; and after the wind there was an earthquake, but Jehovah was not in the earthquake; and after the earthquake there was a fire, but Jehovah was not in the fire. And after the fire there was a still small voice. When Elijah heard the voice, he wrapped his face in his mantle, and went out, and stood at the entrance of the cave.

And there came a voice unto him, and said, "What are you doing here, Elijah?"

And he said, "I have been very zealous for Jehovah Sabaoth; but the Israelites have been rebellious and disobedient, they have thrown down Thine altars, and killed Thy prophets, and I, even I only, am left; and they seek my life to take it away."

Elijah felt that he had failed altogether in his work for God, and was helpless and useless. But Jehovah's answer showed that He had still work for Elijah to do. He bade him anoint a Syrian general named Hazael to be king of Syria; and an Israelite general, Jehu, the son of Nimshi, to be king over Israel; and a certain Elisha, the son of Shaphat, to succeed himself as prophet. Hazael and Jehu would punish the sins of Israel against its God.

"Yet," said Jehovah, "I will leave me seven thousand in Israel, all the knees which have not bowed to Baal, and every mouth which has not kissed him."

So that Elijah was not the only faithful Israelite, and his "I, even I only," was altogether a mistake.

Then Elijah left the cave and the wilderness, and went to look for Elisha, and found him ploughing with twelve yoke of oxen before him, and he with the twelfth. As Elijah passed close by, he threw his mantle upon Elisha. And he left the oxen, and ran after Elijah, and said, "Let me, I pray you, kiss my father and mother, and then I will follow you."

And he left Elijah, and took a yoke of oxen, and killed them, and boiled their flesh with the wood of the plough and yoke, and feasted his servants. Then he set out and went after Elijah, and became his disciple and attendant.

Chapter 4

Naboth's Vineyard

There was a man at Jezreel named Naboth, who had a vineyard close to Ahab's palace. Sometime after Elijah's flight to the wilderness, Ahab sent for Naboth, and said to him, "Give me your vineyard for a kitchen garden, because it is near my palace; and I will either give you a better vineyard for it, or pay you its value in money."

But Naboth answered, "God forbid that I should give you the land I have inherited from my fathers." For in ancient Israel each family held its land as a sacred possession, and it was a sin for a man to sell the family estate and leave his children landless.

But, because Naboth would not sell his vineyard, Ahab went home heavy and displeased, and lay down on his bed, turned his face to the wall, and would take no food. Jezebel his wife came to see what was the matter with him, and he told her all about Naboth and the vineyard. Then she said, "Are you really king of Israel, and cannot have a vineyard when you have set your heart on it? Get up and take food, and be cheerful. I will give you Naboth's vineyard."

So she wrote a letter in Ahab's name, and sealed it with his seal, and sent it to the elders, or chief men, of the city where Naboth lived. And when the elders got the letter, they opened it and read it, and did as Jezebel had written. They proclaimed a fast, as if some great sin had been committed, which would bring trouble on the city. They took Naboth, and put him in a conspicuous place before all the people; and they bribed two scoundrels to bear false witness against Naboth. And the two men came in and sat down before Naboth, and accused him before all the people of cursing God and the king.

Then Naboth was condemned, and carried out of the city, and stoned to death; and the elders wrote and told Jezebel that Naboth was dead. When Jezebel got the letter, she told Ahab that Naboth was dead, and he could take the vineyard; and Ahab went down to take possession of it. But when he reached the vineyard, he found Elijah waiting for him.

And he said to the prophet, "Have you found me, O mine enemy?"

Elijah answered, "I have found you, because you have sold yourself to do evil in the sight of Jehovah. God will destroy all your family, so that they shall no longer reign over Israel; and the dogs shall eat Jezebel by the walls of Jezreel."

Then Ahab was much afraid, and lamented, and tore his clothes, and put on sackcloth, and fasted. And the word of Jehovah came to Elijah, "Because Ahab humbles himself before Me, I will not destroy his family till after he is dead."

Not long after, Ahab was killed in battle, fighting against the Syrians, and his son Ahaziah became king in his stead.

Chapter 5

The War with Moab

Not long after Ahab's death, Elijah was taken up to heaven, and Elisha succeeded him as the prophet of Jehovah. About the same time, the new king Ahaziah died, and his brother Jehoram became king of Israel. Now, in the days of Omri and Ahab, Moab had been subject to Israel; and the king of Moab in Ahab's time was Mesha, and he paid Ahab as tribute a hundred thousand lambs and the wool of a hundred thousand rams. But after Ahab's death, Mesha refused to be subject to Israel, and pay tribute.

Then Jehoram, king of Israel, gathered a great army, and the kings of Judah and Edom came to help him against Moab. After marching for seven days, the armies found themselves in a desert where there was no water, and they seemed likely to die of thirst.

And the king of Judah said, "Is there not here a prophet of Jehovah, by whom we may ask counsel of him?"

One of the Israelites answered, "Elisha the son of Shaphat is here, who poured water on the hands of Elijah."

So the three kings went to ask advice of Elisha, and he bade them bring him a minstrel; and, when the minstrel played, the hand of Jehovah came upon him, and he said, "Thus saith Jehovah, make this valley full of trenches. Ye shall see neither wind nor rain, yet the valley shall be filled with water. And Jehovah will give you victory over the Moabites."

So they dug the trenches, and next morning they were full of water. Now, when the Moabites heard that the kings were coming to fight against them, all the fighting men gathered together on the borders of Moab to meet the enemy. And the same morning they looked across to the valley, and the sun shone upon the trenches, and made the water as red as blood. And the Moabites said, "This is blood; the three kings and their armies have quarreled, and fought amongst themselves, and slaughtered each other. Now therefore, Moab, to the spoil."

Down they rushed in a disorderly crowd to plunder the enemies' camps. But, when they came to the camp of Israel, the Israelites rose up against them, and routed them. Then the three kings marched into Moab, and filled up the wells, and cut down the trees, and destroyed the towns, till they came to a great Moabite city, Kirhareseth, and besieged it, and had nearly taken it. But the king of Moab took seven hundred men, and made a sortie, and tried to break through to the king of Edom and kill him, but they failed.

Then the king of Moab took his own eldest son, who should have succeeded him, and offered him up as a sacrifice to the god of Moab, that he might deliver his people. And for some reason, the story does not tell us plainly why, the Israelites gave up the siege, and returned home.

This is the Israelite account of these wars between Israel and Moab, as it has been kept for us in the Book of Kings. We have also King Mesha's account of wars between Israel and Moab, which was found some years ago, written upon a stone monument. Each writer tells us most about the victories of his own people. I will give you a few verses of King Mesha's story.

"I, Mesha, am son of Chemoshgad, of Dibon, king of Moab. My father reigned over Moab thirty years, and I succeeded him. And I erected this stone to Chemosh [the god of Moab], because he saved me from all plunderers, and gave me victory over all my enemies.

"Now Omri, king of Israel, oppressed Moab many days, because Chemosh was angry with his land... but Chemosh [had mercy] on it in my days.... And Chemosh said to me, Go, take Nebo from Israel, and I went in the night, and fought against it from daybreak till noon, and took it.... And I took from it the vessels of Jehovah, and offered them before Chemosh...."

The rest of the inscription is taken up with an account of Mesha's victories, with a list of the cities he took from Israel, and tells us of his buildings and roads. All these successes of Mesha probably followed the retreat of the three kings from Kirharaseth.

Chapter 6

Naaman

In the time of Elijah and Elisha, there was almost constant war between Israel and the Syrians of Damascus. Bands of Syrians often made raids into the land of Israel, and plundered the villages and farmhouses, and carried off the people for slaves. Once a little girl was carried off in this way, and she became a slave in the household of Naaman, a great Syrian general, and waited upon Naaman's wife. Now Naaman was very much thought of by the king and all the people of Damascus, because he was a brave and skilful general, and by him Jehovah had given victory to Syria. But he suffered from the terrible disease of leprosy.

One day the little Israelite slave-girl said to her mistress, "Would God my master were with the prophet that is in Samaria, the chief city of Israel; he would cure my master of his leprosy."

When Naaman and the king heard what she had said, the king sent Naaman to the king of Israel, with a letter, in which was written: "I have sent you Naaman the Syrian, that you may cure him of his leprosy."

The king of Israel read the letter, and tore his clothes, and said, "Am I God, to kill and to make alive, that this man sends to me to cure a man of leprosy? He is trying to find an excuse for quarrelling with me."

But Elisha heard of it, and bade the king send Naaman to him. So Naaman came with his horses and chariots, and stood at the door of Elisha's house. And Elisha sent to him a message, "Go and wash in Jordan seven times, and your flesh shall be healed, and you shall be clean."

But Naaman was angry because Elisha made so little fuss with him, and said, "I thought he would come out to me, and stand, and call on the name of Jehovah his God, and wave his hand over the place, and cure the leprosy. Are not our rivers in Damascus better than all the waters of Israel? May I not wash in them, and be clean?"

So he turned and went away in a rage. But his servants came and said, "My father, if the prophet had bidden you do some great thing, would you not have done it? How much more, then, when he says, 'Wash, and be clean'?"

Then Naaman went and dipped himself seven times in Jordan, as Elisha had told him; his flesh became like the flesh of a little child, and he was clean.

Then he and all his company went back to Elisha, and he said, "I know that there is no God in all the earth but in Israel; now, therefore, take a present of your servant."

But Elisha would take nothing. Then Naaman asked for two mule-loads of earth, to take home with him, and lay down and build an altar on, because he supposed that, as Jehovah was the God of Israel, He could only be worshipped on Israelite soil; and he begged that Jehovah would pardon him, because, as the minister of the king of Syria, he was obliged to go with his master to the services in the temple of Rimmon, the god of Damascus. And Elisha said unto him, "Go in peace." So Naaman departed for his own country; and we will hope that he sent the little Israelite maiden back to her home and her friends, but the story tells us nothing more about her.

Chapter 7

Jehu

Elijah had been commanded by God to anoint new kings for Israel and Syria. The prophetic anointing would be a sign that these kings were chosen by God. Elijah left this task to be performed by Elisha. In the reign of Jehoram, king of Israel, the Israelites were holding the city of Ramoth-gilead, east of Jordan, against the Syrians of Damascus. Jehoram had been wounded in battle, and had gone home to Jezreel to be nursed, leaving his general, Jehu the son of Nimshi, in command of the army. At this time, Elisha called one of his followers; the Hebrew name for them was "sons of the prophets", members of the guild or order of prophets, and bade him take a vial of oil, and go to Ramoth-gilead and anoint Jehu to be king over Israel. So the young prophet, Elisha's messenger, came to Ramoth-gilead, and went into the room where the generals of the army were assembled, and said, "General, I have an errand to you."

Jehu said, "To which of us all?"

He answered, "To you, General."

Jehu went with him into the house, and when they were alone, the prophet poured the oil upon Jehu's head, and said to him, "Thus saith Jehovah, the God of Israel, I have anointed you king over Jehovah's people, Israel. You shall put all the family of Ahab to death, to avenge the blood of My servants the prophets, and all My servants, whom Jezebel slew."

Then he opened the door and fled, and Jehu came out to the other generals, and one of them said to him, "Is all well? Why did this mad fellow come to you?"

Jehu answered, "Surely you knew who the man was, and what he came for."

But they said, "We know nothing about it; tell us now."

Jehu told them that the prophet had anointed him king over Israel. Then all the generals forthwith laid their robes on the top of the steps as a carpet of state or throne for Jehu, and they blew a trumpet, and shouted, "Jehu is king."

Jehu said, "If you really wish me to be king, see that no one is allowed to go from here to Jezreel, to tell King Jehoram that there is a rebellion against him."

Forthwith Jehu set out for Jezreel in his chariot, with part of the army. And when the watchman on the tower of Jezreel saw Jehu and his men, he told Jehoram that a company of soldiers was coming; and the king sent a horseman to see who they were, and ask what they had come for. But Jehu kept the horseman, and would not let him go back to Jehoram. And the watchman from the tower told the king that the messenger had reached the company, but was not coming back. So the king sent another horseman, and this time the watchman reported, "He came to them, but he is not coming back; and the driving is like the driving of Jehu the son of Nimshi, for he drives furiously."

Then Jehoram had his chariot got ready, and drove out to meet Jehu, and they met in Naboth's vineyard. When Jehoram saw Jehu, he called out to him, "Is it peace, Jehu?"

Jehu answered, "How can there be peace, so long as your mother Jezebel practices witchcraft and all her abominations?"

Then Jehoram turned his chariot and fled, crying, "Treason! Treason!" But Jehu drew his bow, with his full strength, and shot an arrow into Jehoram's breast, and the king sank down in his chariot. Jehu bade Bidkar, one of his officers, throw the body into Naboth's vineyard.

"For," said he, "remember how, when you and I rode together behind his father Ahab, Jehovah said that the murder of Naboth should be punished in Naboth's vineyard."

After this Jehu went on to Jezreel. When Jezebel heard that he had come, she painted her eyes, and put on a grand head-dress, and looked out of the window. As Jehu came in at the gate, she called out, "Is it peace? You murderer of your master!"

Jehu looked up to the window, and said, "Who is on my side?"

Two or three officers of the household looked out; and he bade them throw her down. They threw her down, and Jehu drove over her. Afterwards Jehu sent out to have her buried, and they found nothing but her skull, and the bones of her hands and feet. When they told Jehu, he said, "This is the fulfilment of the word of Jehovah, which was spoken by Elijah, saying, 'In Jezreel shall the dogs eat the blood of Jezebel.'"

When Jehu was king, he put down the worship of the Phœnecian god Baal, and was zealous in the worship of Jehovah. And the kings of the house of Jehu were powerful and victorious, especially Jeroboam II, who gained great victories over Syria and the enemies of Israel, so that under him Israel was almost as great as under David and Solomon, because, as

Jehu

the Book of Kings says, "By him Jehovah gave deliverance to Israel."

Amos, Hosea, and Isaiah

Chapter 1

Amos and Hosea

But Israel did not make a good use of its prosperity. There were many rich men, and powerful nobles; many temples of Jehovah, with their priests and sacrifices. But this wealth and power meant terrible misery: men got rich by making others poor; powerful nobles obtained wide estates by depriving weaker men of their land, as Ahab had taken Naboth's vineyard; so that very many families in Israel were landless, and in poverty and distress. The priests and prophets did not try to stop this wrongdoing, but were often themselves cruel and selfish. Even the worship of Jehovah at the high places or temples was superstitious and corrupt; there were idols like the calves at Bethel and Dan, and other gods were worshipped besides Jehovah.

So when Israel was rich and prosperous under its mighty and victorious king Jeroboam, a prophet Amos came to the great temple at Bethel, and declared to all the people who had come to worship there, that Jeroboam should die by the sword, and the Israelites should be carried away captive to a foreign country.

Amaziah, the priest of Bethel, was very angry, and bade Amos leave the country, and not come to Bethel any more. But Amos and another prophet named Hosea and others went on declaring that Jehovah would not put up with the cruelty and oppression and wickedness of the rulers and priests, but that terrible punishment would fall upon Israel. Not very long after, the king of the great empire of Assyria invaded Israel, conquered the country, captured the capital city, Samaria, and carried the Israelites, the ten tribes, captive to distant countries; and they have never been heard of since.

Chapter 2

The Call of Isaiah

All this while, kings of the house of David had been reigning over Judah at Jerusalem, except that, for a short time, Ahab's daughter, Athaliah, who had married a king of Judah, usurped the throne after the death of her son Ahaziah. Judah was never so rich and powerful as Israel; but under a king Uzziah, who reigned about the same time as Jeroboam II of Israel, Judah was strong and prosperous. Its prosperity was followed by the same misery and sin as in Israel. The people worshipped Jehovah, and offered many sacrifices, and celebrated solemn feasts, especially at the temple Solomon had built at Jerusalem; yet these zealous worshippers of Jehovah were often cruel and grasping oppressors, and mingled superstition and idolatry with their worship.

God raised up prophets in Judah as He had done in Israel, to tell the people that He hated the sacrifices and services of selfish, wicked men, and would punish them all the more severely, because they thought they could bribe Him to let them cheat and oppress their fellows by attending public worship, and making gifts to His priests.

The greatest of these prophets was Isaiah of Jerusalem. He tells us how he was called to be a prophet. He says, "I saw a vision of Jehovah in His temple, sitting on a lofty throne, and His robes filled the temple. Above Him were the seraphim, each with six wings, and they cried one to another, Holy, holy, holy, is Jehovah Sabaoth; the whole earth is full of His glory.

The Call of Isaiah

Then the foundations of the thresholds shook, and the temple was filled with smoke. Then said I, Woe is me! for I am undone; because I am a man of unclean lips, and I live among a people of unclean lips; for mine eyes have seen the King, Jehovah Sabaoth.

"Then there flew unto me one of the seraphim, with a hot stone in his hand, which he had taken with the tongs from off the altar; and he touched my mouth with it, and said, This has touched your lips; your wickedness is taken away, and your sin is pardoned.

"And I heard the voice of Jehovah saying, Whom shall I send, and who will go for us?

"Then said I: Here am I; send me."

Then Isaiah tells us how he was sent to warn the people of the terrible punishment that would overtake Judah for its sin. God told him that the people would not heed his warning, but that yet there would be a holy remnant who would be saved.

So for years Isaiah rebuked the kings of Judah and their nobles and subjects for their sins, and warned them of the coming punishment. Most of the people did not heed his warning. Yet there gathered round him a few followers, who believed in his message, and wished to live according to his teaching.

Chapter 3

The Deliverance from Sennacherib

At last punishment came upon Judah in the reign of a king called Hezekiah. He himself believed in Isaiah, and tried to do the will of God according to the prophet's teaching; but many of his nobles went on in their old ways. A good king cannot make his people good all at once.

After the Assyrians had taken and destroyed Samaria, and carried Israel away captive, the people in Judah and the neighboring countries were very much afraid that the Assyrians would treat them in the same way. Many of them wished to get help from the king of Egypt, and to unite all Syria to defy the Assyrians and fight against them. But Isaiah tried to persuade Hezekiah to keep quiet, and to have nothing to do with the Egyptian alliance against Assyria. At last, however, the Egyptian party in Judah persuaded Hezekiah to unite with his neighbors, and with Egypt to fight against Assyria. Then the Assyrian king Sennacherib marched into Palestine with a great army, took many cities, and defeated an Egyptian army that came to help the allies. How he dealt with Hezekiah we learn from one of Sennacherib's own inscriptions, which says, "As for Hezekiah of Judah, who had not submitted to my yoke, I besieged and took forty-six of his strong cities and numberless smaller towns, by battering down the walls and by assault. I took 200,150 prisoners, young and old, male and female, together with horses, mules, asses, camels, oxen and sheep, too many to count. I shut up Hezekiah himself in his royal city Jerusalem like a bird in a cage."

Sennacherib goes on to tell how he gave the cities of Judah to their neighbors, and how Hezekiah submitted, and sent ambassadors to him, and paid him tribute. But Sennacherib does not tell us what happened afterwards. For the end of the story we must go back to the Book of Kings.

Although Hezekiah submitted to Sennacherib, and sent him much gold and silver, Sennacherib sent an army to take Jerusalem. His generals tried to persuade the people to give up the city to them. They said, "Don't believe Hezekiah when he tells you that Jehovah will save you. Has any god ever saved his people from the king of Assyria? All the countries we have conquered had their gods; and where are they? Did they save the people who trusted them? How, then, can Jehovah save Jerusalem from our king?"

But the people gave the Assyrians no answer, and Hezekiah's officers told him what had been said. And Hezekiah tore his clothes, and put on sackcloth, and went into the temple and prayed to Jehovah, telling Him how scornfully the Assyrians had spoken of the God of Israel. And he sent some of his chief officers to Isaiah for advice and comfort. Isaiah sent him a message that his prayers would be answered, that Jerusalem would not be taken, that Sennacherib would not even come to attack it, but would go back to his own country another way.

That night the angel of Jehovah went forth, and slew 180,000 men in the Assyrian camp, perhaps by some terrible disease; and when those who were left got up next morning, they found them all dead corpses. Then Sennacherib, king of Assyria, set off home to Nineveh and stayed in the East till he was murdered by two of his sons.

Jeremiah

Chapter 1

The Putting Down of the High Places

I have told you how at the high places and other temples idols were worshipped, and other evil practices carried on; and how the prophets condemned such worship. Hezekiah did something to put a stop to it; but, when he died, things were worse than ever. His son and successor Manasseh encouraged the evil worship at the high places, and even placed altars to the sun and moon and stars in the courts of Solomon's Temple at Jerusalem. His son and successor Amon followed in his footsteps. Amon was succeeded by his son Josiah, a child eight years old. Of course, while Josiah was a boy, the government was carried on by some of the nobles and princes.

When King Josiah was twenty-one, God raised up a prophet, Jeremiah, who was a young man like the king. When God called him to be a prophet, he said, "Lord Jehovah, I cannot speak, I am but a youth."

"Then," he tells us, "Jehovah put forth His hand and touched my mouth, and said, 'I have put My words in your mouth.'"

Jeremiah, like Isaiah, was commanded to warn Judah that it would be punished for its sins. So the prophet began to preach against the selfishness, oppression, and idolatry of the men of Judah, especially of the nobles, priests, and prophets. For there were many who made a livelihood out of teaching the will of God, but only a few true prophets who really had the word of Jehovah.

The Book of Kings does not tell us anything about Jeremiah; but we may be sure that he would try to persuade Josiah to observe the law of God. We read that Josiah, when he was twenty-six, set to work to repair Solomon's Temple, most likely because he believed Jeremiah, and was anxious to carry out his teaching.

While the temple was being repaired, the high priest, Hilkiah, came to the king's secretary, Shaphan, and said, "I have found the book of the law in the temple of Jehovah."

Shaphan read the book himself, and then took it, and read it to the king. The contents of this law book were very like those of our Book of Deuteronomy, which threatens the Jews with punishment for such sins as the men of Judah were in the habit of committing.

So when Josiah heard it read, he was much distressed, and tore his clothes. He sent his officers to a prophetess named Huldah to ask about the book. She told them that Jerusalem would be punished for worshipping false gods, but that the evil should not come in Josiah's time.

Afterwards the king gathered the people together at Jerusalem, and read them the book. And the king and the people made a covenant, and solemnly promised to do as the book bade them. Then they set to work to clear out of the temple all the altars and vessels and furniture used for the worship of false gods. They destroyed the temples of false gods everywhere, and they broke down the high places. The king forbade the people to worship any more at the high places, and ordered them to sacrifice only at Solomon's Temple, where he and his officers could see that everything was done decently and in order. So Josiah reformed the religion of Judah as far as public worship was concerned.

Chapter 2

The Fall of Jerusalem

Josiah was killed in battle, and probably people took this as a sign that Jehovah did not approve of his reforms. At any rate, his successors went back to the old evil ways. Jeremiah protested, but they took little notice. Once the prophet came forward in the temple at a great feast, and told the people that Jerusalem and its temple would be destroyed, as Shiloh and its temple had been destroyed long ago.

This saying, that Jehovah's one holy temple would be destroyed, seemed so wicked and blasphemous, that the priests and prophets and people laid hold of Jeremiah, and dragged him before the princes of Judah to have him put to death. But some of the princes were his friends, and protected him.

Yet, at one time and another, Jeremiah was greatly persecuted, because he persisted in warning the people of the punishment that must follow their sins. Once he was beaten, and put in the stocks.

Meanwhile, the punishment of Judah was coming very near. The empire of the Assyrians, who had once ruled over Western Asia, had been overthrown by the Chaldeans of Babylon and their allies, and Judah had to submit to them. And now, as in the time of Isaiah, there was an Egyptian party at Jerusalem who wished to join Egypt and the neighboring countries, and rebel against Babylon. But Jeremiah, like Isaiah, tried to persuade the kings of Judah to keep quiet, and to have nothing to do with Egypt. Sometimes they followed Jeremiah's advice, but, as a rule, they revolted whenever there seemed the least chance of success.

The last king of Judah was Zedekiah, one of the sons of Josiah. He, too, rebelled against Babylon, and Nebuchadnezzar, king of Babylon, came against him with a great army. Jeremiah tried to persuade Zedekiah to submit, and he was inclined to do so. But the princes who wished to join Egypt prevented the king from submitting. They arrested Jeremiah on a charge of intending to desert to the Chaldeans, and let him down into a muddy pit, and he sank in the mud. Most likely they meant to let him starve to death in the pit. But Jeremiah had a friend in the king's household, an Ethiopian, Ebedmelech. When he heard what had happened, he got the king's permission to take Jeremiah out of the pit. Ebedmelech provided himself with ropes, and a number of old rags, and thirty men, and went to the pit, and let down the ropes and rags to Jeremiah. Jeremiah fastened the ropes under his armpits, with the rags between his flesh and the ropes. Then they drew him up out of the pit, but he still remained in prison.

Not long after, the city was taken by the Chaldeans. The city and temple were destroyed, many of the people were killed, and many more were carried away captive to Babylon. Some were allowed to stay in Judah, amongst them Jeremiah, who was released from prison, and treated with great respect. But those who were left in Judah fled into Egypt, and took Jeremiah with them; and the last that we hear of the prophet is that he had to rebuke his fellow-countrymen in Egypt, and especially the women, for their wickedness and idolatry.

The New Israel

Chapter 1

The New Temple

The destruction of Jerusalem and the temple, together with the exile to Babylon, mark the beginning of a new Israel. This new Israel was chiefly the survivors of Judah and Benjamin, especially the exiles at Babylon. After they had been some time at Babylon, God raised up prophets, who told the exiles that they should return to their own land, and that Jerusalem and the temple would be rebuilt. About fifty years after the destruction of Jerusalem by the Chaldeans, Cyrus, king of Persia, overthrew the Chaldean Empire, and took Babylon. He allowed the exiles to return to Palestine, and rebuild Jerusalem and the temple. Some of them went to Palestine, but very many stayed in Babylon. Though they still called themselves Israel, they are generally spoken of as Jews, or men of Judah, and their country as Judaea.

The returning exiles went back to a desolate country, and a ruined city and temple. During the exile, neighboring tribes had taken some of the land of Judah. They wished to have a share in building the temple; and, when the Jews refused, they were angry, and did all they could to injure them and hinder their building.

The foundations of a new temple were laid, to the music of trumpets and cymbals; and the priests sang hymns and praised Jehovah, and the people shouted aloud for joy, because the foundation of the temple of Jehovah was laid. But the very old men, who remembered the former temple, wept aloud, and the shouts of joy were mingled with wailing and lamentation, so that the one could not be distinguished from the other. But the noise could be heard a great way off.

After the foundation was laid, the enemies of the Jews persuaded the king of Persia to stop the building, and it was many years before the Jews could get permission to go on with it. But at last the temple was finished, and opened by a solemn dedication, with feasts and sacrifices and great rejoicings.

Chapter 2

Ezra and Nehemiah

The troubles of the Jews were not over when the new temple was built. They were still poor and weak, and had many enemies. They were not so much given to idolatry and superstition as the old Israelites, but still they fell into many of the sins against which Amos and Isaiah prophesied. In times of distress the rich took advantage of the necessities of the poor to get possession of their land, and to sell their debtors for slaves. Some of the Jewish nobles married heathen wives, and gave their daughters to heathen husbands, so that it seemed likely that soon they would worship false gods as well as Jehovah.

But help came from the Jews who had stayed behind in Babylon. There was in Babylon a Jewish priest named Ezra, who was called "The Scribe," because he was learned in the law; and also a Jew named Nehemiah, who held the high office of cupbearer to the Persian king. Ezra came to Jerusalem with a large company of Babylonian Jews. Not long after, Nehemiah was appointed governor of Judah by the Persian king, and also came to Jerusalem. He built strong walls for the city, so that it could not be taken by the enemy, and he made the rich who had taken land from the poor restore it to the former owners, and he set things in order generally.

Now, Ezra had brought with him from Babylon a book of the Law, something like the book found in the temple in Josiah's reign, but with more laws in it, and better suited to the

New Israel. It was either our Pentateuch that is, Genesis, Exodus, Leviticus, Numbers, and Deuteronomy or something very much like it.

Ezra and Nehemiah gathered all the people together in a large open space before one of the gates of Jerusalem. And Ezra took with him the book of the Law, and stood upon a pulpit of wood, which had been specially made for the occasion, and opened the book in the sight of all the people; and all the people stood up. Then, Ezra blessed Jehovah, the great God, and all the people answered, "Amen! Amen!" and lifted up their hands. Then they bowed their heads, and worshipped Jehovah with their faces to the ground.

Then Ezra read the book to the people, men and women, and all who were old enough to understand; and the Levites, or assistant priests, explained the laws to the people. And Ezra read from daybreak to noon, and went on reading every day for a week.

And the people and their priests and rulers solemnly promised by a covenant to keep these laws, as Josiah and his people promised to keep the laws in the book found in the temple.

For the most part, they and the Jews of later generations kept this covenant, and no longer fell into idolatry, or into the old superstitions. But they were often guilty of other sins, and were so busy attending to all the laws that told them what kind of meat to eat, and how often they should wash themselves, that many of them forgot the teaching of the prophets on kindness and justice.

Yet in many ways they knew more about God and His will than their fathers had done, and kept up in the temple the worship of one invisible, all-ruling God without idols. Till our Lord Jesus Christ came, there was a Jewish people in Palestine, sometimes ruled by their own priests, and sometimes by governors appointed by Persian or Syrian or Egyptian kings or by the Romans. Besides these, there were Jews in Babylon, and Jews in Egypt, Jews almost everywhere throughout the Roman Empire and in the East. And all these Jews were looking for a Savior who should deliver Israel, and bring the whole world to know and serve Jehovah.

A Child's Story of
the Life of Christ

by Helen Brown Hoyt

140

Preface

The story of the life of Christ has been written time and time again, yet it is one that is ever fresh and attractive. Little children love to hear it if it is told in language which their minds are able to grasp, and the aim of this book has been to tell the story so simply that the youngest child can enjoy it because he can understand it.

The account recorded in the four gospels has been closely followed, and the order of events is that accepted by the greatest thinkers and writers. Many of the laws and customs of the times have been introduced to make the text more clear.

The writer does not claim originality, but, knowing that all children love to read or hear a good story, she has tried to tell this old, old story in a way that will make them love it and absorb into their own beings the elements of true living which only the life and teachings of the Christ can give.

Introduction

Far away over the sea, on the continent of Asia, is the land of Palestine, which is also called the Holy Land. If you look for it on the map you will find that it is a very small country. Yet, though it is so small, such great things have happened there that all the world knows of Palestine. This story will tell you why it is called the Holy Land, and why so many people love it.

Very many years ago there lived in Palestine a man by the name of Jacob, who was the son of Isaac, and the grandson of Abraham. He had twelve sons, each of whom was the head of a large family called a tribe. The twelve tribes together made a nation which was known either as the Jews, or as the Children of Israel. Israel was another name given to Jacob after he was a man.

The Jews were better than any other people living at that time, just because they worshipped God. There were a good many people then, as there are now, who did not know about the true God in heaven. They made images, or idols, of wood or stone, which they called gods. They prayed to these idols, asking them to take care of them. They even thanked these gods for giving them life and health, and so many beautiful things. They were heathen, for that is what we call those who pray to idols.

Abraham, Isaac, and Jacob were not heathen; they knew and loved the true God, and taught their children to do the same. But the Jews were not always good. They did wicked things over and over again, but after they had done wrong they were sorry for it, and asked God to forgive them. Then they started over again, and tried to do better.

When Jacob was an old man, he and his children and grandchildren went to live in Egypt, and lived there happily a good many years. But the time came when the Children of Israel were not happy; for the kings who were then on the throne were not kind to them. They made slaves of them, and the Jews had to work so hard and so long that they almost forgot their God.

But at last a child was born who had a different life from the rest of his people. He was named Moses, and was brought up by the king's daughter, in the king's palace. He was very wise and learned. He thought a great deal about his people. He could see how badly they were treated, and how unhappy they were, and his greatest wish was to set them free and take them back to Palestine. The time came when God allowed him to do this.

It was hard to get so many people started, and harder yet to make them do as God would have them. They found fault with everything if things did not please them: with Moses, and even with God. There were many years of very hard work for Moses and their other leaders before they were at last settled in their own country, in homes of their own.

For a great many years God was really their king. He gave them laws through Moses, and all their leaders were chosen by God. They all talked with God, and learned from him what to do for the people. But the time came when they wanted to be like the other nations around them and have a king whom they could see, and who could go before their army when it went to war.

The first king was not a good ruler; but after he died a young man named David came to the throne, and David was a good king. He tried to do as well as he could himself, and tried to teach the people to obey the laws of their God.

David belonged to the tribe of Judah, and was born in Bethlehem. He was only a shepherd boy when he was chosen to be king, and for that reason he is often called the Shepherd King. Although he left his country home and went to Jerusalem to live when he was quite a young man, he never forgot the lessons he learned in the fields of Bethlehem. He wrote beautiful songs that show that while he stayed with the sheep, hour after hour, his thoughts were about God and his goodness. It was thousands of years ago that David lived, yet ever since that time people have read and sung these songs, and we can read them now in that part of the Bible called the Psalms. One of them begins, "The Lord is my shepherd." Perhaps you know it.

After David died, his son Solomon became king. He was very rich, and knew so much that he has been called the wisest man that ever lived. He built for the people a beautiful temple where they could meet to worship God. When this temple was built the people promised to always love and obey the God who had been so good to them and to their fathers. If they had remembered this promise, and kept it, they would have been a strong nation even now; but very soon they began to break God's laws. Some of them even began to pray to idols.

After King Solomon died things grew worse and worse, until at last the Jews were conquered by other nations, their cities destroyed, and the people carried away to other countries. After a time some were allowed to go back to Palestine to live, but there has never been a real Jewish nation since that time, and that was a great many years ago.

But the Jews kept up their courage; for their prophets had told them that they should have a king who should rule the whole world, and who should reign for ever and ever. Prophets are men who tell what is going to happen long before it does come; they foretell things. We have men whom we call weather-prophets. By studying the sky, the clouds, and the winds, they can tell what sort of weather we are likely to have. But these Jewish prophets talked with God, and he told them what to foretell, so they never made any mistakes.

These prophets did not all live at one time; nor did they all tell the same things about the king. One said he was to be born in Bethlehem, and was to belong to David's family. Another said when he should be born; and others told something else about his life. Still another said that before he came God would send a great prophet, who would teach the people how to get ready for the Christ, their king.

At the time of our story there had been no prophet for four hundred years; but the Jews, remembering and believing what the prophets had promised so long ago, were looking for their king. For, if the prophets had spoken truly, it was almost time for him to come. They had forgotten that some of the prophets had said that the king was to be poor, and a man of sorrows.

They expected him to come in great power, and make them a strong free nation again.

Although many Jews were now living in Palestine, they were under the rule of the Roman Emperor. The Emperor had so large a country that he could not look after it all himself; but divided it into what were called provinces and appointed rulers to take charge of them for him. The Jews did not like to obey the Roman Emperor, they did not like the rulers who weve sent to them, and they did so long for their own strong king.

Herod, one of the Roman rulers, who was called a king, was very much disliked, and he began to be afraid that he would lose his throne. So to please the Jews he built them a temple, even more beautiful than the one which Solomon had built for them. That one had been destroyed when the Jews were driven out of their country, and the one which had been built when they had returned was now so old that it was falling to pieces.

The temple was not much like our churches, nor was the service like ours. There was one building of two rooms. In the smaller of these only the High Priest went, and only once a year. In the other any priest could go.

Around this building were four large open spaces called courts, separated from each other by walls. The one next to the building was for the priests alone; the next for the Jewish men; the third for the Jewish women, and the fourth for all who were not Jews. No one could go farther than the court in which he belonged. When we speak of people going into the temple, we mean they went into one of these courts.

The priests were the ministers, who did all the work of the temple, and took charge of the services. In those days the people did more than pray to God to forgive their sins. In the temple was an altar, or sort of table covered with brass. On this altar a fire was kept burning day and night. Twice every day a lamb which had just been killed was burned on this altar, and while it was burning the people prayed to God, asking him to forgive their sins, and to destroy the memory of them as the fire was destroying the lamb. This was called offering a sacrifice.

Another thing the priests did was to offer incense. Incense was made of sweet spices, and was very fragrant. While it was burning the people in the courts outside were praying that their prayers might rise to God as sweet and pure and well pleasing as the incense.

One day, just about the time that our story begins, the work of burning the incense fell to the lot of a priest named Zacharias, who had a wife Elizabeth, but who had no children. Both were very sorry for this, and often when they prayed, they asked God to give them a little son. On this day, as Zacharias alone in the temple was burning the incense, and praying to God, he looked up and saw an angel of the Lord standing at the right side of the altar. When Zacharias saw him he was afraid. But the angel said: "Do not be afraid, Zacharias, for your prayer is heard; God will give you and Elizabeth a baby boy, and you must call his name John. He will bring you joy and gladness, and many other people will rejoice that he is born. For he shall be great in the sight of the Lord, and will turn many from their wicked ways, and teach them to love God. This child is the one whom the prophets said would come to make the world ready for the Christ."

Zacharias could not believe what he heard, and asked, "How shall I know that what you say is true?" The angel answered, "God sent me to tell you about it, and because you have not believed my word you will not be able to speak again until the day when it comes true."

The people outside in the courts waited for Zacharias to come back, and wondered why he stayed so long in the temple. When he did come out he could not speak to them. They knew that something had happened, for he made signs to them, but did not speak. When his week of service was over he went to his home in the hill country of Judea, and there, when the time came, the baby boy was born.

Little Jewish children were not named until they were eight days old. When it was time for this baby to be named, the friends called him Zacharias, after his father. His mother said, "No, he is to be called John." The friends thought it was strange to call him that, for no one in the family ever had that name; and, too, it was the custom to call the first boy by his father's name. They made signs to Zacharias, asking how he would have him called. Zacharias asked for a writing talilet and wrote, "His name is John."

The friends wondered still more when the father also chose that name, but they soon had still greater reason for surprise. Zacharias, who had not spoken for so long, began to talk again. Would you like to know what he said first? He thanked God for what had happened, and then told the friends who were with them that the Christ, the promised king, was coming very soon, and that this child of his was the prophet who would teach the people about their king. This story was told all through the hill country of Judea, and the people asked, "What kind of a child will he be?"

The Birth of the Christ

In Galilee, in the northern part of the Holy Land, is the little town of Nazareth. In this town lived a beautiful young woman, loving and gentle and pure. She was named Mary, and was the cousin of Elizabeth.

A little while before John was born, as Mary was sitting alone one spring day, the angel who was sent to Zacharias came to her and said, "God is very kind to you, Mary, for he has chosen you to be the mother of the Christ child. You must call his name Jesus (which means Savior), for he will save the people from their sins. He shall be great, and be called the Son of God, and shall rule the world for ever and ever."

Mary believed what the angel told her, and gently answered, "Let it be to me as you have said." Then the angel left her.

In the early part of the winter the Emperor of Rome, Caesar Augustus, commanded that all the people should be enrolled, which means that they should have their names written down on a roll of paper. Every Jew of the same tribe must have his name written on the same roll. The Jews were very much scattered, and to do this each had to go to the city or town where the fathers of his tribe had lived, because the tribal roll was there.

The Birth of the Christ

Mary and her husband were both of the tribe of Judah, and Bethlehem was the city of that tribe. You remember, do you not, that David was of the tribe of Judah, and lived in Bethlehem when he was a shepherd boy? Because the Jews were so fond of David they called Bethlehem the City of David.

Bethlehem was eighty miles away from Nazareth, and the roads between the two places were very rough and stony, uphill and downhill. It was a hard journey to take. Mary and Joseph could not travel very fast, and when they reached the city the houses were all full, for strangers from every part of the country had come to Bethlehem on the same errand as theirs. They were very tired when their journey was over, but they found no one there ready to welcome them. There was no room for them anywhere, except in a stable.

There they found a resting place, and there that night God gave to Mary the baby he had promised her, the baby that was the long expected King of the Jews.

The poor people in that country often wrapped a long band around their little babies to clothe them, and this sort of dress was called swaddling clothes. Mary wrapped her baby in swaddling clothes, and since there was no other crib for him she laid him in a manger.

In the beautiful valley just outside the city, where David had taken care of his father's sheep so many years before, some shepherds were watching their flocks that night. They watched them day and night, for it was not safe to leave them alone.

Robbers and wild beasts were about, and the sheep might come to harm if left without care.

The shepherds knew that it was time for the Christ to come, and this night they were probably thinking of him and talking one to another, when all at once a bright light shone around them, and the angel of the Lord came before them. They were very much afraid, but the angel said: "Fear not, for, behold, I bring you good tidings of great joy that shall be to all people. For unto you is born this day, in the city of David, a Savior which is Christ the Lord. And this shall be a sign to you: you will find the babe wrapped in swaddling clothes, lying in a manger."

And suddenly there were with this angel a great many more who sang, "Glory to God in the highest, and on earth peace, good will to men."

When the angels had gone away from them into heaven, the shepherds said to one another, "Now let us go to Bethlehem right away, and see this baby, of whom the angels have been telling us."

They started at once and soon came to the city, for it was not more than a mile away. And there they found Joseph and Mary and the baby.

The shepherds were very happy. They had so longed to have the Christ come: now he had come, and they were looking at him. Do you not think that Mary was happy, too, when she learned from the shepherds how they knew of her baby's birth?

She did not talk much about it, but the thought was a comfort to her for the rest of her life. The shepherds went out and talked with everyone whom they met about the wonderful child, and what the angels had said of him; and thanked God for what they had seen and heard, as they went back to their sheep.

When the child was eight days old Mary named him Jesus, as the angel had told her. When he was forty days old he was taken to the temple at Jerusalem. This was done in order to obey a Jewish law that said that a mother must take her child to the temple and offer sacrifices for him. If she could afford it she must take a lamb and a turtle dove for the sacrifice; if she were poor she could take two turtle doves or two young pigeons. As Joseph and Mary were poor, they took two turtle doves.

There was an old man in Jerusalem, named Simeon, who loved God, and who had so longed to see the Christ that God had promised him that he should not die until he had seen the child. Simeon was in the temple when Joseph and Mary brought in the child Jesus. He looked at the baby, and knew at once that this was the Christ he had so longed to see.

He took Jesus in his arms, and thanked God that he had been allowed to see his Christ. "Lord, now I am willing and glad to go," he said, "for I have seen thy Christ; the Savior who has come to make the world brighter and better." Then he said, as he gave the child back to his mother: "This child is born to be a great help to many people, but others will not believe him.

They will speak against him, and will bring much sorrow to him, and his trouble will cause you sorrow too."

While these things were happening in Palestine, there were in another country in the East some wise men who saw a bright new star in the sky. These men studied the stars so much that they knew those that generally shone as they did old friends, and they knew that they had not seen this before. It seemed to tell them that some great thing had happened. They knew that the Jews were expecting a king, and they decided that this star was sent to tell them that he was born; and they thought they should go to honor him.

So, although they lived a long way from Palestine, they took splendid gifts in their hands and went to find the king. They followed the star until they came to Jerusalem, where Herod the king lived. They were sure that a king would be found in a king's house, so they went to Herod's palace and asked him: "Where is he that is born King of the Jews? For we have seen his star in the East, and have come to worship him."

Herod could not answer them. If he had ever heard of the birth of Jesus, it had not interested him enough to make him remember it. But he called together the learned Jews, and asked them where they expected the Christ to be born. They told him that the prophets had said that he should be born in the little town of Bethlehem.

After Herod had found out all he could about the child, he called the wise men and asked them how long it had been since they first saw the star. He wanted to know how old the child was. Then he sent them to Bethlehem, saying to them, "Go and look carefully for the child, and when you have found him bring me back word where he is, that I may go and worship him also."

The wise men then left Herod and went to Bethlehem, following the star until they came to the house where Jesus was. And when they had come into the house they saw the child with Mary his mother, and they fell down and worshipped him. And when they had opened their treasures they gave him their gifts: gold, frankincense, and myrrh. Frankincense and myrrh are costly perfumes.

This is the first time that any child ever had a Christmas present. And when Christmas comes round year after year bringing with it gifts from those who love us, we will remember this story, will we not? And we will think with love of the little child whose birth we celebrate on Christmas Day.

After giving Jesus their presents, the wise men started home again. But they did not go back to tell Herod where they had found the child, for God had told them in a dream that Herod did not mean what he said, that he did not want to worship Jesus, but to kill him. So they went home another way.

When Herod had heard the strangers asking him where they could find the King of the Jews he had been greatly interested, and a good deal worried. He was afraid that he would have more trouble than ever with the Jews if they had a king of their own. So he, too, wanted to find the child. He had expected the wise men to tell him when they went back to Jerusalem just where he could be found, and there would be no more trouble after that.

But the wise men did not come back to tell him. He waited and waited, till at last he found that they had gone to their homes without seeing him again. Herod was very angry when he heard this. "I must find the child." he said; "it will not do to let him live to be king." One of his plans had failed, but he thought of another.

He did not know how old the child king was. But he was sure that he could not be more than two years old. So as he did not know where to find him, he sent his soldiers to kill every boy in Bethlehem that was two years old, or younger. (The word "child" in our Bibles really means boys; Herod did not need to kill girls in order to be sure of killing Jesus.) The soldiers did as they were told, and there were many sad homes in Bethlehem that day. Bethlehem was a very small town, and there were probably not more than twenty or thirty boys there.

But even this plan of Herod's failed to harm the child Jesus. For on the night after the wise men had started for their homes, an angel of the Lord said to Joseph in a dream, "Take the child and his mother and flee into Egypt, and stay there until I bring you word; for Herod will look for the young child to destroy him."

So Joseph took the child and his mother that very night, and left Bethlehem to do as the angel had told him. In Egypt they were safe, for Herod had no power there, and could not touch them, even if he had been able to find out that they had gone there. Probably he never knew that he had not killed the boy king when he sent his soldiers to the city where he had been born.

They lived in Egypt till the wicked king Herod died. We do not know what they did there, or where they stayed, although many stories are told about them. They probably lived very quietly.

After the death of Herod Joseph dreamed again, and again the angel came to him, saving, "Rise, take the child and his mother, and go back to your own land; for they are dead who sought to kill the child." Joseph obeyed this dream as he had the other.

But they did not go to Bethlehem to live; for they heard that, although the king Herod was dead, yet his son Archelaus, who was ruler there now, was a very wicked man. They went to Nazareth, the early home of Joseph and Mary. There Jesus lived all the years of his childhood, and all but three years of his whole life.

We do not know much about him when he was a boy. The Bible says that he was "filled with wisdom," and that he was "in favor with God and man." We know by this that he was a good boy, and was loved by everyone who knew him.

The people in Nazareth were not thought to be very good, and sometimes, when Jesus was older, he was looked down upon because he had once lived in Nazareth. But if the people were not good the country was beautiful. Jesus probably went to school with the other Jewish boys, and studied Jewish history and law, from the books of the Bible. We can also think of him as playing and working in his father's carpenter's shop, and with his mother in the house.

He learned, too, from other teachers than books. The mountains and lakes, the birds and flowers, the storms, the sunshine, and indeed everything he saw or heard, had lessons for him which he was happy in learning.

This was how he became filled with wisdom; because he saw something to learn in everything about him, and was willing to try to learn the lesson.

The Bible tells of a journey Jesus took when he was twelve years old. Every year in the spring there was a great feast in Jerusalem, called the Feast of the Passover; and Jews from all parts of the country went to it. The women and old men commonly rode on mules or donkeys; sometimes on horses or camels. The young men, with long sticks in their hands, walked beside them and led the animals. Children were not generally taken till they were twelve years old; those who did go ran a part of the way, but when they were tired they were given a ride.

Ever so many people travelled together, and had such a good time on the way! They talked and laughed and sang together, stopped at the springs to get water when they were thirsty, and, as they walked along, picked the fruit and berries they found by the roadside. When they were tired they stopped to rest; for many of them had a long way to go.

Thousands of strangers were in Jerusalem when the feast began. Every house was full, and tents were put up for those who could not find room anywhere else.

When Jesus was twelve years old his parents took him, for the first time, to this feast. It lasted seven days, and then the long procession started home again. Jesus was so much interested in what he was seeing and hearing that when the others left the city he stayed behind. His parents did not know this; they supposed that of course he was with some of their friends in the company, and did not look for him until evening. Then he was nowhere to be found, and no one remembered seeing him all day. Think how troubled his parents must have felt! The boy who had never been away from them was lost, and so far away from home, too! They must go back to Jerusalem to find him.

It took them another day to get to the city, so it was the third day before they saw their boy again. Then where do you think they found him? In the temple, hearing the old gray-haired men talk, and asking them questions so wise that they were astonished to find a boy of twelve years who knew so much.

Do you think his parents were glad to see him? His mother hurried to him and said: "My son, why did you leave us? Your father and I have been looking for you, and have been very sad."

Jesus answered her: "Why did you look for me? Did you not know that I must be about my Father's business?" Jesus did not mean Joseph when he said "my Father," he meant God. He was a young boy, but he was very thoughtful, and he knew that there was work for him to do in the world; and that his work was to teach people how his Father wants them to live. He would have liked to have begun his work even now, but it was not yet time for him to do so. He went back to Nazareth with his parents, and was the same loving, obedient boy that he had always been.

Until a Jewish boy was twelve years old he was called a little boy; but after that he was a young man, and was expected to study and work as the young men did. Everyone must learn some trade, or some kind of work by which he could earn his living. Joseph was a carpenter, and he taught Jesus to do carpentry work: to make houses, tables, yokes for oxen, or anything that is made of wood.

So, busy with his studies and his work, Jesus lived at Nazareth till he was thirty years old. We will leave him there for a while, and see what has become of the son of Zacharias.

John, too, grew to be a thoughtful, manly boy; for his father told him what his work was to be, and taught him what he needed to know, to be ready for it. As he grew older he knew that he could not do good work unless he thought, studied, and prayed much about it. To do this he left his home and his friends, and went, to live all alone in the wilderness.

He could find enough to eat there: locusts, and the honey which the bees left in the rocks and the hollow trees. Locusts are something like our grasshoppers, and even now, in that country, people eat a great many of them. There were caves in the sides of the hills, where John could find shelter from the cold and storms, and from any wild beasts that might be about. His clothing was made of the coarse hair which grows on a camel, and was fastened around his waist with a leather belt.

There in the woods he lived alone for many years with nothing to take his mind from his work. At last the time came for him to preach.

There is a river in Palestine called the Jordan, and it was to the banks of the Jordan that John came from the wilderness and began to preach. He was so much in earnest, and spoke so well, that people liked to listen to him; and before long great crowds from all around came every day to hear him.

They all thought he must be the Christ; but John said: "No, I am not the Christ. I am the prophet from the wilderness whose work it is to prepare the way for the Christ, and tell people about him.

"He is to be so much greater than I am that I am not good enough even to be his servant. Your Savior is coming very soon, but he will not save you unless you are sorry for your sins. You must not say to yourselves: 'God will love us because we are the children of Abraham.' You must be good yourselves if you want to be loved and saved."

Over and over again John said to the people, "Repent, and be baptized, every one of you." To repent is to be so sorry for something we have done that we will ask God's forgiveness and try very hard never to do it again. After they repented he baptized them. You know how pure and clean water makes things that are washed in it. So water is used in baptism as a sign that the one who is baptized wants his heart made pure and clean.

John baptized so many people that he is called John the Baptist, but he told them all that the baptism did not make them good; it only showed others that they meant to try to be better men and women. "When the Christ comes," he said, "He will give you a new heart, and that is what you need to be really good."

We should all pray just as David did so long ago: "Create in me a clean heart, God; and renew a right spirit within me." This is not a very long prayer, but it means a great deal; for when we have been given new, clean hearts we will never again do wrong without being very, very sorry, and praying to be forgiven.

The Ministry of Christ

The Opening of the Ministry

One day John was preaching as usual, when a stranger came to him and asked to be baptized.

John looked at him for a minute, and then said: "I need to be baptized by you. Why do you come to me?" For in that one look something in the stranger's face told John that it was Jesus, the Christ, who had asked to be baptized. Although they were cousins, their homes were so far apart that perhaps they had never seen each other.

John knew that the Savior did not need to repent, for he had never done anything that was wrong. He did not want to baptize him, but Jesus said: "I want you to do it. It is right that you should, even if you do not know the reason why." Then they both went into the Jordan, and Jesus was baptized.

When he came up out of the water something in the form of a dove rested on his head, and a voice from heaven said, "This is my beloved Son, in whom I am well pleased." It was God's voice.

Jesus did not wait to talk to the people then; he went off by himself into the wilderness, where he could be alone with God. He wanted to think about the new life he had just begun. He

163

had no home now, for he had given up his home and everything that was dear to him in Nazareth, to spend the rest of his life in doing good to others, and in teaching them how to be happy.

Forty days and forty nights he spent in this wilderness, thinking much of what others needed, but so little about what he himself needed that in all that time he had eaten nothing. Now he felt hungry. Round about him were some smooth stones shaped much like the loaves of bread they used in that country. They were something like our crackers.

Has not the wicked spirit Satan sometimes whispered in your ear, asking you to do something which you knew was not right? Well, that wicked spirit came to Jesus now when he was so hungry, and said: "If you are the Son of God, you can do anything you want to. Just turn these stones into bread." Jesus was able to do this, for in a few days he did something just as wonderful; but he had been asking God for power to help other people, not to help himself. He did not turn the stones into bread, but answered Satan with a Bible verse which means that although we need to feed our bodies we also need to trust and obey God, who has promised to take care of us.

Satan whispered to him again and said: "If you are the Son of God, why do you not throw yourself down from the high roof of the temple at Jerusalem? God will send his angels to take care of you, for he has promised to do so. They will hold you up in their hands so that you will not get hurt. And when the people see angels taking care of you, and not allowing you to fall, they will believe at once that you are the Christ, and they will worship you." Again Jesus answered with a Bible verse. What he said means that although it is true that God has promised to help us when we are in trouble, it is wicked to do things that are dangerous just to see if he will help us.

Satan now took Jesus where he could see a long way off, and as he thought of all the cities lying beyond the hills, filled with people and riches, Satan said: "All these you can have, if you will obey me. The people will be glad to have you for their king if you will not find fault with their wicked ways. Never mind if they are wicked. Try to please them and me instead of trying to please God."

But Jesus answered him: "Go away from me, Satan, I will have nothing to do with you. It is written, 'Thou shalt love the Lord, thy God, and him only shalt thou serve.'" The wicked spirit found that here was a man whom he could not tempt to do wrong, and he went away for that day. Many other times the evil spirit tried to make Jesus do what was wrong, for the Bible says that he was tempted in every way just as we are, but never sinned. That is why our Savior can help us conquer sin, if we ask him; because he knows just how hard it is for us to do right, and just what we need to conquer Satan, After Satan had gone angels came and comforted Jesus.

Shortly after this Jesus went back to the Jordan, where John was still preaching to a great many people. As John looked up and saw Jesus coming toward them, he said to his hearers,

"Behold the Lamb of God, which taketh away the sins of the world." What did John mean? Just this. Before long, Jesus, a pure, gentle man who had never done a wrong thing, would be put to death like the lamb in the temple service, for the sins of other people. After this happened people need not offer sacrifices anymore; for their sins would be forgiven if they asked God to do it for Jesus' sake.

The next day Jesus passed that way again. John the Baptist was there talking to two of his friends, John and Andrew, and seeing Jesus coming; he said again, "Behold the Lamb of God." This time the two men followed Jesus, who, turning round and seeing them close behind him, asked, "What are you looking for?" They answered, "Rabbi" (which means master or teacher), "where do you live?" He said, "Come and see." They went with him to the place where he was staying, and spent the rest of the day there. Andrew was so much pleased with his new friend that he found his brother Simon, afterward called Peter, and brought him to Christ.

The next day Jesus started on a journey to Galilee, and his three new friends went with him. On the way they met a man named Philip, who lived in the same town as Andrew and Peter. Jesus invited Philip to go with them, and he was very glad to do so. Before he went he found his friend Nathanael, and asked him to join them.

Nathanael did not wish to go when he heard that Jesus was from Nazareth. You remember that the people of Nazareth were not thought to be good, so Nathanael did not think a man from that place could be the Christ. But Philip asked him to go and see Jesus before he decided, and Nathanael went with him. After talking for a little while he said, "Rabbi, you are the Son of God; you are the King of Israel." He was as much pleased with the new friend as the others were, and was glad to join the little company on their way to Galilee. There were six in the company now, — Jesus, and the five men, John, Andrew and Peter, Philip and Nathanael, who were dear friends of Jesus the rest of their lives. They are called his disciples, or learners, because they listened to his teachings and learned from him.

On the third day that they were together there was a wedding in Cana of Galilee, and Jesus and his disciples were invited to the feast. When they came to the house, they found Mary, the mother of Jesus, there. The feast lasted several days, and before it was over the wine gave out. What should they do? It would not do to be without any, yet they did not know where to get more. Mary told Jesus that they had no wine, and although he seemed very unwilling to do anything about it, she was so sure that he would help them that she said to the servants, "Do whatever he tells you."

There were six water pots, or large stone jars, outside the door, filled with water. For it is so hot and dusty in that country that the people need to bathe often, and jars for that use are kept outside the doors of most houses. The tops of the jars are filled with fresh, green leaves, and these leaves keep the water clean and cool. Jesus told the servants to empty all the water from the jars. And then to fill them again with clear water. This they did, filling them to the brim.

Then Jesus said, "Draw some out now, and take it to the governor of the feast." This was the chief guest, who had the direction of much of the feast. The servants did as he told them. The governor took a taste of what they brought him, and said: "How is this? At most feasts they serve their best wine at the beginning, and keep the poorest till the last; but here at the end of the feast they are serving their best wine." And it was so, for Jesus had changed the water in the six jars to the richest of wine.

You remember that although he was very hungry in the wilderness a few days before this he would not turn the stones into bread for his own use. Now it was different; other people were in trouble, not he himself. By using this power which God had given him, he could not only do a kindness to these people, but he could also show them that he was different from the other teachers they had known; that he was the Son of God. And so he did what no one else could possibly have done; it was a miracle. It was the first time Jesus had done anything of the kind, so far as we know; but we shall hear of a good many miracles after this, and we shall find that every time that he used this wonderful power during all his life, it was for this very same reason; to do a kindness to someone. He never used it to make himself more comfortable; and, least of all, to make anyone else uncomfortable.

No one was more interested in what he had done than his five new friends. They had known their Master only a few days, but in that time they had learned to love him; and now they were sure that they had made no mistake in believing him to be the Christ, for no one could do such things as this unless God gave him the power.

After the feast was over Jesus and his disciples went to Capernaum, a busy city on the shore of a lake which is known by three names; the Sea of Galilee, the Sea of Tiberias, and Lake Gennesaret. It was a beautiful lake thirteen miles long and six miles wide; and on it were thousands of boats of every kind. There were the warships of the Romans, which were very tiny in comparison with those of our time. There were the little rough boats of the fishermen, and many pleasure boats.

The country around the lake was beautiful also. Mountains and hills sloped down to the shore, and on these mountainsides anything that was planted would grow; for the soil was very rich. Scattered about were fields of wheat, groves of palms, olives, figs, and oranges. Where nothing else was planted, wild flowers sprang up in great plenty. There are a great many kinds of wild flowers in Palestine, many of them very beautiful, with rich colors. A field of these flowers is said to be a wonderful sight that no one ever forgets who has seen it once.

All along the shores of the lake cities and large towns had been built; and Capernaum was one of the busiest of these cities. Roman soldiers were always there on guard, and strangers were coming and going all the time, for Capernaum was a central place, through which people passed in going from one country to another, and from every direction people came here to trade.

It was a place where Jesus could meet and talk with people of many nations. Later in his life he spent much time in Capernaum; for, besides the work which he could find to do right in the city, it was easy to make short trips into the country around. But now Jesus stayed in the city only a few days, for it was time to go to the Passover Feast at Jerusalem.

You remember how delighted he was when his parents took him for the first time to the Passover, when he was twelve years old, and how he loved to stay in the temple? But this time when he entered the temple courts, he was not at all pleased.

Instead of the quietness and respect which belong to the house of God, there was the greatest confusion. Money was being changed, doves and sheep and oxen were being sold, even inside the temple wall. Such a noise as there was! And all the while the temple service was going on!

Jesus saw some small cords which had probably been used to tie the animals. Out of these cords he made a whip, and drove from the temple the sheep and oxen, and the men who had charge of them. He upset the tables of the moneychangers, and their money rolled about on the floor. Then he said to those who sold the doves: "Take these things away from here, and do not make my Father's house a place of business." His voice was stern, and no one dared to disobey him; so the temple court was soon cleared.

You may wonder why they ever thought of doing such things as buying and selling animals in the temple. The reason was that many of the people who came to worship lived a long way from Jerusalem, and could not easily bring with them the animals for their sacrifices; it was better that they should buy them in Jerusalem and near the temple. Then, too, money had to be changed; for nothing but Jewish money would be taken at the temple, and people from different parts of the world had to bring the kinds of money that were used where they lived.

If these things were true, what was there wrong about it? Why was Jesus displeased? It was not because the things were done, but because they were done in the wrong place; for the temple was built to worship God in, not for a place of business. There was plenty of room outside of the temple, and if they had cared about God's house, and keeping it sacred, as God had told them, they would not have wanted to do their selling there. The priests should not have allowed such things to be done; but probably they got a share of the money that was taken, and so they were willing.

These priests were astonished and angry at what was done. They might lose some money if the buying and selling in the temple was stopped. They had another reason, too: they were the rulers of the people, and they did not like to have this stranger come and take the control they thought belonged to them. So they asked Jesus to give them a sign that he had the right to do such things. He answered them in a way that no one understood then; but years afterward the disciples remembered the answer he gave, and then they knew what he had meant.

Jesus stayed in Jerusalem through the Passover week. The Bible says that many people believed that he was the Christ when they saw the miracles that he did, but it does not tell us what these miracles were. One of these men was a very prominent man among the Jews, named Nicodemus. This man wanted to learn more from this wonderful teacher, but he was afraid to have his friends know that he did so. So he waited till one night after dark. Then, when no one could see what he was doing, he came to the place where Jesus was staying.

Jesus was always willing to teach those who wanted to learn from him, and now he was glad to tell Nicodemus about the new life that everyone must live who wants to please God and make the best of himself. He said that because men did not know the best way to live, God sent his Son into the world to teach them; and whoever believes on him and obeys his teachings has this life that goes on forever and ever. He told him that the coming of the Son of God, like the sunshine, brought light into the world, showing people what was good and what was bad. But as people who have been doing wrong do not like to have the light show what they have been doing, but want to hide away in the dark, so these people would like their own wicked ways and thoughts better than those he had come to bring.

After the Passover was over, Jesus and his disciples left Jerusalem and travelled through Judea, until they came to the place where John the Baptist was still preaching and baptizing. Jesus, too, began to preach. At first only a few people listened to him; soon more and more became interested in hearing him talk. Before long the crowds who had been so fond of hearing John, left him to follow this new Rabbi, or teacher. His disciples baptized more than John did. The friends of John did not like to have the crowds leave their master to follow this new teacher; they went to John, finding fault with Jesus and with the people. But John said: "It is just as it should be. I am not the Christ. My work is almost done, but his will be greater and greater. You must take him for your master, and believe what he tells you. He is the Son of God."

Some of the Jewish teachers, too, were envious because he was winning so many friends. They did not like John very well, but they liked Jesus even less. This was because the people who had trusted them and come to them to be taught were leaving them to listen to these two men. Jesus knew that they did not feel kindly toward him, and he thought it best for him to leave Judea for a while and to go into Galilee.

The Beginning of the Work in Galilee

The shortest road between Judea and Galilee lay through the province of Samaria. Few Jews ever took that way, for there had been a quarrel between the Jews and Samaritans hundreds of years before this time, and they had never become friends again. They hated each other so much that the Jews were unwilling to have anything to do with them, and would much rather take a longer journey than to go through their country. And the few Jews who did go there were not always treated very well by the Samaritans.

After they decided to go to Galilee Jesus and the five disciples who were still with him left Judea early in the morning; for the days were so hot that they wanted to travel as far as they could before the sun was high. They took the shortest way, the one through Samaria. At noontime they came to a well, and Jesus, who was hungry, thirsty, and tired, sat down by the well to rest, while his disciples went into the city to buy food. The well was one which Jacob had built when he lived there hundreds of years before, and it was still in use. It was wide and deep, and held water enough for all the people and their flocks.

As Jesus sat there, weary and alone, a woman of Samaria came to this well to get some water. Jesus spoke to her and asked, "Will you give me a drink?" It was a little favor to ask, was it not? Yet the woman was so surprised to have a Jew speak to her that she said: "How does it happen that you, who are a Jew, are asking a drink from me, a woman of Samaria?" This gave Jesus the chance he wanted, and he told her about the Living Water, which was the spirit of love and kindness which he had himself, and which he would give to all who would ask him for it. The woman asked him to give her some of this water; but she did not know what he meant by it. She thought that if she could have some of it she would never need to go to the well again. Jesus did not explain to her what he meant; he began to talk to her about the wicked life she was leading; for she was not a good woman. She was very much surprised that he should know all about her when he had never seen her before, and she was sure he was a prophet. So she asked him one of the questions about which Jews and Samaritans had often quarreled, whether people ought to worship in Jerusalem or in a temple they had built in Samaria. But Jesus told her that neither was necessary; that if people prayed to God in their hearts they would be heard wherever they were. She was not satisfied, and said that when the Christ came he would tell them what was right. Jesus said, "I, who am speaking to you, am he."

The woman was so anxious to tell her friends that the Christ had come that she forgot her water and went right into the city. On the way she met some of her friends, and said to them: "Come and see a man who told me all things that ever I did. Is not this the Christ?"

The disciples had come back while Jesus was talking to the woman, and had been very much surprised; but they said nothing about it. They had learned that their Master had some good reason for everything he did, although they could not understand it. After she had gone they begged him to eat of the food they had brought him. But he was no longer hungry. The chance to help somebody to be better was more to him than food, or anything else. It was this that made him so lovable.

Very soon the Samaritans came to see him, and were so pleased with him that they asked him to stay with them, instead of going to Galilee. He was always glad to stay where he could do good, so he went with them and stayed there two days. In that time many of the people believed from listening themselves to his teaching that he was the Christ, the Savior of the world.

At the end of these two days Jesus and his disciples started again on their journey. They were together, however, only a short time. The disciples went back to their homes, and Jesus travelled alone through the towns of Galilee.

While Jesus had been doing these things John the Baptist had been getting into trouble. John was a preacher who spoke to anyone whom he saw doing wrong, whoever he was, and wherever he was. One day he told King Herod that he was leading a sinful life, and that both he and his wife were wicked people. This was true, but they did not like to hear John say it. They were so angry that they would have killed John if they had dared. But the Baptist had so many friends that thought he was a great prophet that Herod was afraid to do this. So instead of killing him he took him and put him in prison.

Jesus, you remember, was travelling in Galilee. The people there were glad to have him with them once more. Many of them had seen what he had done at the feast at Jerusalem, and others had heard so much about this preacher who talked so well and did so many miracles that they wanted in know him.

In the course of his journey he came to Cana where he had made the water into wine. While there, one day at noon, a nobleman came to him in great haste. He had come twenty miles, from Capernaum, on purpose to see Jesus and ask him a great favor. He had a son at home who was very, very ill; it seemed as if he must die. But the father had known of the miracles of Jesus, and believed that he could make his child well.

So when he heard that Jesus was in Cana he went to him as quickly as he could, and begged him to go to Capernaum and heal the boy. Jesus said to him, "Unless you see wonders you will not believe." But the father only thought of his sick boy, and said, "Sir, come down before my child dies." The Savior looked at the father who seemed to trust him so, and said, "Go home, your son will live." Did the man believe that Jesus had the power to cure a sick boy twenty miles away, without any medicine? Yes, he believed, and went home, sure that he would find him well.

When he was almost home he met his servants coming to tell him that his boy was well. He asked them when he began to get better, and they told him it was at one o'clock, just the time when Jesus had said, "Your son will live." So the nobleman and all his family believed that Jesus was the Christ, and became his friends.

Though the Jews had only one temple they had in every town places where they met to worship when they did not want to offer sacrifices. These were called synagogues. They had only one room. The men sat on one side of the room and the women on the other behind a screen. There was a raised seat for the preacher and ten "chief seats" where the leading Jews sat.

The service was much like ours. There were prayers and hymns, and a passage was read from the Scripture, or that part of our Bible which we call the Old Testament. The most of what our New Testament tells had not yet happened. Anyone could read this lesson, and could explain it afterward, if he had permission from the ruler of the synagogue, who was the man who had the charge of the service. It was the custom for the reader to stand while he read the lesson, and to sit down in front of the people when he began to talk. The hymns they sang were not like ours, and they had no hymn books. What they usually sang were the Psalms, which we can read in our own Bibles. One man, standing in front of the others, led the singing, sometimes singing alone, while the people joined in the chorus.

Soon after healing the nobleman's son Jesus spent a Sabbath day at his old home, Nazareth. As his custom always was, he went to the synagogue, to read the lesson and talk to the people. They handed him the book from which the lesson was to be read, and he found one of the places where the prophet Isaiah tells about the Christ that was to come, and what he was to do to help the people. You can find just what Jesus read to them that day if you look in your Bibles at the first two verses of the sixty-first chapter of Isaiah.

After reading a few words he handed the book to the man who took care of it, and began to talk to the people. He told them that these words that he had just read were even then coming true; that he was doing just the things that Isaiah said the Christ would do.

For a little while they were glad to listen to him, for he spoke very gently and lovingly. But soon they began to ask one another: "Is this not the son of Joseph the carpenter? We know his father and mother, and we know him. He is no better than we are. What does he mean by saying that he is the Christ? How can he do all these things?" They wanted him to do some miracle to prove that he was the Christ.

When they saw he would do no miracle, but only wanted to talk to them, they grew more and more angry, till at last they were too angry to listen any longer. They rose, took hold of him, and led him out of the room to a high hill, meaning to throw him down and kill him. But Jesus passed through the midst of them and went away, very sad.

Jesus went from Nazareth to Capernaum, and there the people made him very welcome. As soon as they heard of his being in the city they crowded around him to hear him talk. One morning as the people were pressing close about him he stood by the Sea of Galilee. There were two fishing boats on the shore of the lake belonging to his four disciples. The fishermen were not in their boats but were nearby washing their nets. Jesus stepped into one of the boats, which belonged to Peter and Andrew, and asked Peter to push out a little from the land. He could talk more easily if the people were not so close about him. Peter did as he was asked. Then Jesus sat down and taught the people.

When he had finished talking he said to Peter, "Now push out into deep water and let down your net for a haul of fishes." Peter had seen enough of his Master to trust him, and obeyed at once. But when they came to the deep water he said, "Master, we have been out all night, and have caught nothing. Yet, because you have asked me to do so I will let down the net." And he let it down. When he began to pull it in it seemed heavy. He looked; the net was so full of fishes that it had broken. He and Andrew could not pull it in, and called to their friends in the other boat to come and help them. John and James came at once, and together the four men pulled in so many fishes that both boats were full, and began to sink. How surprised they were!

Peter, who had obeyed his Master because he loved him, but who had not believed that they would catch any fish, fell down at his Lord's knees and said, "Depart from me, for I am a sinful man, O Lord." He said this, not because he wanted Jesus to leave him, but because he did not feel good enough to be the friend of this wonderful Christ.

Jesus knew what he meant, and after they had taken their boats to land he asked Peter and the other disciples too, if they would not like to go with him and become fishers of men. How could they be that? By helping to save men as their Master was doing; by throwing a net of love around them, which would draw them away from wicked places and wicked companions; then by teaching them to love God and keep his commandments. When Jesus asked if they would do this, they gladly left their boats and nets and followed him. They stayed with him all the time he was on earth, travelling through the cities and villages with him, hearing him teach the people, and learning many things from him in their long quiet talks. After he left them they still tried to teach the people what they had learned from him.

On the Sabbath day they went together to the synagogue at Capernaum and Jesus taught the lesson. Most of the people of this city loved to listen to him; for he knew how to explain what he had read and made the service very interesting.

This day an insane man was in the synagogue. The Jews believed that if a person was insane it was because a wicked spirit got into him which was stronger than he was and so made him do these strange things. They thought that if the evil spirit could be driven out the man would be like other people.

The people were quietly listening to what Jesus was saying when all at once this insane man called out: "Let us alone. What have we to do with you, Jesus of Nazareth? Have you come to destroy us? I know who you are; the Holy one of God."

Everyone else was very much frightened; but Jesus looked at the man and said to the evil spirit, "Be quiet, and come out of him." The man fell to the floor where he tossed about for a few minutes. When he stood again he was like other people. The evil spirit had gone forever. He was insane no more.

Every person in the synagogue was filled with wonder, and one began asking another: "What does this mean? Where does this man get his power? For he commands even the unclean spirits and they obey him." And in all the country round about in Galilee people talked of what had happened here.

After the service was over Jesus and his four friends went to Peter's house, for they were all to take dinner there. Peter's wife's mother lived with him, and when Jesus reached the house he found her very sick with a fever. He went right into the room where she lay. Her skin was dry and hot, and she was in great pain. The Savior stood over her, took her hand in his, and lifted her up. At once the fever left her, and she was well; so well that she was able to get up and wait on the visitors.

The Great Physician

The Jewish Sabbath ended at sunset on the day we call Saturday, and hardly had the sun gone down this Sabbath afternoon when men and women came in crowds to Peter's door. They had heard of what Jesus had done that day, and everyone had brought with him some sick friend whom he wanted the Savior to help. All sorts of people came; men and women, old and young, those who had been sick a little while, and those who had been sick so long that they never expected to be any better. There were also many with evil spirits, like the one who had cried out in the synagogue that morning.

Jesus was tired. Do you think he felt like seeing all these needy people and doing something for every one of them? He did not think of himself. He thought of their pain, and, laying his hands on all the sick ones, he cured them and drove out all the evil spirits.

Early the next morning, long before sunrise, he slipped quietly away from the house and walked out into the country where he could be alone with God and pray. For Jesus, the Son of God, felt that he needed to ask his Father for help and strength to do his work. But he was not alone long. Peter and the other disciples came to him, and said, "The people have come again this morning for help and are looking; for you." Jesus answered: "We must not stay here any longer, for people in other places need us. Let us go to the next towns that I may preach there also."

By this time many of the men and women who had followed the disciples joined them and begged Jesus not to leave Capernaum. But he could not do as they wished. He said, "I must go and preach the Kingdom of God to other cities, also, for that is my work."

So he left Capernaum and went through other towns of Galilee, healing the sick and teaching in the synagogues.

While passing through one of these cities a man who was a leper saw him and kneeled down before him. Now leprosy is a very dreadful disease or sickness that people in hot countries sometimes have; and one who takes the disease almost never gets free from it. He is called a leper, and is not allowed to touch anybody, for a touch might give the disease to the one who did not have it. He must leave his home and live with other lepers, and if he sees anyone coming near him he must call out so that they will keep away. The Jews always called out "Unclean! Unclean!"

But this leper did not cry "Unclean." He went as near Jesus as he dared, fell down before him and said, "Lord, if you are willing you can make me well." The Savior felt sorry for the poor man; he put out his hand and touched him and said, "I am willing; you shall be well." As soon as he spoke the leprosy left the man; he was well.

Jesus said, "Tell no man how you were cured, but go and show yourself to the priest."

The leper must do that to obey the law of the country, which was somewhat like this: If a man who thought he had leprosy found that it was a mistake and he did not have the disease, or if one who was a leper had been cured of his trouble, he must first go to the priest and prove that he was free from the disease. Then he must go through a form of cleansing, and the priest must offer sacrifices for him. After all this had been done he was called clean and allowed to live with his family again. The lepers went to the priests to be sure that they did not have the disease, because the priests were the ones who were taught to know the disease whenever they saw it; and they were the ones who had a right to decide. There were no good doctors, except among the priests, so the people always went to them for such things as this, just as we go to some doctor.

Jesus told this man to obey the law by showing himself to the priest, and being cleansed, but not to say anything about how he was cured. But the man was so happy and grateful that he could not keep still; he went out and told everyone he met that the Lord Jesus had cured him, and he was well.

The news spread fast. People from far and near came to see the preacher who made more wonderful cures than any doctor they had ever known. Jesus needed rest, and for a few days he kept away from the crowded cities and spent the time in the wilderness.

But in a very few days he was ready for work again, and went to his friends in Capernaum. It did not take long for people to find out that he was there again, and crowds came to hear him from that city, and from all the towns in Galilee and Judea.

Scribes and Pharisees were often among his hearers. The scribes were lawyers; they spent much time in studying the Jewish law, and taught the people what they must do to obey it. They were the men who made the copies of the Scriptures. You know they did not know then how to print with machines as we do now. Every book had to be written by hand with a pen, and it took a long time. The books did not look like ours, but were on long rolls of paper, with a stick fastened to each end, so they could be rolled up smoothly. When anyone wanted to read from a book he must unwind the roll until he came to the place he wanted.

The Pharisees were another very important class among the Jews. Jesus called them hypocrites, for they pretended to be one thing when they were something else. They made long prayers at the corners of the streets where people could hear them; and gave money and food to the poor when they would be seen doing it. They were very strict about some things, but their hearts were bad, and when no one was watching them they could not be trusted. They were dishonest and sly and very unloving. These Pharisees did not like Jesus because he had told them they were not honest men. They wanted to find something to say against him.

One day in Capernaum a number of these people had come to the house where Jesus was preaching. The houses of Palestine are not like ours. Many of them are only one story high, and are covered with a flat roof that can be reached from the outside by stairs. This roof is quite useful; for after the sun goes down in the hot summer days families sit on the roof, and even sleep there. A railing around the edge makes it safe. It is very easy to carry the beds up there, for the bed of that country is only a thin mattress or heavy mat which is spread on the floor when needed, but rolled up and put one side when not in use. In the center of the house there is often a large room called the court, and the part of the roof over this court is made in such a way that it can easily be taken off. It was in the court of such a house that Jesus was preaching.

The crowd had filled the house, and the doorway was blocked with those who could get no farther. Four men came bringing with them a man who was sick with the palsy. Palsy, or paralysis is a disease which takes the life from some part of the body. If one has palsy in his arm, he cannot use that arm to help himself: if it is in his throat, he cannot swallow; if it is in the leg, he cannot walk, or even move their leg. This man had the palsy and because he could not walk his friends were bringing him on a bed to see the Savior.

They tried to get in through the door, but the crowd would not make way. What should they do? They must see Jesus! Their friend must be healed. There was another way to get to him besides going through the door, and that they now tried.

The stairs which led to the roof were usually on the outside of the houses in that country. They would have no trouble in going there, for all the people were crowding the door. So they took the sick man up to the housetop, and, uncovering the roof, they let him down, still lying on his bed, to the court at Jesus' feet.

The Savior knew what trouble they had taken to come to him, and it pleased him to have them show such trust that they were willing to do so much hard work. He stopped his lesson and said to the man who was sick with the palsy, "Son, be of good cheer, your sins are forgiven."

You remember there were many scribes and Pharisees there who were trying to find something to say against Jesus, so that they could prove that he was a bad man, who was making the people believe what was wrong. Now they thought they had found something. They said to one another. "This man pretends to be God; for no one can forgive sins but God." They accused him of one of the very greatest sins that any man could commit. Pretending to be God, or to have the power that belongs only to God, or trying to make people think that God is not so great and good as He really is, was called "blasphemy." The Jewish law commanded that any man who spoke blasphemy, or "blasphemed," should be put to death. What Jesus said would have been blasphemy if anyone else had said it. But Jesus was the Son of God, and to him God had given power which had never been given to anyone before.

Jesus knew what they were saying, and he answered them. "Why do you think evil of me?" he said; "which words are easier to say, 'your sins are forgiven,' or 'arise and walk'? But I will show you that I did not say mere words, but that I, the Son of man, have the power to forgive sins." Then he turned to the sick man and said, "Arise, take up your bed, and go to your house." And immediately that man who was not able to get to Jesus without being carried by his friends rose, rolled up his bed, took it under his arm, and walked away. His heart was full of love and thankfulness to God. The crowd, filled with wonder, left the house soon afterward, saying, "We have seen strange things today."

After the people had all gone, Jesus went out to take a walk. While walking he came to the place where Matthew, a publican or tax collector, was sitting at his work. Jesus stopped and spoke to him, saying, "Will you follow me?" Matthew probably knew Jesus, and was glad to be chosen a disciple of the great Master. He arose at once, left his work, and followed the Christ.

The publicans were the men who gathered the money which the Jews had to pay to the Roman Emperor. Some of them were Romans and some were Jews. Probably many of them were dishonest men, who tried to collect more money than they should, especially from the poor. The scribes and Pharisees thought no publican was honest, and never tried to make one of them a better man. They looked down on them all as wicked men, who should not be allowed to associate with anyone who was good.

They hated to pay the taxes, and hated the publicans who collected them, whether they were Jew or Roman. But they hated the Jews who did this work the most, because they thought they should have more love for their country than to help the Romans get money from them. But Jesus did not think as the Pharisees did, and chose Matthew, who was sometimes called Levi, to be one of his disciples.

Matthew very soon made a feast and invited his publican friends to come to his house and meet the Master and the new companions he had chosen. It was the custom then to allow anybody who wished to go into a house where there was a feast, and look on while the real guests were eating. So the scribes and Pharisees followed Jesus to Matthew's house. When they saw Jesus at the table eating with these publicans, they said to the disciples, "How is it that your Master is willing to eat and drink with these wicked people?" Now Jesus heard what they said, and he himself answered them in these words: "They that are well need not a physician [or doctor], but they that are sick. I came, not to call the righteous, but sinners to repentance."

The Pharisees knew what he meant by this answer. He called them the well and the righteous because they thought they were good enough, and did not need help to be better. He who had come to make people's souls well and happy could do nothing for them because they would not take what he offered to give them. That is why he did not work with them. But the publicans, who knew that they were wicked people and were willing to be made better, were the sick; and Jesus, the great Physician, went among them because he could do them good.

And now it was time again for one of the Jewish feasts at Jerusalem, and Jesus went to the feast. Many of the cities in those times were surrounded with strong walls, and in the walls were gates through which the people went in and out of the town. Jerusalem was one of these walled cities, and had five gates. Near one of them, known as the Sheep Gate, was a pool of water, called Bethesda, which means House of Mercy. Water was never very plentiful in Jerusalem, and all the wells and pools were much prized by the people. But they were especially fond of Bethesda, for the water there was supposed to cure disease.

Someone had built around the pool five stone porches, with steps leading down into the water. Here, sheltered from the weather, the sick people could wait until they could step into the pool. They could not do this whenever they wanted to. At certain times only there was a bubbling motion of the water, which they believed was made by an angel going into the pool. Then, as they thought, whoever stepped into the water first was cured of any disease he had. Of course every sick person wanted to be the first, and as no one could tell when the moving of the water would be, the porches were usually filled with the people who were waiting for the time to come.

It was on the Sabbath day that Jesus, walking by this pool of Bethesda, saw in one of the porches a very feeble man, who had been sick thirty-eight years. His friends had brought him to the pool and left him there alone. The Savior saw him lying there, and knowing how long he had been sick he felt pity for him. "Would you like to be made well?" he asked. The poor man did not know that the one who spoke to him was better able to cure him than the waters of Bethesda, and answered, "Sir, I have no one to put me into the pool at the right time, and while I am trying to get there myself, someone steps in before me." Jesus said to him as he did to the palsied man at Capernaum, "Rise, take up your bed and walk."

Strange enough the man did not say: "I cannot do it. I have not walked for thirty-eight years." He felt as if he could walk now. He rose at once and walked away, carrying his bed with him. The Bible does not say that he even stopped to thank the one who had done so much for him, who was soon lost to his sight in the crowd about the pool.

The man had not gone very far when he was stopped by some of the Pharisees, who thought it was wrong to carry anything in the hands on the Sabbath day. They thought it was wrong to cure the sick, or move them in bed, or even to do any of the little things that make sick people more comfortable. When these very strict Jews saw this man with the bed under his arm they said, "Do you not know that it is the Sabbath day, and that it is against the law to carry your bed?" The man excused himself by saying, "He that made me well told me to take up my bed and walk." It seems as if everyone would have been glad that the man was able to do that, but the Jews were not. They asked, angrily, "Who was it that told you to take up your bed?" The man could not tell them, for he himself did not know.

A little while after this they met again in the temple, and Jesus talked with the man about the kind of life he was living. If he had been a really good man he probably would not have had this trouble, so the Christ said to him, "You are well now, but if you keep on doing wicked things something worse may happen to you. Go, and sin no more." The man left the temple, saw the Jews again and told them that it was Jesus who had cured him. Then they crowded about the Savior, and began to abuse him, because he had done these things on the Sabbath day.

Who do you think spent the day in the way best pleasing to God? The Christ, with a heart full of love, doing what he could to help someone who was in trouble, or the Jews whose hearts were so full of hatred to him because he had done what they called wrong that they wanted to kill him?

Jesus was not afraid of them. He told them that he was only doing his Father's work. It made them still more angry to have him call God his Father. He tried to prove to them that he was the Son of God; that he could not do such things as they had seen him do if his Father did not give him the power. He said that if they would trust him they would see still greater works, and asked them if they did not remember that John the Baptist had called him the Christ. More than that, his Father at his baptism had said, "This is my beloved Son." "You study the scriptures," he said, "because you think they will save you; and they tell of me. Why do you not come to me and learn what I can teach you? I know why you do not come. It is because your hearts are not full of the love of God. How can you believe?" After he had said all he wanted to, he left them.

They did not dare to touch him then, but they did not forgive him, and they made up their minds that they would watch him, and see if they could not find something for which they could punish him. It seems very strange that they would not listen to him, and believe what he taught. Probably if they had been better men they would have been willing to listen, and would have learned to love the man who was always doing so much for others. But they liked to be the rulers of the people, and they were afraid that if Jesus were allowed to teach, the people would leave them, and they would lose their power. They were jealous.

One Sabbath not long after this, Jesus and his disciples were walking through a field of grain in Galilee. The disciples were hungry, and as they walked along they picked some of the grain and ate it. It was perfectly right for them to pick this grain, for the Jewish law said that anyone could pick the ears with his hands if he wanted to eat them, but that no one must cut the grain with the sickle and take it home unless it was his.

"Wherever Jesus went now some of the Pharisees followed to see what he was about. So when these men saw the friends of Jesus eating the grain they said to him, "Your disciples are doing what is not right on the Sabbath."

If the law gave the people the right to pick the grain in this way, why was there any reason why the Pharisees should blame them? You remember that these Jews were very strict about some things, although in other ways they were very bad. One of the things they were very strict about was the keeping of the Sabbath. Their law said that they must not work on the Sabbath, and they said that rubbing off the grain with the hands was work. So they did not allow it to be done on the Sabbath. They could not blame Jesus for breaking the law, because he had not picked any of the grain. But they blamed him for allowing his disciples to do so.

Jesus said to them: "The priests in the temple do more work than this when they offer the sacrifices and burn the incense. Do they break the law? If you had any love in your hearts you would not try to find fault with those who have done no wrong."

The disciples went with their Master to the synagogue, and the Pharisees followed. There was a man there who had a withered hand, one which had dried up and was of no use to him. Jesus saw this man, and the Pharisees saw him, too. They wondered if he would dare to do anything for him on the Sabbath day. The Savior knew that they were watching him, but that did not make any difference. He felt displeased with them because they were so hardhearted, and asked them this question: "Which is right, to do good on the Sabbath, or to do evil? to save life, or to destroy it? If any of you men have one sheep and it should fall into a deep hole on the Sabbath day, will you not take hold of it and lift it out? And how much better is a man than a sheep!" There was no answer. Then Jesus said to the man, "Stretch out your hand." He could not possibly have done so a moment before, but now he stretched it out, and it was like the other. How angry this made the Pharisees! They left the synagogue at once and planned how they could stop the work of this teacher.

The New Kingdom and Its Laws

But though the Pharisees were so unkind to him, Jesus had a great many friends in those days. The crowds that gathered around him grew larger and larger every day. The work was too much for him, and he felt that he must have help. He must train some of his friends to go about as he had been doing, and teach the people. He went out into a mountain, and there he stayed all night, praying to God for strength to do his work, and planning the best way to do it.

When it was morning he went down among his disciples, and chose twelve of them for this kind of work. He called them "Apostles." They were: John, James, Simon Peter, Andrew, Philip, Nathanael, and James, another Simon, Thomas, Thaddaeus, and Judas.

While Jesus had been choosing these apostles men and women had been gathering to hear his morning lesson. It was hard to talk to so many when they were pressing so close to him. So he went a little way up the side of the mountain, where he could be just a little higher than they were, and be easily seen and heard by all. The apostles stayed very near him, anxious now to hear every word their Master said; for were they not going out to teach the same lessons that he did?

In clear tones Jesus taught them all, the apostles and the crowds, the most wonderful lesson the world has ever heard. It is called the "Sermon on the Mount"; and ever since it was given every one who has loved the Savior has loved to read that sermon over and over again.

First he gave them the rules for being happy. These are called the "Beatitudes," and every rule begins with the word "Blessed," which means happy.

"Blessed are the poor in spirit; for theirs is the kingdom of heaven." The poor in spirit are those who are gentle, who are willing to be controlled, who do not get angry with one another; who know they are not as good as they ought to be, and are always trying to be better.

"Blessed are they that mourn; for they shall be comforted." To mourn is to be in sorrow because of some loss or some trouble. It does not seem as if being in trouble could make one happy, does it? Yet it does; for then the heart becomes tender, and feels the need of God. If we never had any trouble ourselves we should not know how to feel sorry for others; we should grow selfish and hardhearted.

"Blessed are the meek; for they shall inherit the earth." Those who are meek are patient when things do not go just right; they think more of the needs of others than they do of their own comfort, and they do not try to get the best of places and the most attention for themselves.

"Blessed are they which do hunger and thirst after righteousness; for they shall be filled." Were you ever so hungry that it seemed as if you could not wait another minute for something to eat? And were you ever very thirsty? Jesus said that people who want to be happy must long to be good, just as they long for food, when they are hungry, and for water, when they are thirsty; if that, they will be sure not to do wrong.

"Blessed are the merciful; for they shall obtain mercy." To be merciful is to show kindness to everybody and everything that is living. It is those who love everybody who are loved by everybody, and only those who do little deeds of kindness whenever they have a chance that can expect to be treated kindly themselves.

"Blessed are the pure in heart; for they shall see God." Only by driving out the bad thoughts that come to us, and filling our minds with good, sweet thoughts, can we keep our hearts pure; if we do not think wrong, we will not do wrong.

"Blessed are the peacemakers; for they shall be called the children of God." Now peacemakers do not tell tales or do anything else to make trouble between others. They try to stop a quarrel, when they know of it, and if anyone speaks harshly to them, they give the soft answer which turns away anger. And all those who do this, who try to make this world better by keeping those around them sweet-tempered, are God's own children.

"Blessed are they which are persecuted for righteousness' sake; for theirs is the kingdom of heaven. Blessed are ye when men shall revile you and persecute you, and shall say all manner of evil against you falsely, for my sake. Rejoice and be exceeding glad, for great is your reward in heaven; for so persecuted they the prophets which were before you." Jesus knew that before a great while his disciples would be ill-treated just because they were his friends, and tried to obey his teachings, and these two Beatitudes were given to encourage them when that time came; to teach them that when one is in the right he need not feel afraid to have people say or do whatever they will. God will help him bear whatever comes.

Jesus called his disciples the salt of the earth and the light of the world. Do you know how useful salt is in saving food and making it taste good? Your mother would not think that she could get along without salt. Neither could the world get along without followers of the Christ, who live by their Master's rules.

But if salt should lose its taste it would be good for nothing at all, but would be thrown away. In just the same way if the followers of the Christ forget to live like him, they cannot do any good.

He said that he would give them light; that means he would make them understand his teachings. Then they must let their light shine; must do good works and let people know that they did so because they had been with Jesus and learned of him. A light is of no good if it is all covered up, and not allowed to shine out. So the light Jesus gave them would do the world no good if they did not let it shine.

"Do not think," said he, "that I have come to destroy the laws you already have. You must obey these laws even better than you have done, and I will teach you how to do it. The law says, 'Thou shalt not kill'; but, in God's sight, angry words and hatred are just as wicked.

"The law says, 'An eye for an eye and a tooth for a tooth'; if any one does harm, he must be paid back in the same way. But I say: 'Resist not evil. If anyone strikes you on the right cheek, turn to him the other also.' Do not pay any one back who does you harm, but bear it patiently, and try to do him good.

"The law says, 'Thou shalt love thy neighbor [or friend] and hate thine enemy'; but I say unto you, 'Love your enemies, do good to them that hate you, and pray for those that ill-treat you. You must do these things to be the children of your Father which is in heaven; for he is good to all whether they love him or not. You do not earn praise if you are kind only to those who love you and are kind to you."

He taught them how to be generous, saying, "When you give money or anything else to poor people, it must not be in the synagogue or on the street corners, where people will see you and praise you for what you have done. You must do it in secret and let no one know anything about it."

He also taught them how to pray: "When you pray you must go to some place where you will be alone with God. Then you must not say over a great many words which do not mean anything to you, but must speak to God as you would to your father, whom you love."

It was in this sermon that Jesus taught the prayer which we all know and call the Lord's Prayer — Our Father which art in Heaven.

He spoke to them about spending so much time in getting money and in laying up treasures on earth where there are moths and rust to spoil, and thieves to steal. He told them to trust their Heavenly Father to take care of them as he did of the birds and the flowers. He said, "Look at the birds flying about in the air; they do not sow nor reap, nor gather the grain into barns for the winter. Yet your heavenly Father feeds them. Are you not much better than they are? And why be so troubled about your clothes? Think of the lilies in the field, how they grow. They do not work; they do not make their clothes, and yet Solomon with all his glory and all his riches was not clothed so beautifully as they.

"If God takes such care of the grass and flowers in the field, which today are growing and tomorrow will be put into the fire, will he not be even more willing to take care of you, and give you food and clothes; even you, who have so little faith? So do not be so anxious about your food and your clothes, for only those who do not know our Father need be anxious about them. Your heavenly Father knows just what you need, and if you love him and think more about doing what he wants you to do than about what you are going to get for it, you will be given all that you need."

Jesus did not mean that they were not to do any work; that the men ought not to earn money and buy food and clothes for themselves and their children. Even the birds must fly around and hunt for their food, although God feeds them. So people will always have to work for the money to buy these things, but they must not be anxious and worry about it. And how foolish it is to spend all our time and thought on getting money which will only buy the things we want while we live on this earth! But if we love God, and try to do those things that make our minds and our hearts better, we shall have something in heaven belonging to us. And this treasure cannot be spoiled by moths or by rust. If we are really God's children, he will give us all that we need, if we do the best we can.

Jesus told his disciples not to judge other people; to be sure that they themselves did everything just right before they found fault with what others did, or blamed them for what seemed wrong. For if you are always judging those around you, people will begin to judge you. They will say that you have no business finding fault with them when you do just as bad, or perhaps worse, things yourself. First be sure you are doing right, then you can help others to be better.

Another thing he said was, that if they asked they would receive good gifts from their Father in heaven. "For," said he, "if your children ask you for bread will you give them a stone, which may look like bread, but which they cannot eat? And if they ask for a fish to eat, will you give them something that will make them sick? And do you not think that if you are willing to give good things to your children when they ask, your Father in heaven will be willing to give you what you need, if you ask him?"

Jesus gave them a rule to learn that is worth so much that it is called the Golden Rule, "Whatsoever ye would that men should do to you, do ye even so to them."

Another thing he said to them was, "Enter in at the narrow door; for the door that leads to destruction is very wide, and the road is very broad, and it is easy to find it." But the way that leads to heaven is narrow, and there is only one door and one way to find it: by coming to Christ and doing what he wishes. It is not so easy at first, perhaps, to get into this path; but it is a happier way, because we have our Father with us all the time.

He showed them how to choose their friends, how they could tell when people were good. "Every tree is known by its fruits," said he. "A good tree cannot bear bad fruit, neither can a poor tree bear good fruit. You do not pick figs from a thorn bush, nor grapes from a bramble bush. So it is with people; a good man out of the goodness of his heart does that which is good, and a wicked man out of the badness of his heart does that which is wicked." So we can know by watching people whether they are trying to be good or not.

It was a long sermon that Jesus preached that day, and this is only a very little part of it. Some day you will want to read it all. If everyone learned these lessons and obeyed them, what a happy world we should have! Jesus himself said: "Whosoever hears these sayings of mine and obeys them, is like a wise man who built his house upon a rock. The rain fell, and the floods came, and the winds blew and beat upon that house, but it did not blow over, for it was built upon a rock. And everyone that hears these sayings of mine and obeyeth them not is like a foolish man who built his house upon the sand. The rain fell, and the floods came, and the winds blew and beat upon that house, and it fell. And great was the fall of it."

The Second Preaching Tour

The lesson for the day was over, and Jesus came down from the mountainside to go into Capernaum; for he made his home there now. As they entered the city they were met by some of the Jewish rulers, with a message for Jesus. There was a Roman captain, called a centurion, who had a much-loved servant. This servant had been taken with the palsy, and was very ill. The centurion had heard of Jesus, and, believing that he could heal any sickness, had sent word by these men, begging the Savior to come and heal the servant.

The Jews were glad to do something to help the centurion, because, although he was a Roman, he had been very kind to them, and had built them a synagogue. They urged Jesus to go. The Savior said, "I will go and heal him," and he started at once.

When he was not far from the house he was met by other friends of the Roman captain, with another message; for as he thought more about it, it seemed that he had asked too great a favor of Jesus. And so he had sent this word; "Lord, trouble not yourself to come, for I am not worthy to have you come into my house. Speak the word where you are, and my servant will be well. For you can command disease to go, and be obeyed, just as 1 tell my soldiers to go or come, and am obeyed."

Jesus was surprised to have this Roman trust him so fully. He turned about and said to those who were with him, "1 have not seen such faith as this among the Jews." To the friends of the centurion he said, "Go back to the house, for the servant is already well." The messengers went back and found the servant well, as Jesus had said.

Early the next morning, while it was cool, Jesus started out again in another direction. This time he went to Nain, a city about twenty-five miles from Capernaum. His apostles were with him, and as was always the case in these days, the crowds followed too.

When they reached the gate of the city they met a procession, of very sad people. A woman of Nain, whose husband had died sometime before, had now lost her only son, and friends were carrying him outside the city to bury him. He must have been a boy very much loved, for there was a long procession following him to the grave, and weeping because he had been taken away from them.

Jesus and his apostles joined the procession as everyone who met them was expected to do, to show that he felt sorry for the family. This poor mother was very, very sad. Jesus, seeing her sorrow and tears, said to her. "Do not weep." Then he did something that surprised everybody: he went up to the frame on which the young man was being carried, touched it, and told those who were carrying it to stop.

They did as he said, wondering what was going to happen next. And what do you think did happen? Jesus said. "Young man, I say to you, Arise." The boy, even though he was dead, heard what the Lord said. He sat up and began to talk. Jesus gave him back to his mother, and then went on his way.

The people who had seen what had happened were afraid and began to tremble. They had seen Jesus cure every kind of disease, but could he even bring the dead to life? Surely no one could do that but the Christ. They thanked God for such a Savior, and said: "A great prophet has come among us. Surely God has visited his people."

The story of what Jesus had done spread about throughout Judea until some of the disciples of John heard it. John was still in prison, but his friends were allowed to visit him there, and some of them told their master what they had heard about the great preacher. John sent them to Jesus with this question, "Are you the Christ that was to come, or must we still look for another?"

Instead of answering them in words Jesus showed them the kind of work he was doing. There were the lame and blind and sick people all around him whom he cured and taught. Then he said to John's disciples: "Go back and tell your master what you have seen and heard; how the blind see, the lame walk, the lepers are made well, the deaf hear, the dead are raised to life. And tell him, too, that the gospel is being preached to the poor." Gospel means good news. John had preached the gospel as long as he was allowed to do it, and Jesus was doing it now, and doing as the prophets had said the Christ would do.

After John's disciples had left him, Jesus spoke to the people in words of the highest praise of John the Baptist, who, he said, was the greatest prophet the world had ever seen. Those of his hearers who were fond of John were very glad to hear the Savior speak so well of him, but the scribes and Pharisees, who did not like the rough preacher from the wilderness, were angry to hear him called the greatest prophet.

Jesus told them their actions were like those of little children who would not be pleased with anything. Because John the Baptist lived in a different way and wore different clothes; because he would not go into their homes and live among them, they found fault with him and said that he was not in his right mind. And yet, when he, the Son of God came, living in the way they did, going to their homes and eating with them, they did not think that was right either, and were no better pleased.

That very day Jesus was invited to take dinner with one of the Pharisees who could not quite make up his mind whether this Rabbi was or was not a prophet. This Pharisee was called Simon, a very common name among the Jews.

If a friend comes to visit us, or if we go to visit a friend, there are some things which we must always do to be polite. It is so in every country, but the rules of politeness are not always the same. In Palestine they were very different from ours. As soon as the guest arrived at the house he was expected to take off his shoes, or sandals, and leave them at the door. Sandals could be taken off very easily, for they were nothing but a sole with one or two straps over the foot and one over the ankle.

After he had taken off his shoes the friend was received by the master of the house, who gave him a kiss of welcome, and then led him to his place at the table. Then a servant brought water and bathed his feet, which was very refreshing to the one who had been travelling in that hot, dusty country. It was not hard for the servant to do this, for the Jews did not sit at the table as we do while eating. They lay on couches which were placed at three sides of the table. They rested on their left elbow and left their right hand free to use. As their heads were towards the table and their feet away from it the servant could easily pass from one person to another, bathing the tired feet. The Jews were very fond of bathing. You remember that at the wedding at Cana of Galilee there were six stone jars standing outside the door for the use of the guests.

After his feet had been washed, either the master of the house or the servant poured sweet-smelling oil on the head and beard of the guest. This was called anointing him. Then more water was brought for him to use in washing his hands. This was one of the things in which the Jews were very particular; the hands must be washed before each meal. There was need of the hands being clean, for every one took his bread in his fingers and dipped it in a dish which was passed to all.

Jesus accepted this invitation to dinner, for he wanted to be friendly with all men and do what he could to please them. He took off his sandals at the door, and then went to his place at the table. But Simon, although he had invited the greatest man that ever lived to visit him, did nothing to care for his comfort; his feet were not bathed, he received no kiss of welcome, no water was brought for his hands.

Jesus did not seem to notice that these things were not done; he took his place at the table with the others, and said nothing. Things were going along as usual at dinner when something happened that Simon had not planned. The door was opened and a woman walked in, a woman who was known in the town to be very wicked. She carried in her hand a box of ointment, a sweet-smelling perfume which was very expensive.

It would not have seemed so strange if some man had walked into the house that way, for you remember that such a thing as that happened very often. But to have a woman do so was very strange, for not even the women of the family usually were allowed at the table when the men were eating.

This woman did not mind the staring and angry eyes that were looking at her, but went straight to the feet of Jesus. She had heard the great teacher some time before this, and his talk had made her so ashamed of herself that since that time she had been living a different kind of a life; and when she heard that he was at Simon's house she made up her mind to go there, too, for she wanted to show that she was thankful to him for teaching her to be a better woman.

She did not feel worthy to be his friend, but she could do for him the work of a servant. As she stood behind him, crying, her tears fell so fast that his feet were wet with them, and she wiped them away with her long thick hair. Even though she was crying, she was very happy to be so near her Savior, and she showed her happiness and love by tenderly kissing his feet. Then she took some of the sweet-smelling ointment from her box and rubbed his feet with that.

All this time Simon looked on, wondering that Jesus did not put a stop to what the woman was doing, and saying to himself: "If this man were the prophet they say he is, he would know what kind of a woman this is, and would not allow her to touch him." Jesus, who was looking at Simon, knew what he was thinking about. "Simon," said he, "I have something to say to you." "Master, say on," answered Simon. Then Jesus told him this story: —

Two men owed another man some money, but neither of them had anything with which to pay their debt. One of them owed what would be about eighty-five dollars in our money, and the other about eight dollars and a half. The man they owed knew that neither could pay him, so he forgave them both; neither need pay anything. Then Jesus asked, "Which do you suppose will love him the most?" Simon answered, "The one who owed the most, I suppose." "You have answered right," said Jesus.

He had not seemed to notice the woman before, but now he turned to her and, still talking to Simon, said: "Do you see this woman? I came to your house because you invited me. You gave me no water for my feet, but she has washed my feet with tears and wiped them with her hair. You gave me no kiss, but this woman since I came in has not stopped kissing my feet. You did not anoint my head, but she has poured ointment on my feet. We all know that she has been a very wicked woman, but she will never be so again. She has done many wrong things but they have all been forgiven, and she is so thankful that her heart is full of love."

Simon saw what the story meant: both he and the woman had done many wrong things, although the woman had been more wicked than he. Neither of them could pay God to forgive them, yet because he loved them he had forgiven them both. The woman was so full of love to the one who had forgiven her that she wanted to do all she could to show it; but Simon had not even been polite. Should you not think that he would have been ashamed, when he thought about all that had happened?

Jesus then turned to the woman and said, "You are forgiven, your faith has saved you; go, now, and be happy." The Pharisees were very angry at the strange teacher who told the woman that her sins were forgiven. They were not glad he could make sick people well, and wicked people good. Because he did not teach what they wanted, they would not believe anything he said, and wanted to put a stop to his work.

But if the Pharisees were unkind to him, he still had many friends. The apostles were always with him now, and there were three or four women who helped them all they could.

From early morning till late at night the crowds pressed around the Savior. Many followed him because they liked to hear him talk, many because they wanted him to heal their bodies. Some followed because the crowd did, and still others, like the Pharisees, were jealous because he was so much loved, and wanted to find something in what he did or what he said that was against the law. If they once did that, they could complain of him to the rulers and have a stop put to his teaching.

One day there was brought to Jesus an insane man. Anyone who had a kind heart would have pitied this man very much, for, besides being insane, he could neither see nor talk. But there was only one who could help him. His friends knew that, and so they brought him to the Christ. When the man left the Savior he could see, he could talk, and he was not insane. The Christ had made a well man of him.

It would do no good for the Pharisees to try to make the people believe the man had not been cured; but they said, "To be sure this man can do great things, but he does not get his power from God; he gets it from Satan." They wanted Jesus to show them a sign from heaven if it was not so, but this Jesus would not do. He said that they had seen signs enough to make them believe him, if signs were to be of any use. He said, too, that many other people had believed and been forgiven, after less teaching than they had had.

As he said these things to them a woman in the crowd called out to him, "Your mother is a happy woman to have such a son as you." To her Jesus answered, "Happier still are those who hear the word of God, and obey it."

After this talk the people thought more of him than ever, and followed him in great crowds. There was not a day of rest for him, and he could hardly get time to eat his food.

Two Wonderful Days

His mother and some of his friends became anxious for fear he would get sick working so hard and taking so little rest. One day they tried to push through the crowd to speak to him about it. Someone told Jesus that his mother and brothers were trying to speak to him, but he said, "Who is my mother, and who are my brothers?"

Then pointing to his disciples, he said, "Behold my mother and my brothers." He did not mean that he did not love his mother any longer; for we know that he loved her very dearly. He meant that it would be wrong for him to give up his work even for the sake of such a dear friend as his mother. He meant that others needed him more than she did; and that he must love and work for them as much as a man would love and work for his nearest friends.

So he went on from one city to another, helping people's souls and bodies. If he were near the lake, when men and women crowded to hear him, he often stepped into a boat, as he did that other day, and pushed out a little way from the shore. There he would sit and teach the people who stood on the bank much more easily than he could when standing among them.

One of his favorite ways of teaching was by parable, that is, by a sort of story. He often explained to his disciples what the story meant, even when he left it for other people to guess. This is one of his parables.

A sower went out to sow his seed, and as he sowed some of the seed fell by the side of the path, and the birds came and ate them up. Some fell on stoney places. These sprang up very soon, because the earth was not deep; but when the sun came up they were scorched, and because they had no root they withered away. And some of the seed fell among thorns, and the thorns grew up and choked them. But others fell into good ground and bore fruit, thirty, sixty, or one hundred times as much as was planted.

The disciples asked him to tell them what this parable meant, and this is the way he explained it: —

"I am the sower; the lessons I try to teach are the seed; the people are the ground. When I said that some of the seed fell by the side of the path, I meant that some of the people hear with their ears, but do not think enough about my words to learn them, and do not try to understand them. So, very soon, the wicked spirit, who is always watching, whispers other thoughts into their minds. The good lessons are forgotten, and cannot grow and bear fruit.

"The stony ground hearers understand my teachings, and try to obey them for a time. But they are not brave enough to keep on trying when it is hard to do right, or someone makes fun of them.

"The thorns are those whose minds are so filled with their work or play, with getting money or having a good time, that thoughts of God and what he wants them to do are almost crowded out.

"The good ground hearers are those who try all the time to know and do what is right, and the more they know and the more they do, the happier and the more useful they become."

Here is another parable that Jesus told them about this time:

"The kingdom of heaven is like a man who sowed good seed in his field. At night, when everybody was asleep, an enemy (someone who did not like him) came and sowed tares among the wheat, and went away quietly, without being seen.

"Tares are weeds which look very much like wheat until the seeds are ripe. There is a little difference, but one has to look carefully to see it. But the seed is very bad; it is almost poisonous. If it is picked and mixed with the wheat it makes the people who eat it sick.

"When it was time for the young plants to show, the servants noticed that some were a little different from the rest. They looked closely, and found that they were tares. They went to their master, and said: 'Sir, did you not sow good seed in your field? How is it that there are tares there?' He answered, 'An enemy has done it.' 'Shall we go and gather them up?' asked the servants. But he answered: 'No, for fear that if you try to gather the tares you will root up some of the wheat also. Let both grow together until the harvest time. Then I will say to the reapers, Gather together the tares first, bind them in bundles and burn them; but gather the wheat into my barn.'"

Jesus spoke other parables. One was about a small seed being planted, and a big tree growing from it. Another was about a little yeast being put into the middle of a pan of flour and working its way through the whole mass of dough. These show what great things may come from little beginnings. We do not know how much good a little act of kindness, even a kind word or smile, may do someone who wants just that thing.

Here is another parable that Jesus did not explain to his hearers, and which perhaps you can think out for yourselves. "The kingdom of heaven is like a merchant looking everywhere for good pearls. When he had found one pearl of great price, he went and sold all that he had, and bought it."

All these and many other parables Jesus spoke to the people one day as he was sitting in the fishing boat on the Sea of Galilee. He taught all day, and when evening came he was tired. "Let us cross over to the other side of the lake," said he to his disciples. They were glad to do as he wished.

It was pleasant weather when they started, but before they had been out very long the clouds began to gather. Fishermen on this lake do not like to see clouds look as these did, for they mean high wind, and a storm that comes very quickly. These fisherman disciples of Jesus knew what the danger was, and got their boat ready to stand the wind and rain as best she could.

Jesus was so tired that he laid his head on a pillow that someone had placed in the stern of the boat, and went to sleep soon after they started. The storm came nearer and nearer: at last it was upon them in all its strength. The rain poured, the wind blew a gale, the waves dashed over the sides of the boat. Jesus slept quietly on, and his apostles, knowing how tired he was, did not wake him. They kept at work, doing all they could to save his life and their own.

The water began to fill the boat; it seemed as if they must all drown. Still Jesus did not wake. At last, so frightened that they did not know what else to do, the disciples touched their Lord, and said, "Master, do you not care whether we drown or not?" Jesus awoke, not in the least frightened, and said. "Can you not trust me yet?" Then he rose, and, looking over the troubled water, he said to the waves, "Peace, be still." In a moment the winds had stopped blowing, the water was perfectly quiet.

The disciples, even though they had seen their Master do many wonderful things, were surprised at the sudden change in the weather. "What kind of a man is this," said they, "that even the winds and the waves obey him?"

The storm was over, and they were soon across the lake. They had no sooner stepped on the shore than they were met by two demoniacs, or insane men, who lived among the caves and rocks on the shore. Insanity had made one of these men dangerous. He was wild, and no one could tame him. Many times he had been tied with ropes and chains, but he had worked on them until he had broken them apart. He wandered among the caves night and day, screaming and cutting his body with stones. He was naked, for he had torn his clothes all to pieces.

When this man saw Jesus coming, even when he was far off, he began to cry: "What have I to do with you. Jesus, Son of the most high God? Do not trouble me." The Savior said, "Come out of the man, you unclean spirit." He then asked the man what his name was. He was not yet in his right mind, and still talked about the many evil spirits that were living in him.

He asked Jesus to send them out of him into some pigs that were feeding on the shore of the lake. There were about two thousand in this herd, and just then the whole herd ran down the bank into the sea, and were drowned. The men and boys that were taking care of them started in every direction to tell everyone in the city and in the country what had happened.

People wanted to know if their story was true, and hurried to the shore to find out for themselves. There they found the demoniac, of whom everyone had been afraid, sitting by the Savior, clothed and in his right mind. They were not afraid of him now, for he was like themselves. But they were afraid of the man who could make the evil spirits obey him, and so they begged Jesus not to stay with them any longer, but to go back to his own country. Think what they lost! For Jesus stepped into the boat again, and did what they asked.

The man whom he had just cured wanted to go with him. But the Master said, "No, go back to your friends and tell them what great things the Lord has done for you." The man obeyed, and he, who a few hours before was wild and dangerous, went through all the cities telling that Jesus had made him well.

The Christ and his apostles crossed the lake again to Capernaum, where they found men and women waiting on the shore, glad to see them back. He taught them as usual, there by the seaside.

While he was speaking to them, a ruler of the synagogue, named Jairus, begged him to go home with him as quickly as he could, and save his only daughter, who was dying. She was twelve years old. "My little daughter is just alive." cried the sorrowing father. "I pray you to come and lay your hands on her that she may be made well." Jesus went with him, but the people, not willing to lose sight of him, followed very closely behind them.

Before they reached the house a servant came to Jairus and said: "Your daughter is dead. Do not trouble the Master." Jesus overheard what he said, and, turning to the sorrowing father, he comforted him. "Do not be afraid," said he; "only trust me and she will be made well."

The whole company moved on toward the house of Jairus, and as they drew near they heard the noise of people groaning and crying aloud. They were mourning for the little girl who had died, in the way the people of that country do even now.

They think that the greater the noise the more will people think they loved the child they have lost.

Jesus stepped into the house, followed by Peter, James, and John, the only ones of the company whom he would allow to go in with him. Then they and the father and the mother of the girl went into the room where she was lying. They found it filled with the mourning people, and Jesus said to them: "Why do you cry, and make so much noise? She is not dead, she is sleeping." They thought he did not know what he was talking about, and laughed at him.

Jesus sent out of the room all but the father and mother, and his three disciples. Then, going over to the bed where the child lay, he took hold of her hand and said, "Little maid, arise." The little girl opened her eyes and began to move. Then she got up and went to her mother. Jesus told the astonished parents to give her something to eat, and left the house with his disciples.

While he was on his way to the house of Jairus another wonderful thing had happened. A woman who had been sick for twelve years was in the crowd. She had been to very many doctors, and had spent all her money in trying to find something that would make her well. Yet she had been growing worse every day. The doctors of that time and in that country were not as good as those who take care of us when we are sick, but very likely this was a trouble that no one could cure, even though he had been a very wise and learned doctor.

Somebody had told her that Jesus of Nazareth could cure any kind of sickness, and she was following to see if he could help her. There was something in his looks that made her trust him. "If I can but touch his clothes," said she, "I shall be well." So she worked her way through the crowd till she was close behind the Savior, and then she put out her hand and touched his clothes. Although in her modesty and her fear that the mighty Teacher would be displeased with her, she only touched the hem, or fringe, at the bottom of his long robe, that touch cured her.

She stepped back into the crowd, and would have gone quietly away had not Jesus turned around and asked. "Who touched me?" Peter and the rest of the disciples said: "Master, the people are all crowding around you and pressing you. Why do you ask who touched you?" But Jesus said, "Someone has touched me purposely, and has been made well;" and he looked about at those near him.

The woman, feeling that he was looking at her, came trembling and fell at his feet. Then, before all those people, she told him why she had touched him, and how she had been made well as soon as she put her hand on his clothes. Was Jesus displeased that she chose that way of being helped? Hear what he said to her, "Daughter, it was your faith that made you well: go in peace, and be free from your trouble." She went away well, and was never troubled again with that sickness, and Jesus went on to Jairus' house, as we have been reading.

Two blind men followed him from the house of Jairus, but he did not stop to give them sight, nor pay any attention to them, although they called to him again and again. "Jesus, Son of David, have pity on us." They followed him even to the house where he was staying, and at last Jesus stopped and turned to them. "Do you believe that I am able to do this?" he asked, "Yes, Lord," answered both at once.

The Savior touched their eyes, saying, "I will cure you because you believe that I can." Their eyes were opened, and when the poor men left Jesus they could see.

Jesus did these miracles, not because he wanted to win praise from men, but because he loved to help those who needed him. He healed their bodies that he might win their love. What he had told Jairus he repeated to the men, "See that no one knows of it." Not one of them did as he asked; they all went out and told the story of what the Savior had done for them to everyone they met.

After giving sight to the blind man that day, a dumb man was brought to the house. He was not dumb after Jesus had spoken to him, for Jesus cured him. The crowd who had followed Jesus about all day were ready to worship him now. They said, "Such things were never seen before in the land." But the Pharisees tried again to make them think that he was not good, but that he was able to do such things only because Satan gave him the power.

The long day had come to an end at last; and as the disciples rested at its close, they thought of all that had happened since the evening before. They thought of the dreadful storm on the lake that Jesus had so easily quieted; of the two demoniacs who met them on the other side, especially of the one who looked so fierce and wild till Jesus had calmed him as he did the angry sea. Then there came into their minds the pleasant trip back across the lake, the joyful welcome of the people, the great joy of the woman who had been healed, and the sorrow of Jairus, which had been turned into joy when the Savior gave him back his daughter. They remembered the happy faces of the two blind men who had received sight, and of the dumb man who went away talking. Was it not a busy day?

The Last Ministry in Galilee

Yet most of the days now were just as busy. From morning till night Jesus went about the cities and villages, teaching in the synagogues, preaching to the people wherever they would come to hear him, and curing every kind of disease. He had hundreds of friends now; he was the most noted Rabbi that had ever been known; for what other one could do such wonders? Twice he had even brought back to life those who were dead, and that was the most wonderful of all. One or two of the greatest and best beloved prophets in the Old Testament times had done this, but in such a different way! They prayed to God for the power to work the miracle, as if for a favor; Jesus raised the dead by his own power, for he was the son of God.

Would not the people of Nazareth, who had tried to kill him the last time he was there, be glad to hear him, now that he had so many friends? He had a great interest in the people with whom he had lived so many years. He was neither angry with them, nor afraid of them; and knowing that he could make their lives happier if they would only let him, he longed to help them.

So one day he went to Nazareth and taught in the synagogue. He taught so well that all who heard him were astonished; they could not help seeing how great a man he was, yet they would not believe that he was the Christ whom the prophets foretold. The old question came up again: "Where did he learn so much? How can he do such wonderful things?

Is he not the carpenter, the son of Mary? Do we not know all his family?" Jesus wondered why they would not believe in him, but he could not help them very much when they felt like this, and so he left them, never to go back to Nazareth again, for they would not trust him.

As he went through one village of Galilee after another, and saw so many people needing to be taught, they seemed to him like sheep without a shepherd. He said to his disciples: "There is plenty of work to be done but there are not many workers. You, my apostles, must go out by yourselves now and work as you have seen me work. Do not go yet among the Samaritans or any other people who are not of your own nation. Go only among the Jews, and as you go, preach, saying, 'The kingdom of Heaven is here.' God will give you the power to heal the sick, cure the lepers, and to raise the dead. You need not take food or money or extra clothing with you; the people among whom you work must give you what you need, for one who works deserves to be paid for it. When you go into a city find some house where you will be welcome; if the people receive you, well; if not, they, not you, will be the losers.

"You will not have an easy time doing this work; people will not treat the disciples any better than they have treated the Master; and many men will hate you because you are my friends, if for no other reason. But, if they trouble you in one city go to another. Do not be afraid of any one; for even if they kill your body they cannot kill your soul. God takes care of such little creatures as sparrows; will he not much more care for you who are worth more than all the sparrows put together? So do not be afraid to let men know that you are my friends, and believe my words. Do not try to make your life an easy one; forget about yourselves and think about what others need, and you cannot help being happy; forget others and think of your own needs and you will never be happy." With these words of advice and comfort Jesus sent his twelve apostles out into the country to do their first work among those sheep who were without a shepherd. They went two by two, so that one could help the other.

About this time Herod heard of the work Jesus was doing, and was afraid. There is a saying, "A guilty conscience makes cowards of us all," and this is what was the matter with Herod now. His conscience was troubling him, and that is why he trembled when he heard of the preacher who could make disease or nature or death obey him. Herod did wrong when he shut John the Baptist in prison, but since that time he had done something even more wicked.

When his birthday came around he celebrated it by inviting a large party of the lords and nobles of the land to his palace. His niece Salome helped to entertain the guests by dancing, and Herod was so pleased with the way she did it that he praised her, and without stopping to think what it might mean, said, "You may ask for anything you want, and I will give it to you."

What would you have chosen? Not what this girl did, I am sure. She did not decide herself, but ran out of the room to talk it over with her mother. Now this would have been a wise plan if Herodias had been a good mother, but she was not. She was a very wicked woman; it was to please her that John the Baptist had been put into prison, but even this punishment had not satisfied the cruel woman. She had never forgiven John for what he had said to Herod about her, and she had tried ever since to have him put to death. There were two reasons why Herod would not do this. He was afraid of the people, who thought John was a prophet, and he himself had learned to like John. Now her chance had come. Without a moment's thought she said to Salome, "Tell Herod that you want the head of John the Baptist brought to you on a platter." The girl went back to Herod and told him what she had decided to have.

Now when he heard what she had chosen he was sorry that he had made such an unwise promise; but he would not break it before all these people. So he sent to the prison, had John put to death, and gave the girl what she asked for. Salome took the gift to her mother.

Herod had been unhappy and troubled ever since that day, for he knew that he did wrong in allowing this good man to be killed. Now when he heard of the wonderful Rabbi who was going about the country healing the sick and raising the dead, he was afraid. "Who is this of whom I hear such things?" he said. "I killed John the Baptist, but it must be that he has risen from the dead and is doing all these great works." He wanted to see the Rabbi to know if his fears were true.

Jesus soon heard the sad news of the death of John, for some of John's disciples came to tell him about it, and to tell him also that Herod was asking about him. Because of these things Jesus did not stay longer in that part of Galilee, but went again to Capernaum. There he met the apostles who had come back to report to their Master what they had been doing, and what success they had had.

They were all tired and needed rest, but at Capernaum so many people were coming and going all the time that they could hardly find time even to eat. So Jesus said to the twelve, "Come apart by ourselves into some quiet place and rest awhile." With joy they sailed away, thinking that as no one knew where they were going they could find a place where they could be alone by themselves. They had missed their Master so much, and they had so much to talk about, and so many questions to ask!

But some of the people on the bank, who had heard Jesus speak, watched to see in what direction the boat went. Toward the northeast! They knew a lovely spot in Bethsaida, a lake town about six miles from Capernaum, and made up their minds that that was the quiet place which the Rabbi had chosen. Following the shore, men, women, and children ran to Bethsaida, and when the Master and his disciples reached the place they found the crowd there waiting for him.

It seemed selfish in the people to do this, for Jesus and his friends needed a rest. But did the Master find fault with them or send them away? O no! They were some of the sheep without a shepherd, and as long as the day lasted he taught them all, and helped those who needed healing. How interested everyone was in him! None of them thought of leaving as long as they could hear this great teacher talk! Evening came on, yet they showed no signs of going.

At last the twelve came to Jesus and said: "Master, send the people away that they may go into the towns and country round about for a place to sleep and to buy food. They can get nothing here, for we are in a desert place." Jesus answered, "They need not go away; we will give them something to eat." Turning to Philip he said, "Where shall we buy bread that these may eat?" Philip answered, "Two hundred pennyworth of bread is not enough for everyone to have a little." This would he about thirty dollars in our money, and as Jesus and his disciples were poor men, thirty dollars seemed to them a great deal of money. They did not know what to do.

"Master," said one, "shall we go and buy bread enough for them to eat?" Jesus asked, "How many loaves have you here?" Peter answered, "Here is a boy who has five barley loaves and two small fishes; but what are they among so many?" The loaves were thin cakes, something like our crackers, made of barley meal, and baked so hard that they were broken instead of being cut.

Jesus said, "Make the men sit down on the grass in groups of fifty and one hundred." This was done, and it was found that there were five thousand men, besides the women and children. It was springtime, and as the people in their bright-colored dress sat in groups on the fresh green grass, they must have looked very pretty.

Then Jesus took the five loaves and the two fishes, and, looking up to heaven, gave thanks. Then he broke them into pieces, and gave them to his disciples. What should they do with them? Pass them around as far as they went? They had seen their Master do so many wonderful things that they did not stop to question him now, but began to serve those who were seated. And they kept on serving them till every one of that great company, men, women, and children, had eaten all he wanted both of the bread and of the fish.

When everyone was satisfied, the apostles gathered up the food that was left, for Jesus had told them to gather up the fragments that remained so that nothing should be lost. After they had gathered them together they found they had enough left over of the five barley loaves to fill twelve baskets.

What did the crowd who had seen this great miracle think? Many of them had heard wonderful stories of what this Rabbi could do; many of them had seen what he had done, and been cured by him; but this seemed to them the greatest work of all. Five thousand and more people fed with only five loaves and two small fishes! Could anyone but the Son of God do that?

They became very much excited, and began to shout: "This is he whom the prophets foretold! Our king has come! Jesus is our king, and we will make him king now!"

Jesus knew that they must be quieted at once, for it would bring trouble both to him and to them should the Roman Emperor hear of any such plan. In one way they were right; he was the king the prophets foretold; but he could not make them understand that he was not their kind of a king. He had not come to help them fight battles, or to sit on a throne in Palestine and have men obey him. He had come to teach men that such things do not bring happiness, that their own wicked thoughts and habits were the enemies they ought to fight, and that the way to serve him best was to do the will of his Father.

And so, while men were still shouting, "We will make him king," Jesus told his disciples to get into their boat, sail to the other side of the lake, and wait for him there. He would stay behind and send the people away. Later he would go with them to Capernaum.

The disciples were disappointed. How different the day had been from what they had expected! And now it was very hard to be sent away by themselves, while their Master stayed behind with these excited people. They did not want to leave him; but he said, "Go," and they obeyed.

It was not long before Jesus had sent away the people, and, tired and, sad, he went up into the mountain to pray. He knew that he could not trust these people. They had wanted to crown him king today because he had done something that pleased them. Tomorrow they would be just as ready to join the Pharisees in treating him badly. They were willing to be helped by him, and they enjoyed seeing him work miracles, but they would not try to understand him. From his Father only could he get strength to keep on with his work, and there on that mountain top he prayed for that strength.

Very early in the morning a storm came up, and he thought of his twelve friends out in the boat. Were they in trouble as they were that other night not so very long ago? If they were, they needed him; he would go to them.

The boat was now in the middle of the lake, tossed about by the waves. The wind was against them, and the disciples could not cross the lake, though they were rowing as hard as they could.

About three or four o'clock in the morning they saw something coming toward them that looked like the form of a man walking on the water. The form came nearer and nearer. What was it? A spirit? They were afraid, and cried out. But hark! What did they hear? A voice, which sounded like the one they had learned to know and love so well, saying, "It is I, be not afraid." They thought it must be the Master whom they saw, and Peter called out. "Lord, if it is you tell me to come to you on the water." Jesus said, "Come," and Peter stepped out of the boat. He, too, walked a little way on the sea; but instead of keeping his eyes on the Lord, he began to look down at the waves, how high and angry they looked! He was afraid to take another step, and, beginning to sink, he cried out, "Master, save me."

Jesus stretched out his hand and caught him, saying, "Why have you so little faith in me? Why could you not trust me?" And he led him to the boat. When they were both there the wind stopped blowing. Then all who were on board came and fell down at the feet of the Christ, and said, "Truly you are the Son of God."

They rowed to the shore of Gennesaret, and very soon after they landed it was known by everybody near that they were there. People carried about in beds those who were sick; they even laid the sick in the streets of the villages, and begged Jesus to let them touch the hem of his garment. As many as did this were cured.

When the five thousand had been sent away without being allowed to carry out their plan of making him king, many of them went to their homes disappointed and angry with him. There were some, though, who spent the night in the valley. In the morning these men looked here and there to find the Rabbi. They thought he could not be far away, for they had seen his apostles sail away without him, and later on had seen Jesus going up the mountain alone.

But after looking about for some time without finding him, they decided to go across to Capernaum. Taking other boats which had come to shore during the night, they crossed the lake. What was their surprise when they got to Capernaum to find Jesus there teaching and curing the sick as if nothing had happened. "Rabbi, when did you come across?" was their morning greeting; and they seemed very glad to see him again.

Jesus did not answer their question; he knew why they were so pleased to find him here, and said: "You are following me about not because you want to learn of me, but because you ate of the loaves and fishes which I gave you. Yet how much better it would be if you wanted to be with me to learn of those things which would make your lives so much better and happier. The loaves and fishes which I gave did not satisfy you very long, but I can fill your hearts with that which will satisfy you forever."

In the synagogue at Capernaum he taught the same lesson, for everyone had heard how he fed five thousand people with five loaves and two fishes, and were talking about it. As Jesus spoke to them about doing God's work, someone asked: "What is God's work? What can we do to please him?" Jesus answered, "Believe on the one God has sent to you."

Someone else said: "Give us a sign that God sent you, if you want us to believe you. Long years ago, when Moses led our fathers out of Egypt to their own country, he gave them bread from heaven to eat, and so they knew that he was sent by God." Jesus answered: "My Father gives you the true bread from heaven, for the Bread of God is he who has come down from heaven to give light to the world." But his hearers did not understand what he meant.

"I am the Bread of Life," said Jesus. He that comes to me shall never grow hungry, and he that believes on me shall never be thirsty. But you will not come to me; you will not believe me though I came down from heaven, not to do my own will, but the will of my Father who sent me. Everyone who believes me shall have the life that goes on forever."

Jesus meant by hunger and thirst that great longing to be good, and to love God, of which he spoke in the Beatitudes, you remember. But the Jews did not understand him, and they began to mutter, and again came the old question: "Is not this Jesus the son of Joseph, whose father and mother we know? How is it that he says 'I came down from heaven?'"

This and other things that Jesus taught were very hard for the people to understand, and many, even of those who had been willing to be called his disciples, would have no more to do with him. Jesus turned to his twelve dearest friends, and said. "Will you also go away?" Peter answered for them all: "Where shall we go? No one else can teach us as you can, and we are sure that you are the Son of God." Then Jesus said, "And yet even one of my twelve chosen apostles is not a true friend." He meant Judas, for he knew that he did not truly love him.

About this time some of the Pharisees came to Jesus to complain of what seemed to them a great fault. It was a Jewish custom, which had been followed years and years, to wash the hands before eating. We have seen that they needed to be sure that their hands were clean, because they must touch the food that the others were to eat. But that was not what the Jews meant by this washing of the hands. They did it as a sign to show that their hearts were washed as clean from sin as their hands were washed by the water.

We know that God told them to do a good many things in just this way, as signs that their sins were forgiven; the sacrifices and the burning of the incense were signs. But this was not one of the things which God had told them about. It was something that their teachers thought they should do. Water was scarce, but, even if they had to go a long way to get it, they must not eat without washing their hands; if there was not enough water for both washing and drinking, they must go without drinking.

These men saw the apostles eating without first washing their hands in this way; so they came to Jesus and said: "Why do not your disciples keep the laws of our elders? They eat without washing their hands." Jesus said: "Why do you not keep the laws of your God, instead of putting the laws of men above God's laws? Yours is not true worship, for you honor men more than you honor God." He did not mean that the Jews were wrong in washing their hands, but that it was wrong to think more about that than about keeping their hearts really clean.

After saying this to the Pharisees, he turned to the people standing near, and said, "Not that which goes into the mouth makes a man unclean, but that which comes out of the mouth." He explained this later: It is not what we eat and drink which makes us wicked, but the bad words and wicked thoughts and actions which come from the heart.

The answer which the Christ gave to these Pharisees made them more angry than ever; they went away decided that something must be done at once to stop this man's teaching, and they did all they could to turn other people against him. This was not so hard to do as it would have been a little while before, for a good many were greatly disappointed that he was not willing to be made their king a few days before.

The Christ in Retirement

So many people were now unfriendly to Jesus that it seemed best for him to leave the country for a while; so with his disciples he travelled to Phoenicia, a country north of Galilee, where the people were not Jews. The Jews were very proud of their race, and called everyone who was not a Jew a "Gentile." Sometimes they spoke of them as "Gentile dogs"; and they thought that they were of very little account.

Into this Gentile country Jesus and his disciples went, thinking that perhaps here they could get the rest they so much needed. They went into a house, hoping that no one would know that they were there. But the Savior could not be hid. A woman who lived there had in some way heard that the one who worked such miracles among the Jews was now in her country.

She had a daughter at home who was no comfort to her, for she was insane. So the mother came to the Christ, and, falling at his feet, said, "Lord, Son of David, have pity on me; my daughter is very ill." But Jesus paid no attention to her. The apostles grew tired of hearing her call, and asked their Master to help her and send her away. Said he, "My work is only among the Jews; she is not a Jew."

The woman heard what Jesus said. To be sure she was not a Jew; the Jews would call her, perhaps, a Gentile dog. Yet she needed help and must have it. Coming nearer she cried, "Lord, help me." "It is not right to take the children's meat and give it to dogs," said Jesus. "True, Lord," the woman answered; "but the dogs eat of the crumbs which fall from their master's table."

Her answer pleased the Savior. Here was a woman too much in earnest to be discouraged when he seemed unwilling to help her. She trusted him through it all, and that trust gave her what she wanted. Jesus said to her: "Woman, great is your faith. I will give you what you ask." And from that hour her daughter was well.

After a few days Jesus and his disciples left this part of the country and went to another, near the Sea of Galilee, though still among the Gentiles. There they went up into a mountain and sat down. The people had never seen Jesus before, yet somehow they knew that here was a man different from any one else they had ever seen. Great crowds came to him, bringing with them all their friends that were not well. There were lame, blind, dumb, and deformed, and many others, and Jesus healed them all.

These Gentile people who had never seen the Christ's miracles before, wondered very much at what they saw when Jesus made the lame men walk, gave those who were blind their sight, and made those who were deformed straight and strong like other people, and they praised the God of the Jews, who could help men to do much more wonderful things than their heathen gods ever did for them. Some even thought that Jesus was himself the God of the Jews, and they were not very far from right, for he was the son of God, and the Savior of the world.

One man who was brought to the Savior was both deaf and dumb. Jesus took this man away from the rest of the people; he put his fingers in the deaf ears, then spat and touched the tongue that could not speak. "Be opened," he said; and at once both ear and tongue obeyed him; the man could hear and talk. Jesus asked him and the others he cured, as he had so many times asked the Jews, not to tell how they had been made well. But the more he asked them to be quiet the more they spread the news about.

For three days the crowds stayed with him, forgetting everything but the pleasure in being there. At the end of the three days Jesus called his disciples, and said to them: "I feel sorry for these people. They have been with me for three days, and are now hungry, and they have nothing left to eat. If I send them away hungry, they will be faint before they reach home, for many of them live a long way off."

His disciples must have forgotten just then about the other time that Jesus fed thousands of people with just a very little food that a boy had with him, for they did not say that he, their Master, could feed them, but asked, "Where in this mountain can we find bread enough to feed so many?"

"How many loaves have you?" asked Jesus. They answered, "Seven loaves, and a few small fishes." The Master then commanded the people to sit down on the grass, took the seven loaves and the fishes, broke them in pieces and gave them to his disciples to set before the people.

After every one had eaten all he wanted, the disciples found that the food that was left filled seven baskets full. For the second time Jesus had made a little food grow into enough to feed thousands of people; for there were more than four thousand fed this time.

When the people were satisfied, he sent them away, while he and his disciples went down to the shore of the lake. The twelve were not sent away by themselves this time; the Master entered the boat with them, and together they set sail for Galilee.

Jesus loved Galilee, and he longed to be once more with his own people and have them friendly to him. He had been away for some weeks now, and perhaps he thought they had missed him and would be glad to have him with them once again. So he and the twelve sailed across the lake to their home land.

But no sooner had the boat come to the shore than some of the Pharisees met him, and told him that if he were the Christ he must show some sign to prove it. This Jesus was not willing to do. He had proved it to them a great many times, if they had been willing to believe him. Asking for a sign from heaven was only a way to excuse themselves for not trusting him, after they had seen so many of his wonderful works, for they had seen enough of his miracles to make them believe what he said, if they had not set their hearts against him.

Jesus could do nothing for people who would not believe him, and so with a sad heart he left them and went again to another part of the lake shore. As they were crossing the lake he warned his apostles not to trust the Pharisees, and not to believe their teaching, for they were deceitful men, and would not allow the truth to be told to the people.

The boat landed at Bethsaida, and as soon as they got to the shore a blind man was brought to the Savior. Jesus took the man by the hand and led him outside of the village, There he spat on his eyes and laid his hands on them. Then he asked the blind man if he could see anything. "Yes," said the man, "I see men, but they look like trees walking." The Savior then touched his eyes again, and told him to look up. He did so; men looked like men now, and everything was clear to the eyes that had been blind; the man could see. Jesus then sent him away, saying, "Do not go back into the town, and do not tell anyone in the town what made you see." You remember that this was what he told a great many of those he cured.

Leaving the man, Jesus and his disciples went on their journey, travelling toward the north country again. As they walked slowly along, talking together by the way, Jesus asked the question, "Whom do men say that I am?" The apostles, while on their preaching trip, had heard what people were saying about this famous Rabbi, and they were ready to answer. "Some say you are John the Baptist," said they, "and others think that you are one of the old prophets come back to life again." "Whom do you say that I am?" asked Jesus. Peter answered, "You are the Christ, the Son of the living God."

This answer made the Master happy. This little band of twelve men believed in him if no one else did; and he said: "Simon, you are truly blessed. You have learned this, not from what any man has told you, but because the Father himself has taught you. With friends such as you are my work will go on, even when I am taken away from you."

Then he began to talk with the disciples of things that made them very sad. He said that he would not be with them very long; that in a short time he would go to Jerusalem and there would have to suffer many things from the priests, the scribes, and the Pharisees, who were so very unkind to him, and were trying so hard to find some wrong in him. "They will have things their own way, and will kill me," said he, "but on the third day I will rise again."

It made the apostles very unhappy to hear such sad news. Must their dear Master leave them in that way and never be their king? Could he not save himself from harm? Peter who was very apt to speak without thinking, said, "Lord, this shall never happen to you." But Jesus knew more about it than Peter did; he knew that these things must be; that, though he was king, his throne was in the hearts of men, not in Jerusalem, and that only by his death could he be the Lamb of God, and take away the sins of the world. It was not pleasant to think that such a thing could happen, but he knew that it must be, and that it was right.

So he turned and answered Peter as he did the tempter in the wilderness: "Go away from me, Satan. I do not like to hear you talk so," said he, "for it shows that you want to please yourself, and that you want to have things done in your own way, not as God wills. 1 must suffer these things, if I do what is right; and any man who follows me must do as I have done. He must teach what is right and live right, even if, like me, he has to lose his life for it. But then it is better to lose one's life than to lose one's manhood by doing wrong; for what would a man really gain if he should gain the whole world but lose his own soul?"

One evening about a week after this talk with his apostles Jesus took Peter, James, and John with him into a high mountain to pray, leaving the rest of them at its foot. The disciples finished praying, and as they waited for their Master they began to grow sleepy. At last their eyes were so heavy that they could not hold them open; their heads nodded, and they fell sound asleep.

Jesus prayed a long time, and as he prayed he was transfigured before them. By that we mean that he was altogether changed in his looks. His face shone and glistened like the sun, and his clothing was whiter than any cloth that was ever made, as white as the light of the sun.

Two men were with him, speaking about those things of which he had talked with his disciples: his going to Jerusalem and being put to death there. These men were Moses and Elijah. Moses, who years before had given to the Jews the ten commandments and their laws; and Elijah, one of the prophets whom they most loved. How the Jews worshipped the memory of these men who were now talking with Jesus!

The bright light, or something, waked Peter, James, and John in time to see this glorious sight, and they did not know what to make of it. As they looked the forms began to vanish. They wanted to hold them back, and Peter, without really knowing what he said, called out, "Lord, it is good for us to be here; let us make three tabernacles (or booths), one for you, one for Moses, and one for Elijah."

But even while he was speaking they lost sight of what had so astonished them; a cloud wrapped itself about the bright forms, and they could be seen no more. But hark! did they not hear a voice from the clouds? Surely they did, and the voice said, "This is my beloved Son, hear him." It was the voice of God.

The disciples were so afraid that they hid their faces on the ground; but in a moment they felt the soft touch of their Master's hand and heard his sweet voice saying to them, "Rise, and do not be afraid." Lifting up their eyes they saw no man but Jesus only. Moses and Elijah were gone, but their Savior was left with them, and the Father in heaven had told them to listen to his teachings.

As they walked down the mountain side the next morning to join the other disciples, Jesus said to them: "Do not tell anyone what you have seen just now. Wait till I have gone from you, then you may tell them." How sorry they were to hear him say that! Why could they not go back to tell the people of what they had seen? One of the reasons the scribes gave for not believing in Jesus was that the prophets had foretold that Elijah should come before the Christ. Now if they, who had just seen Elijah, could tell the scribes that he had come, would they not change their minds? Would they not then believe that their Master was the Christ?

But the Master knew best, and he said, "No." He made them understand that nothing would change the minds of the scribes; that John the Baptist was the Elijah who had been promised. Yet though he had come and the people had known him, they had not believed in him, but had allowed him to be put to death. They would treat the Christ in the same way, even if the disciples should tell what they had seen. So Jesus said, "Tell no one until after my death."

As they got to the foot of the mountain they found the other disciples in trouble. They were surrounded by a great crowd of people who seemed to be very angry and excited, and were talking in loud tones. One man among them had his son with him: a boy who was not only deaf and dumb, but who had been very ill.

When the father saw Jesus coming he took his boy to him and said: "Master, I beg you to help my boy, for he is my only child. I have asked your disciples to cure him, but they cannot do it." Even while he was talking the boy was taken with an ill turn, and fell to the ground, where he lay tossing about.

Jesus asked the father how long he had been in this way, and the father answered: "Ever since he was a little child; and when he has had these bad spells he has sometimes fallen into the water, sometimes even into the fire, and I am afraid he will be killed. If you can do anything to help him, will you not do it?"

Jesus said: "Do you trust me? There is nothing I cannot do for one who trusts me." "I do trust you," answered the father with tears in his eyes. "Help me to trust you even more." Then Jesus spoke to the boy who was tossing on the ground, and at once his body became quiet. He lay there so still that the people said, "He is dead"; but Jesus took his hand and lifted him up. He was not dead, he was a well boy, neither deaf nor dumb, nor unlike other children.

The days Jesus had planned to spend in the northern country were now over, and once more the little band started for the south. They travelled through Galilee quietly, without stopping to teach or to cure the sick, for Jesus did not want the Pharisees to know that he had returned.

Very soon after they had come to Capernaum a man came to the door of the house where they were staying, and asked Peter if his Master was not going to pay the tax. This tax was one which the Jews took from their men once a year after they were twenty years old. It was taken in the springtime, and the money was used to pay some of the expenses of the temple service. Peter at once answered "Yes," and went into the house to get the money.

Jesus stopped him, and asked him: "What do you think, Simon? From whom do the kings of the earth take taxes, from their own children or from strangers?" "From strangers," said Peter. "Then," said Jesus, "the children are free. I do not need to pay this tax, for it is money given to God, the King. I am the Son of God, and need not pay taxes to him. Still, that no one may think he has reason to find fault with us, go to the seaside and throw out your hook. Catch the first fish that comes up, and when you have opened his mouth you will find a piece of money; take it, and pay the tax for yourself and me."

While they had been on their way, some of the apostles had talked about who should be the greatest in the Master's kingdom; for they believed that Jesus was the promised king of the Jews, and they could not think of him as any different from other kings. Very many times Jesus had tried to explain it to them, but they could not seem to understand that he would rule the world through his life and teachings, but not sit on an earthly throne. They still hoped that before long he would live in a king's palace in Jerusalem, and that they, his twelve most intimate friends, would be his chief officers.

Jesus did not seem to notice what they were saying at the time, but when they were together in the house at Capernaum he asked, "What were you talking about on the way?" No one wanted to answer him; they were all ashamed to have him know about it, and kept still. But they did not need to answer the question, for Jesus knew what they had been saying.

Sitting down, he called them to come around him, and said: "In my kingdom the one who wants to be first of all shall be last of all, for not the selfish but the unselfish are the great ones. To be great is not to have a high office and make other people serve you; it is to be a servant yourself, to be ready at any time to help those who need you."

He then called a child to him, and when he had taken the little one in his arms he said: "Whoever wants to be great in the kingdom of heaven must be like this little child, loving and obedient and trustful. This child does what he knows how to do without thinking whether he has a high or a low place, and all the time he is growing stronger, and better able to fill any place which God may give him. This is the spirit which everyone must have who belongs to my kingdom; for unless you become as little children you cannot enter into it."

Though Jesus did not go out to work among the people, he was not idle in these days. There was so much the twelve needed to know before they could do his work, that he spent his time in teaching them. Some of the words he said to them are very precious to us now. He taught them that the one who did anything for the love of the Christ would have his reward in the love of his Father in heaven. Even as little a thing as giving a cup of cold water to someone who was thirsty was enough to win that love, if they only gave it because they wanted to do something for the Christ who had done so much for them. Anyone, even the youngest and weakest can get this reward, for it is not given in return for our doing great things, but in return for our great love. And the love of our heavenly Father is the greatest reward that anyone can have.

He showed them what a terrible thing it is to make any one do wrong, and how carefully we should guard against it. He said to them that it would be better for a person to give up everything in this world, rather than to do what was displeasing to the heavenly Father.

He told them that just as a man was glad to find a lamb which had been lost, even though he had a great many more, so the Father was unwilling that anyone, even a child, that trusted him should be lost.

Another thing he said to his disciples was that if two or three people met together to pray for something they wanted very much, he would be there with them, though they could not see him, and would give them what they asked for. Of course we must understand that God will not give us something that is bad for us just because two or three ask him, any more than a good father on earth will give his children something that will hurt them, even if they all ask for it. Sometimes we think God does not answer our prayers, because he does not give us what we ask for. But perhaps what we have been praying for would be very bad for us, and the best answer our Father could give us was to say "no."

After he had told them all these things Peter asked him how often he ought to forgive his brother, if he did him wrong. "Until seven times?" he asked, thinking he had said a great many. But Jesus replied, "I do not say 'till seven times,' but until seventy times seven." And then he told them this parable: —

The kingdom of heaven is like a certain king who began to look over the accounts which he kept with his servants. One of them he found owed him ten thousand talents. That was a very, very large sum of money, probably more than twelve million dollars. The servant did not have enough money to pay such a bill. So the king commanded that he should be put in chains, and that his wife, his children, and all that he had should be sold to get the money to pay the debt.

The servant could not bear to think that his family must be sold as slaves; he fell down at the king's feet and begged him not to do it, saying, "Lord, if you will have patience with me, I will pay you all that I owe you." He looked so troubled and begged so hard that the king had pity on him, and told him he need not pay the debt; he would forgive him all he owed. He then commanded the officers to let him go free.

This same man, when he had gone away from the king, found another who owed him sixteen dollars. This man was poor and could not pay even so small a sum. The king's servant took this poor man by the throat, and said. "Pay me what you owe me!" His debtor cried to him as he had to the king: "If you will be patient with me I will pay you all." But he would not, and had the man put into prison until he could pay the debt. The king's servant had just been forgiven a great debt, and had a chance to show a kindness to someone else. But he would not.

Now other servants of the king who saw this told their master all about it. When he heard the story he was very angry. He sent for his servant, and said to him: "You wicked servant! I forgave you all that great debt because I was sorry for you. Ought you not to have had pity as well on the man who owed you?" Then he ordered his officers to take the man to prison, and to keep him there till he paid his debt.

After telling this story Jesus said, "So will my heavenly Father do to you if you do not from your hearts forgive those who wrong you."

Autumn Visits to Jerusalem and Perea

Day after day Jesus spent in this quiet way, training his disciples for their work. At last it came time for the Jewish Feast of Tabernacles. This was held in Jerusalem, in the autumn, a little earlier than our Thanksgiving. It lasted eight days, and while it lasted none of the Jews lived in their homes, but made for themselves tabernacles, or booths, of the green branches of trees. These booths were put up all over the city: on the house tops, in the courts, or in the streets.

Jesus had not been in Jerusalem now for a year and a half. When it was time to go to this feast some of his relatives urged him to go with them. "You have disciples there who want to see what you are doing," said they. "No one who wants the world to know what he is doing does things in secret. If you can do such wonderful things as are told of you, you should show yourself where everyone can see you." They said, "If you can," for even they, his relatives, did not believe that he was the Christ.

But Jesus was not yet ready to go to the feast, and he told them to go without him. "The people do not hate you, for you think as they do," said he, "but they do hate me, for I find fault with the way they live. The time for me to show myself to the people at Jerusalem has not yet come." So they started for Jerusalem, leaving him behind. A little later, when the right time had come, he went to the feast with his disciples.

The people at the feast were asking: "Where is Jesus? Is he not coming to the feast?" Not seeing him they began to talk about him among themselves. Some of them said, "He is a good man." "No," said others, "he is teaching the people what is wrong." His friends did not dare to talk much about him, for they were afraid of the leaders of the Jews, the Pharisees, who hated him.

One day, in the middle of the feast, to every one's surprise, Jesus walked into the temple and began to teach. No one knew how he got there, but there he was. He talked so well that even his enemies could not help liking to hear him, and they wondered how a man who had never studied in their schools could know so much.

Jesus heard the questions and answered them himself. He told them that he spoke about the things that he had learned from his Father in heaven, and that anyone that knew God must know that his teachings were true. The reason why they did not understand him was, he said, because they did not really know and obey God, even though they made a great show of loving him and obeying his laws.

"If it is God's law which says 'Thou shalt not kill,' why are you planning to kill me?" They were much surprised that he should know of their plan to kill him, and tried to make him think it was not so. But Jesus knew it was true.

"I did one good deed which you will never forgive," he said. "If your priests do work on the Sabbath, in order to be sure that the law that Moses gave you is not broken, why are you angry with me because I made a man entirely well on the Sabbath? You call it something very wicked, and yet it was only an act of kindness. Why are you not fair to me, and judge me by what I really do?"

His words astonished those people who knew of the secret plans of the Jews, and they asked: "Is not this the man they are trying to kill? How does he dare to say such things to them? Do the rulers think that he is really the Christ? But we know where this man comes from, and no one is to know where the Christ comes from. He cannot be the Christ. And yet when the Christ comes will he do more or greater miracles than those which this man does?"

Many of the people, hearing all that he was saying to them, were ready to believe that he was really their king. "When the Christ comes will he do more wonderful things than this man?" they asked. The leaders, when they heard the people, thought it was time to put a stop to it.

There were seventy of these leaders who belonged to what was called the Sanhedrin, which was the highest Jewish court. They were the ones who kept watch to see that the laws were not broken. They arrested anyone who did what they thought was wrong, and they punished those whom they arrested, unless the punishment was to be death. If they wanted to take the life of any prisoner they must ask the Roman court for permission to do so. Almost every man in this Sanhedrin hated Jesus.

This court sent officers to arrest Jesus. But the Master went on talking, though he knew that the officers were only waiting for a good chance to take him. They were afraid to take him when there was a crowd around him, for the people loved to hear him talk. "I will be with you only a little longer," said he. "Then I will go to him who sent me. You will want me then, but you cannot find me; for where I am going you cannot come." The people wondered what he could mean by this, and asked: "Where will he go that we cannot find him? Will he live among the Gentiles and teach them? "But he meant that he was going to his Father in heaven, and those who hated him could never go to live with him there.

Every day, while the feast lasted, Jesus went into the temple and taught. There was one part of the service at this feast which everyone loved. Early in the day, before the morning sacrifice, a priest went from the temple with a golden pitcher in his hand, to the pool of Siloam. This pool was outside the walls of Jerusalem and the priest went in and out of the gate, called the Water Gate, followed by a happy band of worshippers. The pitcher held a little more than a quart of water and, when the priest had filled it with water from the pool, he marched at the head of the procession back again to the temple. As soon as he entered the temple courts, other priests began to blow trumpets; and they kept blowing them until the water had been poured into a basin on one side of the altar. At the same time, wine was poured into a basin on the opposite side, and everyone began to sing the psalms which were always sung at that service. When they came to the last words, "Give thanks unto the Lord, for he is good, for his mercy endureth forever," everyone waved a branch of palm and willow tied together which he held in his hand. This was done to remind the people that God had given their nation water to drink when they were in the wilderness.

On the last day of the feast, perhaps just as these things were being done, Jesus called out, as he was standing in the temple: "If any man is thirsty, let him come to me and drink. He that believes on me shall have living water." He meant the same by this as he did when he spoke in just the same way to the woman at the well of Samaria. He meant the spirit of love and service which God would give to all who truly loved his Christ.

Some of the people said, "Surely this is the Christ," and although there were many who said, "No, he is not," there were so many who showed their liking for him that no one dared to arrest him. Even the officers who had been sent to take him felt that he was different from other men. No one laid hands on him, and he passed out of the city into the Mount of Olives, which was a high hill only a little way from Jerusalem.

The officers went back to the Sanhedrin without their prisoner. "Why have you not brought him?" asked the Pharisees; and the officers answered: "We could not do it; we never heard anyone speak as he did." "Has he deceived you, also?" "He has not deceived any of us," was the reply of the Pharisees.

Jesus had one friend among the Sanhedrin, and that was Nicodemus, the man who came to him in the nighttime at the Passover feast, two years and a half before. Nicodemus had grown braver since that night when Jesus had told him about the new life; he was not afraid to stand up for the great Teacher now, even if he were the only one in the Sanhedrin to do so. He said, "Does our law judge a man without giving him a trial? without giving him a chance to speak for himself, and tell what he is doing?"

This question made the other men very angry with Nicodemus, but it broke up the meeting, and every man went to his own home. They knew in their hearts that Jesus had not broken a single law, and that they had no right to arrest him. They must give up their plan for a while; but they made up their minds to watch him more carefully, and to arrest him if they could possibly find an excuse.

The next day they brought to him a woman who had broken a Jewish law, for which the punishment was stoning to death. They asked Jesus what they ought to do with her. They thought they had given him a question that was hard to answer, for they knew how kind and loving he was, and stoning was a cruel death. But he said, "Let the one among you who is without sin cast the first stone." The Pharisees thought of their wicked lives and one by one left the temple. When they were all gone Jesus said to the woman, go and sin no more.

Jesus spent the night on the Mount of Olives. He loved to get away from the noise and the crowd and the close air of the city into the pure, fresh air of the hills. It was a great comfort to him to be able to go there every night, and still lose none of the services at the temple.

The temple always looked very beautiful when the great lamps were lighted, and one day of the feast, as the people looked with pride on the sight, Jesus said, "I am the light of the world; he that follows me shall not walk in darkness, but shall have the light of life."

The Pharisees answered, "You say that about yourself, but it is not true." Then said Jesus: "It is written in your law that if two men agree in telling the same thing, it is true. I am one that says I am the Son of God, and the Father that sent me is another that says the same thing. So, by your own law, the saying must be true."

"Where is your father?" said they; and Jesus replied: "You neither know me nor my Father; if you had known me, you would have known my Father also; but, because you will not believe me, you will die without being forgiven for your sins." Then they asked, "Who are you?" and he answered, "Even the same that I said to you in the beginning. When you have killed me, then you shall know that I am the Son of God, and that I do nothing by myself, but speak those things that the Father has taught me. He that sent me is with me; my Father does not leave me alone in my work, for I always do what pleases him."

While he was speaking these words, many began to believe that he was telling the truth, and to them Jesus said, "If you will only keep on believing what I tell you, I will teach you how you can free yourselves from your sins." They did not like to be told that they were not free from sins, and, as Jesus went on telling them of some of their faults, they became so angry that they took up stones to throw at him. But Jesus passed through their midst, and walked out of the temple.

We suppose that Jesus with his disciples went back to Galilee for a short time, but they did not stay very long. The Savior had done everything he could for the people there; he had cured the sick, fed the hungry, and given life to the dead. But because he was a poor man, and had not made himself the kind of king they expected, there were very few people in Galilee who loved him and believed that he was the Christ.

There was another feast in Jerusalem in a few weeks, and he travelled toward that city again. He planned to rest awhile in Samaria, and sent a messenger ahead to engage rooms for himself and his apostles in a Samaritan village. It was two years and a half since the woman at the well had asked him, "Where ought men to worship God, in Mount Gerizim or at Jerusalem?" but it was still the question that made trouble between Jews and Samaritans. Anyone who believed that Gerizim was the right place of worship was thought to be a friend of the Samaritans, and was made welcome to their homes. But they knew that Jesus and his friends were on their way to worship at Jerusalem, and, for that reason, the messenger could find no one willing to give them room.

How angry this made James and John! In their anger they said, "Lord, shall we not call down fire from heaven and burn this city?" But the loving, gentle Savior, who always forgave his enemies, said, "No," and without an unkind word they went on to another village.

As they travelled along he asked one man after another to follow him, but they made excuses. One man wanted to wait until his father died; another wanted to go back home and say good-bye to his family. But the Master said that whoever became his follower must not let anything stand between him and them.

One man said, "Yes, Lord, I will follow you wherever you go." Jesus answered, "The foxes have holes, and the birds of the air have nests, but the Son of Man has not where he can lay his head." He had no home where he could take his friends; they must be as poor as he was, if they wanted to be with him and do his work.

There were some men beside the twelve who loved him so much that they were willing to do this, and Jesus chose seventy of them to go, two by two, as the apostles had gone, into all the cities and towns where he planned to go later. He told them as he had the twelve, to go just as they were, without taking food or money or extra clothing. They were to teach the people and heal the sick, and those whom they helped must give them the things they needed. The seventy men started at once, and Jesus and his twelve disciples travelled on, crossing the river Jordan into the country called Perea.

When these men came back to their Master again they were very happy. They had much to tell him of the way in which they had been able to cure the sick, and to help those who needed them so much.

"Wherever he went some of the scribes and Pharisees followed, asking him questions, not because they wanted to learn from him, but because they hoped that he would say something against either the Roman or the Jewish Law. Then how quickly they would arrest him! Jesus knew their plan, but it did not trouble him. He answered all of their questions, and did it so wisely that they could find no fault with what he said.

One day one of these scribes, who had studied the law all his life, and who felt that he was both wiser and better than Jesus, asked, "Master, what shall I do to get this new life of which you teach, — this life that never ends?" Jesus said, "What is written in the law?" The scribe knew everything in the law by heart, and answered, "Thou shalt love the Lord thy God with all thy heart and with all thy soul and with all thy strength and with all thy mind, and thy neighbor as thyself."

Jesus said, "You have answered right; when you do that you have begun that life." Then the lawyer asked, "And who is my neighbor?" Jesus answered this question with a story.

A certain man went down from Jerusalem to Jericho. The road between the two places was rough and dangerous. Great caves and rocks on the sides of the road made good hiding places for robbers and other wicked men, for from them they could rush out at the people who were passing, and rob them.

This often happened, and as this man was passing along the road, the robbers rushed out at him. They fought with him and robbed him of everything he had, even to the most of his clothes. Then they left him, cut and bruised and almost naked, lying half dead by the side of the road. There the poor man lay, not able to do anything to help himself.

There were a good many Jewish priests living at Jericho, and soon one of them came along. Probably he was on his way to or from a service at the temple. He could not help seeing the wounded man, but he passed by as if he had not seen him, crossed to the other side of the road, and kept on his journey. He did not even give him a look of pity.

Soon another Jew came along. He also helped in the temple service, and should have been willing to do God's work wherever he found it. He, too, saw the man in trouble, but, after looking at him for a minute, he went along as the priest had done, without trying to do anything for the poor man, although he knew that he might die if someone did not help him.

Before long a Samaritan came riding by. As he drew near he saw the man lying there by the side of the road, helpless. He knew that he was a Jew, and that probably he hated his race; but he felt sorry for him because he was in such trouble.

Going up to the place where the man lay, he put some oil on his cuts and bruises and bound them up as well as he could. Then he put the man on his own mule and walked beside him till they came to a house where they both could get shelter. He took care of him that night, and in the morning, when he was obliged to go away, he gave the man who kept the house some money, saying, "Take care of him, and if you need to spend more money than this I will give you the rest the next time I come along." Then he went on his way.

Jesus told this story, and then turned to the lawyer, saying, "Which now of these three, do you think, was a neighbor to the man who fell among the robbers?" The scribe answered. "He that took pity on him." Then Jesus said, "Go and do the same." If the lawyer had asked the question because he really wanted to know the answer, Jesus would have been glad to teach him. But he knew what the man wanted, and that is why he told the story instead of answering him.

Two or three miles outside of the city of Jerusalem was the village of Bethany, and here lived a family who loved Jesus, and of whom he was very fond. In the family were two sisters, Mary and Martha, and their brother Lazarus, and they were very glad to have Jesus make his home with them whenever he could do so.

Martha was the house keeper, and because she wanted everything very nice when the Savior was there, she kept about her work, and did not take much time to talk to him. But Mary was different; she was so fond of hearing Jesus talk, that whenever he was in the house she dropped her work and sat at his feet that she might not lose a word of what he was saying.

One day when Martha was tired and fretted because Mary had not come to help her, she went into the room where her sister was sitting and said: "Lord, do you not care that my sister has left me to do the work alone? Tell her to come and help me."

Jesus did not send Mary away, but said to Martha: "Martha, you take too much care and fret yourself about many things that are not important. There is only one thing that is really needful, and Mary has chosen that one thing that will never be taken away from her." The one thing was loving to be near the Christ, and to learn of him.

As Jesus and the disciples were walking about Jerusalem one day they saw a man who had been blind ever since he was born. There are a great many blind people in those hot countries, more than in our cooler climate, for the heat and the brightness often bring on a disease of the eyes. There are no schools, or homes, where they can be taught to work so that they can earn their own living. There are very many poor people there, too, many more than we have here, and most of them much poorer. And most of these very poor people, some of whom are sick, or lame, or deformed, sit and beg for money by the sides of the roads. Very many of the blind people do this also, and this man was one of those who begged in Jerusalem. He had begged for so many years that everyone in the city seemed to know him, and to look for him in his usual place.

As they passed by him the disciples asked, "Master, who sinned, this man or his parents, that he was born blind?" They asked this question because many people thought that blindness, or any sickness, or trouble of any kind, was a punishment from God for somebody's sin, and the disciples wanted to know if this belief was true.

Jesus answered: "It was neither his sin, nor his parents' that made this man blind. His blindness was not a punishment from God, but the power and goodness of God shall now be shown by giving him sight. I must do the works of God while I can, for the night is coming when I cannot work. As long as I am in the world I am the light of the world." He knew that the Sanhedrin would not rest until they had killed him, and that is what he meant by "the night is coming when I cannot work."

When he had finished these words he spat on the ground and made some clay; then he spread the clay on the blind man's eyes, and said to him, "Go wash in the Pool of Siloam." The blind man did as he was told, and when he came back he could see as well as anyone.

When the neighbors of the man, and those who had always known him, saw him with his eyes no longer blind, they did not know whether it was he or someone else. One said to another, "Is not this the man who sat and begged?" Some answered, "Yes, it is he." Others said, "I do not know; it looks like him." The man himself said, "I am the very one."

"Then how were your eyes made to see?" they asked. Said he: "A man that is called Jesus made clay, put some on my eyes, and told me to go to the Pool of Siloam and wash. I went and washed, and came back seeing." "Where is he now" they asked. But this the man could not tell them; he was blind when Jesus spoke to him, and he had never seen the Savior.

All this happened on the Sabbath day, and the man who had been blind was taken to the Sanhedrin to see what they would say about it. Again he told with joy the story of how he had received his sight. The Jews were very much troubled. It was a wonderful cure. No one had ever heard of such a thing as giving sight to a man who had been born blind. Some of them even began to wonder if they had made a mistake, and he really was the Christ. "But," said some of them, "he is not a good man; if he were the Christ he would keep the Sabbath." Others said, "But how could a bad man do such a wonderful deed?" and some were almost ready to believe in him.

Turning again to the man who stood before them, they asked: "What have you to say of this man who opened your eyes?" "I say that he is a prophet," he answered.

There were a good many of the rulers who would not allow themselves to think that Jesus was the Christ, and as an excuse these began to say that the man had never been really blind. They called in his parents and asked them if he was really their son who had been born blind, and if so, how it was that he could see now.

They answered that they knew that he was their son, and that he had been born blind, but how it was that he could see now they did not know. "He is old enough to tell himself, ask him," they said.

These people had a good reason for not wanting to tell all they knew about it. Like all good Jews they loved to go to the synagogue service. The Pharisees had sent out a notice that anyone who believed on Jesus, and said that he was the Christ, should be put out of the synagogue, and should not be allowed to worship there anymore. And so the parents, afraid that they might say too much, told the rulers to ask the young man himself, if they wanted to know what had been done.

The Jews knew what the young man would say, but they called him to the again, and tried to make him think it was not Jesus who had given him sight. "God gave you your sight, praise him for it," they said. "It could not have been Jesus, for we know that he is a bad man."

"Whether he is a bad man or not," said the man, "I do not know. This one thing I do know, that once I was blind, and now I can see." They then asked again, "What did he do to you?"

271

Pleased as the man had been to answer this question the first time it was asked, he would not answer it now. "I have told you already what he did, and you would not hear; why do you want to hear it again? Will you also be his disciples?"

The Pharisees did not like this answer. They, the great Sanhedrin, who had studied all their lives, who were themselves the teachers of the people, were they asked to learn of this teacher whom they so hated? They began to talk angrily, saying: "You are one of the kind to be his disciples. We are the disciples of Moses. We know that God spoke to Moses, but we do not know where he came from."

"It is a strange thing that you do not know where he came from," answered the man, "when he can do such a wonderful thing as open my eyes. We know that God does not hear sinners, but if any man worships him and obeys him, God will hear him. Since the world began no one ever heard of a man who could open the eyes of one who had been born blind; and if this man were not from God he could not do it."

How angry the Pharisees were at this answer! What did the man mean by talking to them in this way? Raising their voices they called out, "Does a man like you, a sinner, try to teach us?" They then sent him away with the punishment which his parents so feared; he would not be allowed to go again to worship in the synagogue.

When Jesus heard what they had done he found the man whom he had cured, and said, "Do you believe on the Son of

God?" Said the man, "Who is he, Lord, that I may believe?" And then Jesus told him that he had already seen him, and was even then talking with him. As the man looked at him he knew that he was talking with his Savior, and that his Savior was the Son of God. Saying, "Lord, I do believe," he fell down and worshipped him.

As they talked together Jesus said, "My coming into the world has done two things; it has made those who were blind see, and it has made those who think they can see, blind." There were some Pharisees standing near to hear all that was said, and one of them asked, "Do you mean to say that we are blind?"

Jesus answered them: "If your eyes were blind and you could not see, it would be no fault of yours; but it is a sin when your minds and hearts are so blind that you will not let yourselves believe me. If I had not come to teach you how to live better lives, you would have had some excuse for your sins. But since you have heard my words and have seen me do things that no other man can do, and yet will not believe me, there is no excuse for you.

"The kingdom of heaven is like a sheepfold (a place where sheep are gathered together at night). He that does not go through the door into the sheepfold, but climbs in some other way is a thief and a robber. He that goes in by the door is the shepherd of the sheep. I am the door. If any man goes into the sheepfold through me he is safe, as the sheep are safe in the fold."

They did not seem to understand what he meant, and so he explained it to them. Heaven is the sheep fold; the people are the sheep. The Christ is the door, and all who want to go to heaven must go through the door. This they can do by believing the Christ and obeying him.

Those who teach any other way of going into heaven are thieves and robbers, because they are taking from the people the best things of life.

He told them another parable to show them that his greatest wish was to do them good. In this parable he called himself the shepherd of the sheep, and other teachers hired men, who do not care for the sheep because they do not own them.

He said: "I am the Good Shepherd, and the good shepherd is willing to give his life for the sheep. But the one who is hired to take care of the sheep, who does not own them, cares nothing for them. If he sees a wolf coming, he leaves the sheep and runs to look out for himself. Then the wolf catches the sheep and scatters them. I am the Good Shepherd, and will give my life for the sheep."

How sweet and loving his voice was! Many of the people — who heard him talk believed that he was telling the truth. They thought they would like to belong to this good shepherd, and that they would like to go to heaven by this door. But some said, "He is insane; why do you listen to him?" "But," said those who were ready to believe him, "what he says does not sound like the talk of an insane man. Can one who is insane give sight to a man that has always been blind?" And they almost began to quarrel among themselves.

Very soon after Jesus had spoken these words, it was time for another of the Jewish feasts. This was the Feast of the Dedication, which, like the other feasts we have studied about, lasted one week. This feast was held in the winter time. As he walked in the temple one day, some of the Jews came around him and asked: "How long shall we have to wait without knowing whether you are the Christ or not? If you are the Christ, tell us so plainly."

Jesus answered: "I have told you so many times, but you would not believe me. The miracles that I do ought to answer your question, but you will not believe me because you are not my sheep. My sheep hear my voice, and I know them and they follow me, and I give them the life that will last forever. My Father, who gave them to me, is greater than all else, and no one shall be able to take them away from my Father or me, for I and my Father are one."

The Jews then took up stones to throw at him. What did the Savior do? Did he speak to them in anger? No, he gently said, "Many good deeds have I done for you, through my Father; for which of these are you stoning me?" It would seem as if those words would have made them drop their stones in shame and ask him to forgive them, but it did not.

They answered, "It is not for good works that we stone you, but because you, a man, call yourself God." Jesus said: "If I do not do the works of God, then do not believe me. But if I do, then believe the works that you see, even if you cannot believe me. Then you will know and believe that the Father is in me, and I in him."

Again the Sanhedrin tried to arrest the man who called himself the Son of God, but they could not do it. Jesus left the temple and crossed the Jordan into the country where John the Baptist used to preach. Many of the people followed him even there, saying, "He is greater than John, for John did no miracle. Everything that John said about this man is true." And many believed on him there.

These new friends asked him to teach them a prayer, as John had taught his disciples. Jesus then taught them the same prayer that he had taught the disciples in Galilee, the Lord's Prayer. He told them not to give up praying because God did not seem to answer them at once; for the Father loved to have them keep asking, and would give them what was best for them, just as they were willing to give good things to their children.

The people of this part of the country crowded around him just as the people of Galilee had the year before; for no one could hear him talk once without wanting to hear him again. Some probably believed that he was the Son of God, but no doubt others heard him talk, and then forgot him.

As he was teaching the people one day, a Pharisee asked him to dinner. Why he invited him we do not know. Perhaps he liked to hear him, and wanted to know him better; but probably he wanted to draw him away from the people and get him to say something of which he could complain to the rulers.

Whatever his reason, Jesus went with him, sat down to the table, and began to eat. You remember the custom the Pharisees had of washing their hands before they ate, and how they did it? Jesus did not wash his hands as he sat down to this dinner, and the Pharisee found fault with him. But Jesus wanted to teach the people that these customs were not of much importance, if only the real commands of God were obeyed. It was much more necessary to be honest and kind and loving, than to wash one's hands just because it was a custom.

So when the Pharisee found fault with him he told him and the others who were with him at the table what he thought about these things. They did not like this, and tried to say things that would make him angry, so that he would say more than he meant to say. But they did not succeed; he went away from them and told his friends not to trust the Pharisees, for they were hypocrites, who said one thing when they meant another.

But he said: "Do not be afraid of them, even if they arrest you and try to kill you. God, who takes care of even the sparrows which are worth so little will surely take care of you. Yet even though they should kill you, it is only your body that they hurt, for they cannot touch your soul, that part of you which is to live forever."

Two brothers who lived in that part of the country had quarreled about some money that had been left to them; one of them took more than the other thought was right. One day, while Jesus was talking to a very large crowd of people, the brother who did not think he had his share of the money said to him, "Master, speak to my brother, and tell him to divide the money with me."

Jesus answered him, "Who made me your judge, or gave me the right to divide your property for you?" That was not what he had come to earth to do. But he had come to teach, and while the people were thinking about property, for they had all heard the question, he taught them a lesson. "Do not long to own what you see other people have," he said, "for a man's happiness does not depend upon the number of things he owns."

There was once a rich man who owned a great piece of land and planted it. Everything grew well one year, and at harvest time there was so much to gather that the man did not have room enough to put it all. He thought to himself: "What shall I do? My barns are too small. Where shall I put all that has grown this year?"

He might have given some away, might he not? But he did not want to do that, he wanted to keep it all himself. So he said: "I will pull down my barns and build others which will be large enough to hold all that I have gathered. Then I will say to my soul, 'Soul, you have enough for many years; take your comfort now; eat, drink, and be merry.' "But God said to him: "You foolish man, you will die this very night; then who will have those things that you have stored away?""

Jesus waited a minute, and then said, "So is everyone who is rich in money and other treasures, but is not rich in God's love."

After finishing this story Jesus taught his disciples many things that he had taught the people of Galilee in the Sermon on the Mount. He told them not to be too anxious about their food and clothing, for God, who cared for such tiny things as birds and flowers, would surely care for them. "Let your greatest wish be to live as one of God's children ought, and all these things will be given to you. Do your best every day, and then, whenever God calls you to live with him, you will be ready to go."

He was teaching in the synagogue one Sabbath day, and with the worshippers was a woman who was very much deformed. For eighteen years her back had been bent like a bow, and nothing on earth could make it straight. The loving heart of the Savior felt pity for the poor woman. He called her to him, and, laying his hands on her, said, "You are free from this trouble."

No sooner had he said this than the woman felt a difference in her back and found that she could stand straight again; that she was no longer deformed. It made her very happy, and she thanked God for what had been done.

But the ruler of the synagogue was very angry that this had been done on the Sabbath. So he said to the people: "There are six days in the week in which men ought to work. Come on one of those if you wish to be cured!"

Jesus turned to this man and said: "You hypocrite, does not each one on the Sabbath untie his ox and lead him away to water? If there is such need of doing this that it is not wrong to do it on the Sabbath, should not this woman be freed from the trouble she has borne eighteen years, even on the Sabbath day?" These words made the Pharisees ashamed of themselves, and the people shouted for joy because of the glorious things that were being done.

Wonderful Teachings

Jesus went through the cities and villages teaching men and women how to enter the kingdom of God. Every day he was drawing nearer to Jerusalem, for it was almost time for another Jewish feast. A party of Pharisees met him when he was not far from the city, and said to him: "Go away from here. You are not safe, for Herod is looking for you, and if he finds you he will kill you." Jesus answered, "You may go back to Herod and tell him that I will work cures as long as I live; but before long my work will be done. I must go to Jerusalem, for that is the place where a prophet ought to die."

Then, as he thought of the city which he so loved, and wanted so much to help; as he thought of the unkind way in which he had already been treated, and of the cruel punishment which would come to him there, he cried: "Jerusalem, Jerusalem, who kills the prophets, and stones those who are sent to you; how often I would have gathered your children together as a hen fathers her brood under her wings, and you would not let me! And now it is too late!"

Jesus was invited to the house of one of the chief Pharisees, one Sabbath day, to eat bread, and here he was watched every moment. It was a very common custom in that country, as we have seen, for people who are passing a house to walk in at the open door. While they were at the table this Sabbath day, a man who was ill came into the Pharisee's house. Jesus looked at the man and said to the scribes and Pharisees, "Is it right to heal on the Sabbath?" There was no answer.

He took the man, healed him, and let him go. Then he again spoke to those about the table, asking, "Which one of you, if one of your animals should fall into a deep hole, would not pull him out on the Sabbath?" They would not answer this question, either, for they knew that they would all do that. And, if they would do so much for a suffering animal, how could they blame him for saving a suffering man? So they said nothing, and Jesus began to talk to them in parables.

There were certain places at the table which were given to the guests who were the most worthy of respect. Jesus noticed that at this feast the guests chose these places for themselves. No seat of honor was left for him, the chief guest. And so he spoke this parable.

"When you are invited by any man to a wedding, do not sit down in the highest place, for perhaps a more honored guest than you has been invited. Then he who invited you both will say to you, 'Give your place to this man,' and with shame you will have to take the lowest place.

"But when you are invited go and sit down in the lowest place. Then when he who asked you to come says, 'Friend, go up higher,' you can take another place, and be respected by all who are at the feast." It is better to begin at the bottom and go up than to begin at the top and go down.

That was the first lesson that he taught. The second shows who ought to be invited to share our good times. Jesus said: "When you make a dinner or a supper do not invite your friends or relatives or rich neighbors, who will later make a feast and invite you back again. But call in the poor, the deformed, the lame, and the blind, who do not have many good times. They cannot pay you back, but the Lord will reward you." A great many people have learned this lesson now, but very few knew it then. Just think how many kind things are done for the poor people among us today! There are a good many Thanksgiving dinners given to the newsboys, the sailors, the children in the homes for orphans and in the hospitals. The poor children in many cities are given days or weeks in the country and by the sea. All these things, and many more, because Jesus taught this lesson of love.

The next lesson was given in this parable. A certain man made a great supper, and invited many guests. When the supper was ready he sent his servant to say to those who had been invited, "Come, for all things are ready."

That was another of the customs in those days. People were invited some time beforehand, and then when everything was prepared the servant went around again to tell those who had accepted the invitation to come. They had no clocks and watches, and perhaps that was one reason why they did so.

These guests had said that they would accept the invitation, but when the servant went to them the second time they began to make excuses. The first said he had bought a piece of ground that he wanted to go and see, and must be excused. Another said, "I have just bought five yoke of oxen, and I must try them to see if they are as good as they ought to be; I shall have to be excused." Still another said, "I have just been married, so I cannot come."

All the guests had some kind of an excuse, and when the servant went back to his master and told him of these things he was very angry, for he had prepared good things for the feast. He said to the servant, "Go out quickly into the streets and lanes of the city, and bring in the poor, the deformed, and the lame, and the blind."

The servant did this, and then said to his master, "Lord, I have done as you commanded, and yet there is room." The master said: "Go out again and bring in more people till the house is filled, for none of those who were invited shall taste of my supper."

This is the story of what had happened in the Savior's own life. The gospel he had come to teach was the feast of good things which had been made ready, and the Jews' were the invited guests who had found every kind of excuse for not coming to it. The publicans and the common people were the lame and the blind who had been willing to come to Jesus, and they had received the blessings which the Pharisees would not take.

Yet, though these Jewish rulers did not want to be friends with the Savior themselves, they found great fault with him, because he went so much among these publicans, even going to their homes and eating with them. At one time, when the scribes and Pharisees were complaining of the company Jesus kept, he told them three stories, to show why he did what they thought was so bad.

He wanted to show them that God cared even for those who had been very wicked, if they only were sorry for their sin, and that he cared for them really more than for those who had never done anything that was very bad, but who thought they were very good, and were not sorry for the wrong things they did. These were the stories.

What man is there who has a hundred sheep who, if he should lose one of them, would not leave the ninety-nine wherever they were, even though it should be in the wilderness, and go after the one that is lost until he finds it? He is willing to hunt through the woods and over the mountains, for he knows that it is weak and timid, and that it will be very much frightened, and may get hurt, out alone among the wild beasts. He is willing to take great trouble, if he can only find the sheep which has wandered away from the flock. And when he has found it he is very joyful, and lays it gently on his shoulder, and carries it home to the sheepfold.

And when he gets home he calls his friends and neighbors together, saying to them, "Be glad with me, for I have found the sheep which I had lost." Jesus said that in the same way there is joy in heaven over one wicked person who truly repents, more than over ninety-nine persons who are not so very bad, and who think they need no repentance.

Repentance, you remember, is being so sorry for what we have done that we will try very, very hard not to do the wrong thing again. Do you remember the story Jesus told the Pharisee, Simon, when the woman anointed his feet? He said that the one who had done many wrong things, but who had repented and been forgiven, would love God better than one who had been a better man, but who was not sorry for what wrong things he had done.

You know, the more we love anyone the more willing we are to please him, even when it takes a good deal of time and trouble; and if we truly love our heavenly Father, we shall want to be as sweet, loving, and obedient as possible, because we know it pleases Him.

This was the second of these three stories. What woman, who has ten pieces of silver, if she should lose one piece, would not light a lamp and sweep the house, and look carefully till she finds it? And when she has found it she calls her friends and neighbors together, saying, "Be glad with me, for I have found the piece of silver that was lost."

So I say to you, there is joy among the angels of God in heaven over one sinner that repents.

The third story was one which has been loved by a great many people ever since Jesus told it to these Jews so long ago. It was the story of the prodigal son.

A certain man had two sons, and the younger one said to his father, "Father, give me my share of your money and property, for I want to go away from here." The father did as the boy wished, and, not many days after, this younger son gathered together all that he had and took a journey into a far country.

He fell into bad company there, and spent his money for wicked pleasure, and spent it very fast. The time came when he had not enough left to buy even the food he needed, and he went and worked for a man of that country, who sent him into his fields to take care of the pigs. There were many days when the young man was hungry enough to eat the food given to the pigs.

One day, while at work, as he thought of his happy home, and how foolish he had been to leave it, he said to himself: "How many hired servants of my father have bread enough and to spare, while I am suffering here from hunger. 1 will leave this place and will go home to my father and will say: "Father, I have been wicked. I have broken God's laws, and have done many things that I am ashamed to have you know. Let me be one of your hired servants."

The more he thought about it the more decided he became, until at last he left his work and started home.

Now when he was still a long way off, the father, who dearly loved his boy, saw him coming and ran to meet him. He put his arms around his son's neck and kissed him. The young man, who was ashamed of the life he had led, said: "Father, I have been wicked. I have broken God's laws, and done wrong to you. I am not worthy to be called your son."

But the father said to his servants: "Bring here the best robe and put it on him, and put a ring on his hand, and shoes on his feet. Kill the fatted calf, and let us be merry; for this my son was lost and is found."

His orders were carried out, and the household began to celebrate the coming home of the younger son.

Now the older son was in the field, and as he came toward the house he heard the music and dancing. He called one of the servants and asked what these things meant. The servant said, "Your brother has come home, and your father has killed the fatted calf because he is so glad to have him back safe and well."

The older son was angry and would not go in. His father came out and urged him to come in and be glad with them that his brother had come back. But he would not go. He said: "I have stayed here all the time, doing as well as I could for you, and you never made a party for me; you have not killed as much as a kid for me, that I might be merry with my friends. But as soon as my brother, who has been away wasting your money, has come back, you have killed for him the fatted calf."

The father answered: "Son, you are always with me, and all that I have is yours. Still it is right we should be merry now, and very happy; for your brother was lost, and is found."

Jesus spoke these three parables to show the Jews why he worked among the publicans and wicked people. They were the sheep that had strayed away, and the treasure that had been lost. They were the younger son, and had indeed been more wicked than their brothers, the scribes and Pharisees. They had not wanted to obey the law of God, their Father, and to serve him, but had wandered away and wasted their lives in doing just what they liked.

But now they were learning how foolish they had been, and were coming back to their Father, asking him to forgive them, and take them to be his workers. And the Son of God was teaching them to do his Father's work.

Soon after this he told two other stories, quite different from these. In the first one he showed how the people who care for money, and what it will buy in this world, plan carefully for the time that is coming. The man of whom the story is told was not honest in his planning, and the Savior did not praise him for that. But he did say that those who serve God should try to plan for the future, as well as others; and should try to make themselves liked by their companions.

The other story was about two men. One was very rich and had everything he wanted; the other was a beggar who, poor and sick, sat on the steps of the rich man's house, and begged for the scraps of food that they were going to throw away.

But there is another side to the story. After telling about the two men while they were living on this earth, he told them that in the other world the poor beggar was to have the highest place, for he had served God in his poverty better than the rich man, with all his money. He showed the people that having good things in this life does not mean that good things will come to us in the other life, unless we are good, and love and serve God.

A messenger came hurriedly to Perea, one day, to find the Savior, saying, "Lord, your friend Lazarus, whom you love so dearly, is very sick, and his sisters, Mary and Martha, have sent for you." Now, although Jesus was so fond of this family, he did not go at once to Bethany to help them, but stayed two or three days longer where he was, in Perea.

For two days he said nothing about going away, but, at the end of that time he said to his disciples, "Let us go into Judea again." They answered: "Master, do you not remember that the Jews almost stoned you the last time you were there? Are you going to risk it again?"

Jesus told them that he was, for his work in Judea was not yet done, and then said, "Our friend Lazarus is sleeping; I must go and wake him out of his sleep." The disciples thought that Lazarus must be better if he could sleep, and answered, "Lord, if he is sleeping he is better."

Jesus said: "He is not sleeping in the way you mean; Lazarus is dead. I am glad, for your sakes, that I was not there when he died; you will have greater reason than ever for believing in me. Come, let us go to him."

The disciples were almost afraid to have their Master go back into Judea, and Thomas said to the others, "We will all go and die with him."

When they reached Bethany they found that Lazarus was dead, as the Master had said, and had been in the grave for four days. You remember that Bethany was only a few miles from Jerusalem, and many Jews had come from that city to comfort Mary and Martha. They were a sad and lonely family now, for they loved the brother who had been taken from them, and they missed him very much.

Martha heard that Jesus was on the way, and went out to meet him; but Mary sat still in the house. When Martha came to the Savior, she said: "Lord, if you had been here my brother would not have died. But I know that God will give you whatever you ask of him."

Jesus said to her, "Your brother shall rise again." Then he spoke to her words which have, ever since that time, cheered people when their friends have been taken away from them; for he told her that one who believes in him shall never die; for though he dies on earth, he is living somewhere else, and will live forever.

These words were a comfort to Martha, for she believed them, and she went back to the house to tell Mary about it. She called so softly that no one else could hear what she said, "Mary, the Master is come, and is calling for you."

As soon as Mary heard this glad news she rose quickly and went to see Jesus, who had not come into the town, but was waiting in the place where Martha had left him. Now when the Jews who had come to this home to comfort the sisters saw Mary rise in such haste and go away from the house, they followed her, saying, "She is going to the grave to weep there."

Mary went away, and when she got to the place where Jesus was waiting she bowed down at his feet. She was crying so hard that she could scarcely talk, but she said, "Lord, if you had only been here my brother would not have died." And when the loving Savior saw her crying, and the Jews who had followed her crying too, he could not keep back the tears from his own eyes. Jesus wept, for he, too, had lost a friend whom he dearly loved.

The Jews noticed this, and some of them said, "See how he loved him." From others came the question, "Could not this man who opened the eyes of the blind have kept his friend from dying?"

The Savior asked, "Where have you laid Lazarus?" And they replied, "Come and see." Still weeping, Jesus went to the grave. It was a cave, and a stone lay upon it. The Master said, "Take away the stone," and someone took it away.

Then, raising his eyes to heaven, Jesus prayed in these words, "Father, I thank thee that thou hast heard me. And I knew that thou hearest me always, but because of the people who stand by, I said it; that they may know that thou hast sent me into the world."

When he had finished this prayer he called in a loud voice, "Lazarus, come forth." The people looked on in wonder. Could it be possible that Lazarus would hear that voice, and obey? But no, it could not be, for he had been dead and buried for several days. While they were still talking in this way Lazarus walked out of the grave, a living man.

Many of the Jews who had never before believed in Jesus changed their minds when they saw what he had done for Lazarus. But some of those who saw it went to the Pharisees and told them about it.

At once a meeting of the great council, the Sanhedrin, was called, and the question was put: "What shall we do? for this man surely works many miracles. If we let him alone all the people will soon believe on him. Then the Romans, fearing that we will try to make him king, will take away even the freedom that we now have."

The High Priest then rose and said: "You are not very wise about this thing. Is it not better that one man should die than for the whole nation to be punished?" Before the meeting was over it was voted that Jesus should die, and the command was sent out that any man who knew where this teacher was must tell of it, that he might be arrested.

The council even planned to kill Lazarus, too. "For," they said, "everyone who sees him will know that he was raised from the dead, and will believe that Jesus, who raised him, is the Christ."

The Last Journey to Jerusalem

Jesus did not stay any longer in the cities, but went with his disciples into Ephraim, which is near the wilderness. Here he stayed until it was time for the Passover feast. Then he and his disciples started again for Jerusalem.

As they passed through a certain village of Samaria, they saw a company of ten men; nine Jews and one Samaritan. The men did not come very near the travelers, for they were lepers, and did not dare to disobey the law of the country. No one could help feeling pity for the lepers, they were so lonely. Driven from their homes, with no hope of ever being allowed to go back to their friends; suffering with this dreadful disease, which no doctor on earth knew how to cure, they wandered about.

But however much people pitied them there was only one who was able to help them. Perhaps these lepers had heard that Jesus of Nazareth could heal any trouble, even their dreadful disease; perhaps they had heard that he would pass that way, and were looking for him. Now, when they saw him coming, even while he was far away, they began to cry, "Jesus, Master, have pity on us."

The Savior, hearing their cry, said: "Go, show yourselves to the priest." They turned about to obey him, and as they walked along looked at one another, and then at their own flesh. What joy! Their skin was no longer dry and white, and full of sores; it looked as it had when they were well. Could it be true that they were lepers no longer? Yes, it was really true; Jesus had made them well.

Now the Samaritan, when he saw that he was well, went back to the Master, and, falling down at his feet, thanked him again and again for making him well. Seeing only this one man, Jesus asked: "Were there not ten who were cured? Yet none of them have come back to thank God except this stranger. Where are the nine?"

And where were they, the Jews who had been made well? Hurrying as fast as they could to show themselves to the priests. They longed to hear them say that they were well; they longed to live like other people again. They longed so much to be at home with their friends that in their hurry they forgot to thank the One who had made them well. How different their lives would have been if the Savior had not been so kind to them! And yet they did not say a word of thanks to the One who had made this difference! Do we ever forget to thank God for what he does for us?

As Jesus and the twelve travelled toward Jerusalem they were joined by other groups of people who were on their way to the feast; and as they walked together Jesus taught one lesson after another and answered the questions that were asked him. The Pharisees asked when the kingdom of heaven should come, and he told them that this was a kingdom which was not seen, for it was in the hearts of those who belonged to it.

Here is one of the parables he told on that journey. Two men went into the temple to pray; one was a Pharisee, and the other a publican. The Pharisee stood with his head up and proudly said: "God, I thank thee that I am not as wicked as other men are, or even like this poor publican. I go without food twice every week, and I give away a tenth of all that I own."

But the publican, standing away from the others in the temple, did not even lift up his eyes toward heaven. He put his hands on his breast and said, "God be merciful to me a sinner."

"I tell you," said Jesus, "that God was better pleased with this man than he was with the other who boasted of his good works." Those who are the greatest in their own eyes are often the least in God's sight. If we are kind and generous to others because we love them we will not always be thinking how good we are to them.

As the company passed along the road little children were brought to the Christ, that he might put his hands on them and bless them. The disciples wanted to send them away, for they thought their Master was too busy to be troubled with children, but Jesus would not allow this to be done.

He called the little ones to him, and laying his hands on their heads in blessing, he said those words that so many children have learned since then, and that every child loves if he has ever heard them.

"Suffer the little children to come unto me, and forbid them not, for of such is the kingdom of heaven."

Jesus always loved the children. Do you remember that time, after his disciples had been quarreling about who was to be the greatest man in the new kingdom that they thought Jesus was going to have in their country? Then Jesus took a child in his arms and said that it was only those who were loving and obedient like a child; those who knew they did not know much, and were willing to learn, that would be members of the kingdom, and that wanting to be great was sure to make them the lowest.

When they had gone a little farther on, a rich young man came up to the Savior and kneeled at his feet, saying, "Good Master, what shall I do that I may have the life that goes on forever?" Jesus said to him: "Why do you call me good? There is none good but one, that is God. But if you want to live forever, keep the commandments. You know them. Do not kill. Do not steal. Do not tell things that are not true. Honor your father and mother. Love your neighbor as yourself."

The young man answered and said to him: "Master, I have kept all these commandments ever since I was a little boy. What more must I do?" Jesus knew that this was so, and said to the young man: "If you want to be perfect, go and sell all that you have and give it to the poor, and you shall have treasure in heaven. Then come and follow me."

Now this young man was very rich, and probably cared more for his money than for anything else in the wide world. Jesus knew this, and knew that until he was willing to give up everything that was dearer to him than love for God, he could not be a true disciple of his. And so, though he loved the young man, he asked him to do this thing which was so hard for him to do. The young man said no more, but went away very sad. He felt that he could not do what the Master had asked of him.

Turning to the other travelers Jesus said, "How hard it is for people to give up their riches and the things that are dear to them, to follow me!" And he showed them that it was only when God gave them new hearts that such a thing was possible.

Peter then spoke for himself and the other disciples, and said, "Lord, we have left all to follow you; what shall we gain by doing it?" Jesus answered: "There is no man who has left home or parents or friends or wife or children, for my sake, who shall not receive in this world many times as much as he has lost. And in the world to come he will have the life that never ends." Then he told them another story.

The kingdom of heaven is like a man who owned a large vineyard; that is, a place where grapes are grown. When he went out very early one morning to find men who would work for him in this vineyard, he found some who agreed to work all day for a Roman penny. This was worth about sixteen cents of our money, and was what such laborers usually received for a day's work.

About nine o'clock in the morning he went out again, and seeing others standing in the marketplace doing nothing, he said, "You can go into my vineyard, and whatever is right I will give you." At twelve o'clock and at three o'clock he did the same thing.

Even as late as five o'clock in the afternoon he found men in the marketplace who were doing nothing. He asked them, "Why do you stand here all the day idle?" and they answered, "Because no man has hired us." He then told them, as he had the others, that they might work in his vineyard, and that he would pay them what was right.

In that country they called the day over at sunset, and as that was usually six o'clock, they stopped their work then. So when it was time to stop work that evening, the master said to one of his head workers, "Call the men in and pay them for what they have done, beginning with those who came last."

The men who had worked but one hour came in, and each of them received a penny. Those who came to work at three o'clock were called next, and they also had a penny apiece; and so did every man who had been at work in the vineyard that day.

Now, when those who had been at work since early morning heard that everyone had been given the same money, they were angry. They thought they should be paid more than those who had only worked a part of the day, and they found fault with the man who hired them.

"Friends," said he, "have I not given you all that I promised you? I have not wronged you, for you agreed to work for a penny a day. Take what belongs to you, and go home. Is it not right for me to do as I wish with my own money? Are you angry because I want to be kind to these other men?"

In this parable Jesus taught that the Father will always reward good, honest work; not always according to the amount we have done, but according to our willingness to help. Just as a mother thanks her little daughter for trying to help her, even though the little girl could not do much work, nor do it very well.

Jesus now took his disciples apart from the others, and as they sat together, resting, he spoke to them once more of what was going to happen to him. "We are on the way to Jerusalem now," said he, "and there I shall be given up to the chief priests and scribes, who have said that I should be put to death at once. But on the third day I shall rise again."

It is strange that the disciples could not understand what their Master meant, but they did not, and even now they were wondering who would have the highest places in the kingdom.

The mother of two of them, James and John, came to him at this time, and asked that her two sons might have the highest places, those next to Jesus himself.

The ten other disciples were very angry with these two, when they heard what they had asked; for they all wanted the same thing, and they thought their Master would probably give these places to those who had asked for them first. Very possibly they felt that they would be much more worthy of them than the two who had asked. At any rate they did not think James and John had any more right to them than they had.

Again Jesus tried to teach them that the one who would be the greatest must be the least. He must be willing to forget himself, and think of others, even as the Christ, their Master, who all his life worked for others instead of having others work for him.

After a short rest Jesus and the twelve started again on their journey. As they came near to Jericho they saw two blind men sitting by the wayside, begging. Though these men could not see what was going on, they could tell by the sound that a great many people were passing.

One of the two, named Bartimæus, asked what it all meant, and they told him that Jesus of Nazareth was passing by. Bartimæus knew that name, and knew he had spoken to other blind men and given them sight. So now he called out. "Jesus, son of David, have pity on me."

He called so loudly that people tried to quiet him; but he would not be quieted. Jesus stood still and commanded that the blind man should be brought to him. Willing people called to Bartimæus, 'Be of good cheer; rise, he is calling you."

Then they led both him and his friend to the Savior, who said to them, "What do you want me to do for you?" They answered, "O Lord, we want our eyes opened." The Savior touched their eyes and said, "Your belief in me has made you well." The blind eyes could see now, and the two men followed the Savior, praising God for what had been done for them. And all the people, when they saw it, also praised God.

The travelers, who were now a large company, arrived at Jericho. This was a busy city where there was a great deal of buying and selling going on; and as a certain share of the money taken in this way belonged to the Roman government, very many publicans lived in the city to collect this money.

One of the most noted of these publicans was a man named Zaccheus. When he heard that Jesus was passing through the city he wanted to see him. He was a very short man, and could not see over the heads of people, but he was so very anxious to see this Rabbi, of whom everyone was talking, that he ran ahead and climbed a tree on the road along which he knew Jesus must pass.

As the Savior drew near, he looked up and saw the man in the tree. "Zaccheus," said he, "make haste and come down, for I want to stay at your house today." What an honor for Zaccheus! He did not need to be called twice, but came down as quickly as he could, and with joy welcomed the Savior to his home.

The people frowned, and muttered, "He has gone to be the guest of a man who is a sinner." Perhaps Zaccheus was a wicked man; perhaps he had not always been honest; but the loving spirit of his guest made him want to be good and honest, and to begin a different life right away.

So he said, loud enough for all to hear him, "Lord, half of my goods I will give to the poor, and if I have taken anything from any man dishonestly, I will give him back four times as much as I have taken."

Jesus said to him, "This day is salvation come to this house. I came to earth on purpose to seek and to save that which was lost." The Savior knew that a man who was willing to do as much as this to undo his wrong actions had started in the right direction. He was saved, for he would be a better man forever after this.

But even though he had done Zaccheus so much good, and had made an honest man of him, the people were displeased to think that Jesus should be friendly with a publican. Did he not claim to be their king? Was he not even now on the way to Jerusalem, where he would set up his throne? That is what they thought and what they hoped.

Knowing their thoughts, Jesus told them this parable. A certain nobleman went into a far country to receive for himself a kingdom; then, after he had been made king, he expected to return. Before he left home he called to him his ten servants and gave to each of them the same amount of money, saying, "Make the best use you can of it until I come back."

Now his people did not like this nobleman, and sent this message to the far country. "We will not have this man rule over us." No attention was paid to the message. The nobleman received his kingdom and returned.

Again he called his servants, to whom he had given the money, that he might find out what each one had been doing. The first man came gladly, for he had done his best with the money that had been given him. He passed it to his master, saying, "Lord, here is your money, and ten times as much more as you gave me." To him the nobleman said: "Well done, good and faithful servant. Because you have been faithful over a very little, you shall now be ruler over ten cities."

The second man, too, was glad to come, for he had done his best. He said, "Lord, here is five times as much as you gave me." The nobleman praised him also, and said, "Well done, you shall be ruler over five cities."

The next man came unwillingly, for he had done nothing with his master's money. He hung his head in shame, as he said: "Lord, here is your money which I have kept laid away in a napkin. I was afraid of you, for I know how strict you are, and how much you expect everyone to do."

"If you knew that I expected a great deal," said the nobleman, "why did you not try to make my money earn all it could, so that, when I came back, I could have received all that belonged to me?" Then he said to those that stood by, "Take all that the man has away from him, and give it to the one who has been the most faithful."

In this parable the Christ himself is the nobleman, and heaven is the faraway country. Those to whom he was talking were the servants, and so are we, for the Christ has not yet come back from the faraway country. We must make the best use of everything he has given us if we want to hear him say to us, "Well done, good and faithful servant."

After the rest at Jericho the travelers were ready to climb the long hill that lay between them and Jerusalem. It took five or six hours to do this, and they gave themselves time enough to finish their journey before sunset, for it was Friday, and at sunset the Jewish Sabbath began.

Bethany was between Jericho and Jerusalem, and when they came to this little village Jesus and his disciples, leaving the rest of the party, went to the home where he was always welcome, the home of Martha and Mary. There he quietly spent his Sabbath day, happy in knowing that he was among friends that loved him.

The Passover did not begin until the next Thursday at sunset, but many Jews from the country had already arrived at Jerusalem, and were asking each other, "Do you think Jesus will come to the feast?" They may have been answered by some of those who travelled part of the way with Jesus, who told them that he was even then at Bethany.

The Last Week of the Christ's Earthly Life

Saturday

On the evening of Saturday, for the Sabbath was over at sunset, his friends at Bethany made a feast for him. As Martha was doing the work, and Mary and Lazarus were both there, we think it was probably in their home.

A great many of the Jews had come to this feast for two reasons: They wanted to see Lazarus, who had been brought back to life; and they wanted to see Jesus, who could do so great a miracle.

As the guests sat at the table, a delicious perfume began to fill the air, and looking at Jesus they saw what had made it. Mary had taken a beautiful box which held a pound of very costly ointment, had broken this box and poured the ointment on the head and feet of Jesus, and was then wiping his feet with her long hair.

Ever since the apostles had gone about with their Master they had lived like one family. All the money was kept in one bag, and was used to pay the bills for any or all of them. Judas was the apostle who took care of the money bag, and he was now the one who spoke first.

He felt angry, and said, "Why is this ointment being wasted? Why was it not sold and the money given to the poor?" He said this, not because he cared for the poor, but because he was a thief, and if the money had gone into the bag, he could have had part of it for himself.

Jesus said to Judas: "Let her alone; why do you trouble the woman? You will have the poor with you always, but you will not always have me. She has done well. What she has done will be told in memory of her wherever people learn about me.

Sunday

Early on the morning of our Sunday a company of people took palm branches in their hands and went out of the city to meet Jesus. At Bethany, too, a crowd had gathered to see the one whose name was on everyone's lips. For all those Jews who were at the grave of Lazarus when the Master brought him back to life had often told the story of what they had seen.

Jesus sent two of his disciples ahead to another village, saying: "When you get to a certain place you will find a colt tied by the door in a place where two roads meet; a colt on which no man has ever sat. Untie him and bring him to me. If any man asks you why you are doing this, you must say, 'The Lord needs him,' and then the man will let him go."

The disciples went as he told them, found the colt tied by the door, and untied him. A man who stood by said, "Why are you letting the colt loose?" The disciples answered, "The Lord needs him." The owner said no more, and the friends of Jesus took the colt to their Master. After they had thrown their coats on its back to make the softest saddle they could for him, Jesus sat on the colt and rode to Jerusalem.

He was followed by the people who had been waiting for him at Bethany and by the large company who had come from all the towns of Galilee and Judea to the Passover feast. It seemed as if his followers were enough to protect him from the wicked plan of the Jews. Once again there were thousands of people who were ready to own him as their king and to crown him.

How proud these men were to be in his company! One tried to do more than another to honor him! Some threw down their clothing to make a soft carpet on which he might ride; others cut down branches of palm trees and carpeted the road with them.

When the great company came to the foot of the Mount of Olives both those that went before and those who followed after waved their branches, and with a loud voice sang praise to God for all the mighty works they had seen. And this was their song: "Hosanna to the Son of David! Blessed is he that cometh in the name of the Lord! Hosanna in the highest!"

They soon reached the top of the mountain, and Jerusalem was in full sight. Every Jew loved Jerusalem, and Jesus loved it dearly, even though he had never been well-treated there.

Now, as he looked at the city, and thought what he could have done to save it, he felt so sad that he cried, "Jerusalem, if you had only known what was best for you! But it is too late. The day is coming when you and your children shall he destroyed, and there will not be one stone left upon another."

This really came true in less than fifty years after the death of the Christ. The Romans marched against the city, tore down the walls, killed men, women, and children, and left nothing but ruins behind them.

The procession moved on through the gates into the city. Though the people of Jerusalem expected to see a great many strangers there during Passover week, they wondered what it meant to have this great army march through the city, doing honor to a man who was poorly dressed, and sitting on a little untrained colt.

The whole city was interested, and asked, "Who is this?" The crowds with Jesus answered, "This is Jesus, the prophet of Nazareth in Galilee."

Now the rulers of the Jews were troubled when they saw and heard all these things. They were afraid it would be impossible for them to carry out their plans, if so many people had become the friends of Jesus. Some of them called out, "Master, tell your disciples to stop their shouting." But he answered, "If these should keep quiet, the very stones of the city would cry out."

When the crowd arrived at the temple they separated, for not all were clean and ready to go into the temple. Jesus went in, and stayed there until evening, when, with the twelve, he went back to Bethany to spend the night.

Monday

Monday morning, on the way to Jerusalem, Jesus saw, a little way from the roadside, a fig tree. It seemed to be a strong, healthy tree, and he hoped to find some fruit on it, for he was hungry. But when he came to it he found nothing but leaves. Jesus said to it, "No man shall ever eat fruit from this tree again," and passed on.

His heart was sad as he entered the temple, for there in the court of the Gentiles he saw the same sights that had troubled him three years before. Moneychangers were doing their work, and men were buying and selling cattle. He would not allow them to carry on their business while he was there, and drove them out again as he had before. As they saw how quickly he was obeyed, the scribes and Pharisees looked on in wonder and hatred. But they did not dare to touch him, so many of the people had become his friends.

All day long Jesus worked in the temple. The lame and the blind came to him and were healed; hundreds of people crowded about him to hear his words. When the children who had seen the procession the day before, and had learned the song of the crowds, saw Jesus in the temple, they began to shout the same words, "Hosanna to the son of David." The priests and scribes did not like this, and said to Jesus, "Do you hear what these children are saying?" Jesus answered, "Yes;

have you not read that from little children often comes the most perfect praise?"

Tuesday

Monday night was spent in Bethany again. On Tuesday morning, as they went again to Jerusalem, the disciples noticed that the fig tree they had passed the day before was dried up from the roots and withered away. Peter said, "Master, see how quickly this fig tree has withered away."

Jesus said, "If you have faith in God, you can do greater things than that." But he did not want them to think that they could ask God to destroy anything because they did not like it; so he told them when they prayed to be sure and forgive all who had done them wrong, that the Father in heaven might forgive them. "But if you do not forgive, your Father in heaven will not forgive you."

As soon as they came to Jerusalem, Jesus went into the temple. As he was walking through the courts some of the Jews came to him, and asked, "What right have you to come here and do these things, and who gave you the right?" They meant such things as cleansing the temple and teaching there.

Jesus said: "You answer my question, and I will answer yours. Was the baptism of John from heaven or of men?" This means, was John really a prophet of God, or did he pretend to be one when he was not.

The Pharisees did not know how to answer the question. "For," thought they, "if we say he was from heaven, he will say,

'Why, then, did you not believe him?' But if we say he was from men, we fear the people, for everyone thinks that John was surely a prophet." And so they answered, "We cannot tell." Jesus said: "Neither will I tell you who gave me the right to do these things."

"A certain man had two sons, and he said to the first, 'Go, work today in my vineyard.' The son answered, 'I will not,' but afterward he repented and went. The father went to the second son and said, 'Go work today in my vineyard.' This son answered, 'I am going, sir,' but he did not go. Now which of those sons best pleased the father?" They answered, "The first."

Jesus said: "The publicans and sinners are like that son, and they will enter the kingdom of heaven before you do. For John came to tell you what you needed to do, and you did not believe him and do it. The publicans and sinners did believe him; you did not repent, but they repented."

Then he told them another parable. There was a certain man who planted a vineyard and put a hedge or fence around it. Then he made a place where the grapes could be made into wine, and built a tower where the workmen could stay to guard it. Everything was done to make it safe, and to make the work easy. He then rented it to men who were to take care of it, and went into a far country.

When it was time for the fruit to be ready he sent his servants to get what belonged to him. But these men who had rented the vineyard had not worked, and they had no fruit to give. They took the servants and beat one, killed another, and stoned another. The owner sent other servants to look after things, and they were treated just as badly.

Last of all he sent his son, saying, "Surely they will respect my son." But when these men saw the son coming they said among themselves: "Here is the son, who will sometime own this vineyard. Let us kill him and take it for ourselves." And they caught the son and killed him, and threw his body out of the vineyard.

"What," said Jesus, "will the owner of the vineyard do to these wicked men?" The scribes answered, "He will destroy them, and rent his vineyard to other men who will do better." Jesus said, "That is what God will do to you, for he is the Lord of the vineyard, and you are his servants, who are planning to kill his Son."

He spoke another parable about a king who made a feast when his son was married, and invited a great many guests. When the dinner was ready he sent his servants to tell those who were invited to come to the feast, but they would not come. He sent still other servants to tell them that everything was ready, and it was time for them to be there. But the guests paid no attention. One went to his farm and another to his shop; by some the servants were very roughly treated, and at last were killed.

The king heard of it and was so angry that he sent his armies to kill the murderers, and burn their city. Then he said to other servants: "The wedding feast is ready, but the guests who were invited were not worthy to eat it. Go out into the streets and call in every one you meet."

This the servants did, bringing in the good and the bad. At the door everyone was given a robe which he was asked to wear at the feast.

When the king went in to see the guests he found one man who would not take the robe that was offered him, and was there in his old clothes. The king said, "Friend, how did you come here without a wedding robe?" The man said nothing, for he had no excuse. Then said the king to his servants, "Tie him hand and foot, and take him away and punish him."

The scribes and Pharisees knew that in all these parables Jesus meant to show them how unworthy they were. They could hardly keep their hands off of him, but they were afraid to touch him when he was among so many friends. They went out to think up some questions they might ask which would lead him into trouble, however he answered them.

Before long they sent some men to him who pretended to be very friendly, and said: Master, we know that you are truly good, and will answer every question in the way that pleases God, whether it pleases men or not. So we want to ask you this question: "Is it right to pay taxes to the Roman Emperor, or not? Shall we pay them, or shall we not?"

They spoke kindly, but Jesus was not deceived. He knew that, though they seemed so friendly, their hearts were full of hatred. He knew also why they asked that question. They did not see how he could answer it without making enemies. If he said "No, do not pay the taxes," they could give him to the Romans to be punished. If he said "Yes, you ought to pay them," he would displease most of the Jews, who hated to pay the tax, and who thought they would never have to pay it after their king came.

Jesus said: "Why do you tempt me? Bring me a penny." Then, after they had given him one, he asked, "Whose face and title are these on the penny?" They said, "Caesar's." Then said Jesus, "Give to Caesar the things that are Caesar's, and to God the things that are God's."

After this wise answer they left him, and went away, trying to think of some other question to ask. They tried one after another, but his answers were all given in such a way that they could find no fault in them. It seems strange to us that the very ones who were looking so eagerly for their king should be so unwilling to accept him when he came. But they forgot that their king was to be poor and humble; they thought of him only as a great soldier.

It was only a little earlier, on this same day, that he reminded them of an old story that they all knew. When Solomon was building the great temple, the workmen came upon one stone of so queer a shape that, after trying it in a good many places, they decided that it was a mistake, and threw it away. But when the great work was almost done, the most important stone was missing. After long hunting they found the one that they had thrown away, tried it, and found that it fitted! They knew what he meant. They had treated him as worthless, but they would find that he was the Christ, the Son of God, and their great Judge.

When he was asked, "What is the greatest commandment of all?" Jesus answered: "Thou shalt love the Lord thy God with all thy heart, and with all thy soul, and with all thy mind. And the second is like it: Thou shalt love thy neighbor as thyself." This was a wonderful answer, for if we do these things we shall never break one of the commandments. If we love God with all our heart we will never want to worship idols, or take his name in vain, or break his Sabbath. And if we love all those around us as well as we do ourselves, we will never want to do anything to hurt them or even to make them uncomfortable.

Then he turned to the Pharisees and asked them this question: "What do you think of the Christ? Who is he? "They answered, "The son of David." "How can he be," said Jesus, "for David called him his Lord." No one was able to answer him a word, nor did anyone dare to ask him anymore questions.

Jesus turned to his disciples and to the people who crowded about him, and said: "The scribes and the Pharisees teach you the law of Moses, and that you must follow; but do not follow their actions. They teach, but do not themselves do as they teach; they lay heavy burdens on other men's shoulders, but they themselves will not carry them; they do all their deeds to be seen by men."

Then he told these wicked scribes and Pharisees what he knew about them; that, instead of being good teachers for the people, they did them harm; that, though they made a great show of loving God, their hearts were very wicked. Jesus was always loving and kind even to wicked people, if they were sorry for their sins, and were ready to try to do better; but he spoke very hard words to these hypocrites, words that they could never forget, words that have shown all the people in the world who have read this story how deceitful these men were. And how angry it made them!

The fact that they were angry shows that they were not sorry for their sins, for if they had been willing to become better men they would have been grateful to the Savior for showing them that they needed forgiveness, and for showing them the way to receive it. Their anger would have left them, as they thought over their lives, and they would have come to Jesus to be forgiven, and would not have tried to kill him for telling them the truth. Someone said once that when two persons were disputing he could tell which was wrong by seeing which one became angry first; and it is certainly so very often.

Jesus then went out of the temple. As he passed through the Court of the Women, he saw the people putting gifts of money into the boxes which were kept there for that use.

Everyone was expected to give as much as he could, and there were many who were able to put in a good large sum.

But as Jesus passed the box a very poor woman put in two mites. We have no money as small as a mite; the two mites were only about half a cent, which was a very small gift. But Jesus said to his disciples: "Truly this poor widow has done more than anyone else here; for though the rich have given more money than she has, they still have plenty left, while she has given all she had."

This teaches us that if we give away only what we do not need ourselves, it is not being really generous, and the Lord will not be so greatly pleased with our gift. It is the giving until we have to go without something we would like to have, or the giving away something we would like to keep, that makes us really generous. And it is this kind of giving that our Savior loves, and rewards with his blessing.

A great many people think that those who give great sums of money should be thanked and praised, but that those who only give a little bit are not worthy of praise. But it is not the largeness of the gift, but the love that prompts it, that should be measured. Even a child can give a gift with a great deal of love in it.

During the day, Philip and Andrew came in to ask their Master if he would talk with some Greeks who were waiting in the Court of the Gentiles. Of course, these Greeks were not allowed to go into the court where Jesus was teaching, and so he gladly went out to them. The Bible does not tell us what they said to him, but the answer that he gave them makes us think that, perhaps, knowing the wicked plan of the Jews, they invited Jesus to go to their country, where he could do his work and be safe. Jesus might have done this, and have saved his life, but he did not. He said to these Greeks: "Unless a grain of wheat falls into the ground and dies, it does little good; but if it dies, it bears much fruit. He that loves his life shall lose it; but he that loses his life in this world shall have the life that is everlasting. What shall I say? Shall I ask my Father to save me from this trouble? No, I came to this earth for the purpose of saving the people, and if my death will make them believe that I am the Son of God and that what I have tried to teach them is true, I am willing to die."

Then he prayed, "Father, glorify thy name." He stopped speaking. What was that sound that everyone heard? Some said that it thundered; others, that an angel had spoken to Jesus. But some of his dearest friends, who stood near him, heard a voice from heaven say, "I have both glorified it, and will glorify it again."

Do you remember that when he was baptized a voice from heaven said, "This is my beloved Son, in whom I am well pleased?" And do you remember that other time, when he was on the mountain top with Peter, James, and John, that the voice said, "This is my beloved Son, hear ye him?" It was this voice which spoke now for the third time. Jesus said to those that heard it, "This voice came, not because of me, but for your own sakes, that ye might believe."

Though they had just heard this proof that Jesus was the Son of God, many of the Jews would not yet believe him. Some of the rulers did believe in their hearts that he was the Christ, but they were afraid to say so, for fear that the Sanhedrin, the great council, would put them out of the synagogue. They loved the praise of men more than the praise of God, and they were afraid that they would lose some of the honor that the common people had been paying them, if they should join this poor, humble man from the little town of Nazareth, and his fisherman disciples.

As Jesus and his disciples went through the temple gate on their way out this afternoon, the disciples, looking back with pride, said, "Master, see what beautiful stones these are, and what great buildings!" The Master said, "Yes, they are beautiful buildings, but the time is coming when there shall not be left one stone upon another."

The disciples said no more at the time, but as they sat down to rest on the way to Bethany, they asked, "Master, when are these things you spoke of coming?" He did not tell them the exact time, but he said that before that happened there would be great trouble in the land. They, his friends, would be badly treated and put into prison, and some even killed. It would be hard to be his followers, and some would give up trying, so that they might have an easier life. But he told them that if they would always try to follow him, no matter how hard it was, they should be saved at last. He told them to be always ready, for they did not know when their Lord would call for them. He said much that we cannot yet understand; but there is enough for us to know what he wishes us to do while we are waiting for his coming.

He told them that if a man left his house in charge of his servants, and went away, without saying when he would come back, the servants, if they were faithful, would be always ready, and always on the watch for their master.

So, in just the same way, our Master has left us, and given us some work to do. We must be careful to do the work, and to be on the watch for his coming, if we are faithful servants. But he says in another place, that it would not please the master to find that his servants had stopped their work, and had been always standing at the door, wondering and guessing when he would come. So we must be careful to do our work, while we are waiting.

He told several other parables that would make them always remember the lesson. One was about ten virgins, or young women, who went out to meet a bridegroom. It was the custom at a Jewish wedding for the groom (the man who was to be married) to go with some of his friends to meet the bride at her home, where she was dressed in her wedding clothes, waiting for him.

Then the young friends of both the bride and the groom, with torches and music, went with them to their new home. After all the wedding party had gone into the house, the doors were shut, and no one else could get in. Then the marriage took place, and the feast that followed lasted for many days.

Five of the ten virgins in the parable were wise, for, not knowing how long they would have to wait for the bridegroom, they filled their lamps, and took some extra oil with them, for fear the lamps should burn out. The other five took only the oil that was in their lamps.

They had to wait so long for the groom that every one of the ten virgins fell asleep. At midnight they were aroused by hearing someone call out, "The bridegroom is coming." Up they jumped, and looked to see if the lamps were all right. No, they had gone out. As the wise maidens took the extra oil and filled their lamps, the other five said, "Give us some of your oil." But the wise ones answered: "No, we cannot do it. There is not enough for us and for you too. Go to those who sell oil, and buy some for yourselves."

So the foolish virgins, who had not been careful to see that they had enough oil, went to those who sold, bought more, and filled their lamps. But before they were back at the house the bridegroom came. All those who were ready went with him and the bride, in the procession, to his house. Then the door was shut.

When the foolish maidens had filled their lamps, they, too, went to the bridegroom's house. But they were too late. They knocked on the door, but no one would let them in, and they must go sadly away.

In this parable Jesus is the bridegroom, we are the friends who are waiting for his coming. Love for him is the oil which we must burn in our hearts, which are the lamps. If we have not enough of this love to keep our hearts as bright as they should be until our Savior is ready for us, we cannot enter his home to be with him.

We do not know when he will come, and we must be careful and watchful so that we may be ready. There will not be time to get ready after we know he is coming. We cannot borrow the oil of love from those around us, for, no matter how kind and loving our friends are, they are not so loving as our Savior was, and, even if they were, they could not help us be loving if we were not willing to try ourselves all the time.

Another parable that he spoke was very much like the one of the man who went into a far country and left his money for his servants to take care of. But in this case the servants did not all have the same amount of money, as they did in the other story. One had five talents (a talent is a very large sum of money); another had two; and a third had only one.

But the servants did the same with this money. The one who had the five talents did business with it, and gained a great deal more money with it. The one who had the two tried as hard, and really did as well as the other, though the amount of money he gained was less.

But the third one in this story, as in the other, did not try at all. He said he was afraid of his master, and so had hidden the money in the ground, where he could find it and return it when the master came home. And then he gave him back just the same money that he had received.

The lesson, too, was the same as in the other story. Though we cannot all do the same kind or amount of work, there is something for everyone to do, and he must do the best he can.

Another parable was about the time when we shall all have finished our work on earth, and shall stand before our Father in heaven, to hear whether he thinks that work has been good or bad. He called the Father the King who, when his servants came before him, separated them, putting some on his right hand and some on his left.

To those on the right hand he said: "Come, you blessed, into the home which has been prepared for you; for I was hungry and you fed me; I was thirsty and you gave me drink; I was a stranger and you took me in; I was naked and you clothed me; I was sick and you visited me; I was in prison and you came to see me."

Then said those on the right hand: "Lord, when did we see you hungry and fed you; or thirsty and gave you drink? When did we see you a stranger and took you in? or naked and clothed you? Or when did we see you sick or in prison, and visited you?"

The King answered, "Because you have done these things for my children on the earth you have done them for me."

Then turning to those on his left hand, the King said: "You cannot stay here with me, for I was hungry and you did not feed me; I was thirsty and you gave me no drink; I was a stranger and you did not help me; naked and you did not clothe me; sick and in prison, but you did not visit me."

Then these people answered the King, saying: "Lord, when did we see you hungry or thirsty or a stranger or naked or sick in prison, and did not try to help you?" And the King answered,

"Because you did not do these things for my children on earth you did not do it for me."

After he had finished this long talk with his disciples Jesus said to them, "There are only two days now before the Passover feast, when I shall be taken away from you." It was with sad hearts that they went back to Bethany that night. And now we come to a very sad part of the history. One of Jesus' own disciples, Judas Iscariot, decided to give him up to the people who hated him so, if only he could get some money for doing it. He had the purse and carried all the money, and loved it more than he loved his Master.

There was a meeting of the Pharisees that same evening, Tuesday. They were very angry, and were planning what they could do with this Jesus, who dared to talk to them as he did in the temple that day. They were still determined to kill him, but they did not know how to do it, for he seemed to have so many friends.

They had just decided that it must be done secretly, and not until the feast was over, and the people from the country had gone home (for they were the ones who would defend him), when Judas came before them, and asked them, "How much will you give me if I tell you where you can find Jesus?" They were glad to make any kind of a bargain with him, for they knew that he would show them a place where they could find Jesus alone, without any of his friends near him. So they offered Judas thirty pieces of silver, or about seventeen dollars. Judas agreed to do it for that sum of money, and left them. From that time he watched for a chance to sell his Lord.

Wednesday and Thursday

We do not know what Jesus did on Wednesday. The Bible says that he went every morning to the temple, and taught all day, and perhaps he did the same this day. But nothing is told of what he taught, or of anything that happened. A good many who have studied about it think that this Wednesday was an exception, and that he spent it quietly at Bethany with those who loved him so. We hope so, for it was his last quiet day.

Thursday was the last day of the Passover feast, and in the evening the Passover lamb was eaten. Every Jewish family had a lamb this day, which the father took to the temple. There it was killed, and the priest burned the fat upon the altar. The father then took the rest of the lamb home, where it was roasted and eaten with bitter herbs. If a family was too small or too poor to eat a whole lamb, two or three families ate one together.

We have seen before that Jesus and his twelve disciples formed a sort of family, and they were to eat the Passover together at this time. So on Thursday morning Jesus said to Peter and John, "Go to Jerusalem and prepare the Passover that we may eat it." The disciples said, "Where shall we go?" for they knew of no place where they would be welcome.

Jesus answered: "When you come to the city you will meet a servant carrying a pitcher of water. Follow him into the house where he enters, and say to the master of the house, 'The Master wants your guest chamber for a place where he can eat the Passover with his disciples.' He will show you a large upper room, furnished with tables and couches. Use that room, and make the supper ready."

The two disciples went to the city and found everything as the Master had said, and prepared the Passover supper. When evening came Jesus and the other disciples joined them. There seems to have been a little trouble about choosing their seats, and deciding who should have the seat of honor; for they did not yet know the lesson their Master had tried so often to teach them. He taught them this lesson once again, in a way that they never forgot.

Not only was there trouble about the seats, but no one was willing to take the part of the servant, and wash the dusty feet before they began to eat. We have seen that this was one of the things that should be done, because the people then did not wear shoes and stockings as we do now, but only sandals, fastened on their bare feet. A walk of several miles over the dusty roads would make them very uncomfortable, and if they had had a servant, one of the first things he would have done for them would have been to wash their feet.

Jesus waited until they were all seated, and it was certain that no one was willing to do this servant's work. Then, rising from the table, he took off his outer garment, got a basin of water, and began to wash their feet, and to wipe them with the towel which he had put around his waist in the way the servants did.

The disciples must have been very much surprised and ashamed to see their Master doing the work, but no one seems to have said anything until it came Peter's turn to be washed. Perhaps they were too much ashamed to speak. But Peter said, "Lord, why do you wash my feet?" His Master said, "You do not know now why I do it, but you will know some time."

Peter was not willing to let it be done, and said, "You shall never wash my feet." Then Jesus said, "If I do not wash them you cannot love me, for my friends are willing to obey me."

Now Peter did love his Lord dearly, and, though it was not right for him to hold back, even if he could not bear to have his Master do for him the work of a servant, yet he did so because of his love and respect for Jesus. So, if being washed by his Master showed that he truly loved him, he was more than willing that it should be done, and he said, "Lord, wash not only my feet, but my head and my hands." Jesus understood Peter. He knew that this disciple loved him, and was trying hard to be like his Master, loving and pure; so he said, "He that is clean needs only to have his feet washed; and most of you, my disciples, are clean, but not all." Judas was with them, and Jesus knew of the bargain he had made with the Jews; that is why he said, "You are not all clean."

After he had washed the feet of the twelve, Jesus put on his robe again, and sat down, saying: "Do you know what I have done to you? You call me your Master and your Lord, and that is right. If I then, your Lord and Master, have washed your feet, you ought to be willing to wash one another's feet; for I have given you an example, that you should do to others as you would have them do to you. The servant is not greater than his master; you will be happy when you have learned this lesson."

The lesson was, not that everyone must wash the feet of others, for that is not the custom now, as it was then; but that we must be ready to do anything to help our friends, even the humblest, most disagreeable services.

The time was now drawing near when the Savior of the world must give up his life for the people. He looked troubled and sad as he said, "One of you is going to betray me." To betray means to give someone up to his enemies. Was it not too bad that one of those men whom Jesus had most taught and loved should turn out to be so wicked?

The disciples looked at one another, wondering who it could be: first one and then another asked Jesus, "Lord, is it I?" Judas was one of those who asked this question, but probably the rest of the disciples did not hear the answer, for Peter motioned to John who was lying close to Jesus, with his head on the Master's breast, to ask him who would do so dreadful a thing.

Then John asked, "Who is it, Lord?" Jesus answered, "It is the one to whom I shall give a sop, after I have dipped it." Dipping the sop was another Jewish custom. On the table there was one large dish of food, and usually each one at the table put his fingers into this dish and took from it what he wanted. But sometimes one person would dip a piece of bread into the dish and then pass the bread, and what came out with it, to someone else; that was the sop, and that is what Jesus now passed to Judas. As he gave it to him he said, "What you are going to do, do quickly."

The other men at the table did not know what their Master meant. Some of them thought that because Judas carried the moneybag he had been sent out to buy something for the feast, or to give something to the poor. But Judas knew what Jesus meant, and went out at once. It was now dark night.

After Judas had gone out, and only those were left who truly loved the Master, came what we usually call "The Last Supper." Jesus took some of the bread that was on the table, and after he had thanked God for giving it to them, he broke it in pieces and gave it to his disciples, saying, "Take this and eat it; for it stands for my body, which will be broken for you." Then he took a cup of wine, and after again giving thanks, passed the cup to his disciples, saying, "Drink ye every one of this; for it stands for my blood, which is shed to wash away your sins."

From that time until now, in the church service, people eat the bread and drink the wine in memory of their Lord's death. We call it the Communion Service, or the Lord's Supper.

After this Jesus and his disciples sang a hymn. We can know what this hymn probably was, for the Jews always sang certain Psalms after they had finished eating the Passover, and those were probably what were sung now. They were Psalms 115-118, and you can read them yourselves in your own Bibles.

After singing the hymn they left the house and went to the foot of the Mount of Olives, where there was a garden where Jesus had often been before. As they went along the Master talked to his disciples, and said some of the words that have been the most precious to all who love him. He began by telling them that his death was to come very soon.

"Little children," he said, "I shall be with you only a little while longer. I am going where you cannot follow me now; but sometime you will come to be with me. There is one thing that 1 want you to be sure and remember, and that is, to love one another as I have loved you. If you do that, everyone will know that you have learned from me."

Peter said: "Lord, where are you going? Why cannot we follow you now?" His Master answered sadly, "This very night you and all the rest of my friends will leave me and will be ashamed to own that you ever knew me." Peter then said, in his quick way: "No, Lord, though everyone else should be ashamed of you, I will not be ashamed. I am ready to go to prison, or I will die to save you."

His Lord knew him better than he did himself, and said: "You will die to save me, Peter? I tell you that before the cock crows in the morning you will deny me three times; you will say that you are not my friend, and never knew me." Peter could not believe that it would be so, and said earnestly,

"Though I should die with you, I will not deny you." All the rest of the apostles said the same thing.

But we shall see that their Master knew them best, after all.

Jesus tried to comfort his friends, for they were all feeling very sad. "Let not your hearts be troubled," said he; "you believe in God, believe also in me. I am going to my Father's house, and there is room there for you, too. I will go and prepare a place for you, and then I will come again and take you with me, that where I am, there you will be also. I am the way, the truth, and the life. No man can come to the Father unless he loves me, and comes in that way. He that learns what I have taught, and keeps my commandments, is the one that loves me; and he that loves me shall be loved by my Father, and I will love him.

"I am the vine, you are the branches; unless the branches cling to the vine and draw their life from it, they cannot bear fruit; neither can you do good works unless you cling to me. Remember my command, that you love one another. The world will not love you, for the same reason that they have not loved me. They will put you out of the synagogue; they will put you in prison; they will even kill you, because you cling to me. But, when the time of trouble comes, remember what I have told you, and remember that you are not suffering any more than your Master did before you. I shall not be here to help you; I shall be with my Father; but if you ask the Father to help you for my sake, he will do it."

With these words and many more Jesus comforted his loved friends, and told them what to do after he had left them. Then, lifting up his eyes to heaven, he prayed to the Father, and asked him to keep these men pure; to help them remember what he had taught them, and to give them the power to go into the world and teach other men what they had learned. He prayed, too, for all who should afterward be led to love and trust him, through these his friends. When their earthly work was done, as his was now, he asked that they might also be taken to live with the Father in heaven.

They had now reached the little garden near the foot of the Mount of Olives, where they were going. This garden was called Gethsemane. Jesus had often taken his disciples there, and he loved it dearly. When they had come into the garden, Jesus said to the disciples, "Sit here, while I pray." Then, taking Peter, James, and John, he went a little farther on, and said to them: "My soul is very sorrowful. This trouble seems more than I can bear; stay here and watch."

He went on still farther alone, and fell on the ground, praying: "O Father, if it be possible, save me from this great sorrow. Yet, not my will, but thine, be done." The three disciples heard this much of the prayer; but when their Master returned to them for comfort, he found them, not watching, but fast asleep. They were his three dearest friends, but even they were not ready to help him now, when he so much needed their help. He said to Peter: "Simon, could you not watch with me one hour? You will need to watch and pray, or you will fall into temptation. You want to do right, but you are very weak."

Again he left them to pray for strength; again they heard him say, "Father, if this trouble cannot pass from me, and I must bear it, thy will be done." He came to his disciples once more, and found them sleeping.

For the third time he left them and prayed in the same words, while they slept. When he came back the third time, he said to them, "Sleep on now, and take your rest; for the time is come when the Son of man shall be betrayed into the hands of sinners."

But their sleep for that night was over; and in sleeping when they should have stayed awake they had lost their last chance to help their Master. It seems as if we would have stayed awake with our Master, if we had been there with them. But we do not know what we would have done, and we must not blame them. They were very weary; the hour was late; and they had spent a hard and sorrowful day.

Friday

Not very long after Jesus had returned to his disciples for the third time, perhaps very soon, they heard him say, "Rise, let us be going; for he that will betray me is near." They were on their feet before he finished speaking, and at the same moment saw Judas coming toward them, and with him a crowd of men armed with swords and sticks, and carrying torches.

Judas had been busy since he had left his friends in the upper room. He saw them leave the house, and followed them until he was sure where they were going. He knew the garden well, for he had often been there with his Master and the other disciples.

As soon as he was sure that they were going to the place he knew so well, he rushed to tell the priests and the Pharisees, that now was the time to seize Jesus, for there was no one with him but a few disciples. The Jews quickly gathered together a band of men, armed them with swords and heavy sticks, and put Judas at the head of this company. Then Judas led the men to the place where he had so often sat and listened to his Master's words.

He had given the men this sign, "The man whom I kiss is the one you want; hold him fast." As they drew near, Jesus walked toward them, and Judas kissed him, saying, "Hail, Master." Jesus did not push him away; he did not even speak unkindly to him; but, looking with eyes full of sorrow and pity at the man he had chosen for his friend, the Master said, "Judas, betrayest thou the Son of man with a kiss?"

The disciples, who were now wide awake, saw that their Master was in danger. They had two swords among them, and Peter said, "Lord, shall we strike them with our swords?" Without waiting for an answer, he struck a servant of the High Priest, and cut off his ear. Jesus said: "Put up your sword into its place, Peter. Do you not know that I can, even now, pray to my Father, and he would give me a great army of angels? But I must finish my work. I must die to save the world." And he touched the ear of the man and healed it.

Then, turning to the armed men, he asked, "Whom seek ye?" "Jesus of Nazareth," they answered. "I am he," said the Savior. The men were so astonished to have him give himself up without trying to defend himself or let his apostles defend him, that they fell backward.

Again the Savior asked, "Whom seek ye?" and again they answered, "Jesus of Nazareth." Jesus said: "I have told you already that I am he. If therefore you seek me, let these, my friends, go. Why did you come out as against a thief, with swords and clubs? I sat with you every day in the temple, and you did not lay a hand on me."

They now took hold of Jesus, bound him, and led him away. Though all the disciples had boasted that they would never leave their Master, every one of them ran off and left him alone with these cruel men.

Friday

They took him first to the house of Annas, the High Priest, and then to Caiaphas, his son-in-law, who was the one who really did the work of the High Priest at this time. He was the man who had said that it was better that Jesus should die, and was one of those who had tried the hardest to stop the teaching of the Christ.

Peter and John had by this time come back to see what was being done with their Master. John, who was known at the palace of the High Priest, was allowed to go inside; but Peter could go no farther than the outside door. John went out and spoke to the woman who had charge of the door, and asked her to let Peter go in also. As she showed him in the woman asked, "Are you not one of this man's disciples?" "No, I am not," said Peter. Then he went in and stood at the fire with some of the servants to warm himself, for it was cold.

All this time Jesus was standing before Caiaphas, who was asking him questions about his disciples and about his teaching. The Savior said: "I have taught where everyone who wished to do so could hear me; I have said nothing in secret, but have taught in the synagogue and in the temple where all the Jews come together. Why do you ask me what I have taught? Ask those which heard me, what I have said to them."

When he had spoken these words one of the officers which stood by struck him with the palm of the hand, saying, "Why do you answer the High Priest so?" Jesus said: "Did I say anything wrong? If I did, tell us what it was; but if not, why did you strike me?"

The chief priests tried hard to find someone who could tell of some law which Jesus had broken, or of something wrong he had tried to teach. But they could not do it until, at last, they found two or three men who were willing to tell lies about him. But, as the stories of these men did not agree, there was nothing in them to prove the prisoner guilty.

Caiaphas stood up, and looking at Jesus, asked, "Have you nothing to say about these stories which they tell of you?" Jesus did not answer. The High Priest then said: "Answer me. Are you the Christ, the Son of God?" Jesus said, "I am." Upon hearing these words, Caiaphas said to the rest of the council: "We do not need to hear anything more, for we ourselves have heard what the man has just said. What do you think of him?" They all shouted, "He is guilty; he must be put to death."

Now all this happened before the sun rose, though by law the Sanhedrin could not try a prisoner until after sunrise. So they had to wait till that time before a vote could really be taken. Jesus was put in charge of some officers, who treated him so badly that we cannot bear to think of it. They blindfolded him, then struck him, and asked, "Tell us who struck you"; they spit in his face; they said everything they could think of to make fun of him and hurt his feelings.

As soon as the sun rose, which was about six o'clock, the officers led their prisoner into the regular courtroom. To get there they had to pass through the porch where Simon Peter was standing with some of the servants. When we last saw Peter, he was warming himself at the fire; but after he was warm he had gone out into the porch to wait until the trial was over.

He had been there only a short time when a girl said to the others, "This fellow is one of the men who were with Jesus of Nazareth." Peter, who knew that those who were around him were unfriendly to his Master, was afraid to own him. "I do not know the man," said he. About an hour later a man who had been watching Peter carefully, said, "This fellow must have been with Jesus; for I saw him in the garden with him, and you can tell by the way he speaks that he came from Galilee." Again Peter said, "I do not know this man of whom you speak."

Just then the cock crowed, and Peter, who but a few hours before had boasted that he would go to prison with his Master, or even die for him. remembered what his Lord had said when he made that boast, "I tell you that, before the cock crows, you will have denied me three times."

Now just at the moment when Peter has said "I know not the man," Jesus, who was being led to the courtroom, passed through the porch and heard what his friend and disciple said. As Peter raised his eyes, his Lord turned and looked at him. It was the same loving face that had looked at him for the last three years, but with such a sad and grieved look that it almost broke Peter's heart. He never forgot that look. It was too late to be sorry, but he went out and wept bitter tears.

The court was ready to take the vote at once. The question was asked of Jesus: "Are you the Christ? Tell us." Jesus answered: "If I tell you, you will not believe me; and if I ask you, you will not answer me, or let me go. The time is coming when the Son of man shall sit on the right hand of God." Then they all said, "Are you the Son of God?" He told them that he was, and that, at the end of the world, they would see him coming in power with the angels with him to be the judge.

They said, "That is enough; he has spoken blasphemy; we do not need to hear anything more." The vote was then put, and it was decided that he should die.

Now, as they could not put him to death without having permission from the Roman Governor, and as no other punishment but death would satisfy them, they made their plans to take Jesus at once to the Roman courtroom, where he should be judged by Pilate, the Roman Governor.

Pilate lived away from Jerusalem the most of the time, but he happened to be in the city now, for so many strangers came to this Passover Feast every year, that he thought it was the safest plan to be on hand in case there was any trouble to settle. The whole multitude rose and followed the officers who led Jesus through the streets to the courtroom which was in Pilate's house.

Judas had known all that was going on, and when he saw that the vote had been taken, and that Jesus must really die, he was sorry for what he had done, and tried to undo it. He brought back the money that had been given him for betraying his Lord, and offered it to the chief priests and scribes, saying, "I have been very wicked and have betrayed a man who has done no wrong." "What is that to us?" said they; "that is your business."

They would not take back the money, and, much as Judas loved money, he did not want that which had cost his Master's life. Throwing it down on the floor, he went out of the room, very miserable and unhappy. By his mean act he had gained thirty pieces of silver, but in gaining it he had lost his own soul. He was never seen alive again. The Bible says he went out and hanged himself.

The priests were not willing to put the money into the temple boxes, because, as they said, it was "the price of blood." So as they did not know what else to do with it, they bought a piece of land, which they used as a burial ground for strangers, whom they did not wish to bury in their own tombs.

Jesus was led into Pilate's house, but the priests and scribes stayed outside. It was Passover week, the week when they made a great show of being holy. Though they were wicked enough to want to kill a good man, they were not wicked enough to step into the house of a Gentile! So Pilate came out to them, asking: "What has the man done? What have you to against him?"

They answered, "If he were not a wicked man, we would not have brought him to you." Said Pilate, "Take him to your own court, and judge him by your law." The only thing they could prove in their own court, as we know, was that he called himself the Son of God; but they knew that Pilate would laugh at such a charge as that, and so they had to make up some other story to tell him.

They said: "We found this fellow trying to lead the people into disobedience, telling them not to pay taxes to Caesar, and saying that he himself is their king. We think that he ought to be killed, but it is not lawful for us to put any man to death." Were they telling the truth? Do you remember what Jesus did say when they asked him about paying the taxes to Caesar?"

While Pilate was outside, talking to the people, Jesus stood in the courtroom. Pilate now went back to him, and asked him, "Are you the king of the Jews?" Jesus said, "Do you ask this question because you want to know, or because these people say that I am?" "Am I a Jew?" said Pilate. "The chief priests of your own nation have brought you to me. What have you done?"

Jesus said: "I am not the kind of king that you mean; if I were, my servants would fight for me, and I should not be given up to the priests. Mine is a very different kingdom; it is not of this world." Pilate asked, "Are you, then, a king?" "Yes," said Jesus, "I am a king. I came into the world for the purpose of ruling men; I came to teach them the truth, and everyone who is true believes my words." "What is truth?" asked Pilate. But, without waiting for an answer, he went back to the Jews who still stood outside, waiting patiently for him to return. Pilate had found no reason why they should want to harm this gentle, loving man, who showed so plainly that he did not want to make any trouble. So he said to the chief priests and scribes, "I find no fault with the man." They cried out, "He is stirring up the people with his teachings throughout all Palestine from Galilee to Judea."

When Pilate heard them say "Galilee," he saw a chance to clear himself from deciding what should be done. He was glad of the chance, and asked: "Is the man a Galilean? Then he must be taken to Herod." Herod, the ruler of Galilee, was also in Jerusalem at this time, for he had come to the feast. He was very glad to see Jesus; he had wanted to do so for a long time, because he had heard so much about him. He hoped that he should see him work some of his wonderful miracles, of which he had heard.

Herod asked questions of Jesus, and the priests and scribes told the same wrong stories about him that they had told Pilate. But the Savior stood there, neither answering the questions nor denying the stories. Herod and his soldiers laughed at the idea of this prisoner being a king, and began to make fun of him. Then Herod sent for a king's robe, put it on Jesus, and sent him back to the Governor of Judea.

Again Jesus stood before Pilate. Pilate went out once more to the people and said: "You have brought this man to me, and you say he is stirring up the people to disobey the Roman government; but I have examined him, and so has Herod, and neither of us thinks that he has done anything worthy of death. Therefore I will have him whipped, and then let him go."

The Jews showed that they were not satisfied. It was the custom at the Passover feast for the governor to set one prisoner free; and to please the people the choice was usually left to them. At this time there was a very wicked man in prison, named Barabbas, who was both a murderer and a robber. Pilate now said, "Whom do you want to have me set free, Barabbas, or Jesus who is called the Christ?" They all cried out at once, "Barabbas!"

Pilate, who wanted to set Jesus free, spoke again, "What shall I do with him whom you call the king of the Jews?" The people cried out, "Crucify him!" "Why, what evil has he done?" asked Pilate; but they only cried the louder, "Crucify him!"

They meant, "Let him die on the cross," and that was the most cruel punishment ever known. The body was fastened to a heavy wooden cross by great nails, which were driven through the hands and feet, and the pain was terrible. The cross was put in an upright position, and the prisoner was not taken down until he was dead. It was too dreadful a punishment for the most wicked man that ever lived.

When Pilate saw that they were determined, and that he could not make them do what was right, he called for water, and, washing his hands before them all, said; "I am not guilty of doing this great wickedness. You must take it upon your selves." The Jews, glad to know that Pilate would let them have their way, said, "Let the blame rest on us, and on our children, forever."

The blame did rest on them and their children, and punishment came very soon. Forty years later, when the Roman army left their once beautiful city, not a single building was left standing, and all the people who were not killed at the time were driven away from their homes. Many of them were taken captive by the Romans, and afterward put to death.

Then Pilate set Barabbas free, and sent Jesus away to be whipped, as was always done before a man was crucified. The soldiers hurried their prisoner away, and, after they had whipped him, began to make fun of him as Herod had done. Because purple is the king's color, they found an old purple robe, which they put upon this king of the Jews. They made a crown out of some thorns, and pressed it down upon his forehead until the blood came. They bowed before him, as if he were a king, saying; "Hail, king of the Jews!" They struck him on the head, and spit on him.

When they had had all they wanted of this cruel mocking, they took him back to Pilate. The Governor determined to try once more to make the Jews willing to let him set Jesus free. He went out with him before the people, and said: "I bring him out to you that you may know that I find no fault in him. Behold the man!"

Jesus showed how much he had already suffered; was it not enough to satisfy these wicked Jews? No; again they cried out,

"Crucify him!" Pilate said, "Then take him and crucify him; for I find no fault in him." But both Pilate and the Jews knew that they could not put a man to death without the permission they were trying so hard to get.

The Jews then said, "We have a law, and by our law he ought to die; for he made himself the Son of God." Pilate was still more afraid. He did not dare to crucify the Son of God. He was afraid for another reason, too; for, while he was in the courtroom, his wife had sent this word to him, "Have nothing to do with that just man, for I have been troubled all day because of a dream that I had about him."

So he turned again to Jesus, and asked, "Who are you?" The prisoner made no answer. "Will you not speak to me?" said the Governor. "Do you not know that I have power to crucify you and to set you free?" Then Jesus did speak. "You could have no power at all against me, except it were given you from above. Those who gave me up to you have sinned more than you have." Pilate then made up his mind to let Jesus go free.

The Jews saw that he was about to do this, and cried: "If you let this man go free, you are no friend to Caesar; for whoever calls himself king speaks against Caesar." Hearing this cry, Pilate changed his mind once more. If the Jews complained of him to the Emperor, another Governor might be put in his place, he would rather do wrong than have that happen.

Once more he tried to make the Jews pity their suffering Christ. "Behold your king!" said he; "shall I crucify your king?"

"We have no king; but Caesar," shouted they. What an answer from those very people who hated to be under the Roman power, and were so very unhappy because they were obliged to obey the Roman Emperor.

There was nothing more that Pilate could do unless he was willing to give up his position for the sake of doing what was right. That he was not willing to do. So he gave the order that Jesus should be crucified.

The Death and Burial of the Christ

It was nearly nine o'clock on Friday morning when Jesus was led out of the city to be crucified. He had to carry his own cross a part of the way, but later on a man whom they met was ordered to carry it for him. A great company followed him, and many of the women cried aloud. Turning to these, Jesus said: "Daughters of Jerusalem, weep not for me, but weep for yourselves and for your children. The days are coming when you will wish that your children had never been born, and that the mountains and hills would hide you from the trouble your eyes shall see."

There were two thieves who were to be crucified this same day, and they also were in the procession. They marched out through the city gate to the place called Calvary, and there the cruel work was done. Jesus was nailed to the cross which stood in the middle, and the thieves were placed one on his right hand and one on his left.

The Savior did not speak until the cross was being lifted; then he said, "Father, forgive them, for they know not what they do."

Soldiers were left to guard the crosses; but these men felt no pity, and began at once to cast lots to see what share each should have of the clothes which had been taken from the men who were being crucified.

A title, or sign, had been written to place over each cross, telling what the man's name was, and what wicked thing he had done. Over the cross of Jesus, Pilate had put this sign: "Jesus, of Nazareth, the king of the Jews." This was written in three different languages, so that everyone could read it. When the rulers of the Jews saw this sign, they were not willing to have it stay there, and went to Pilate, saying: "The sign is wrong. Write not The king of the Jews, but that he said, I am the king of the Jews." But Pilate had done all he wanted to for them, and would not change it.

People came from the city to see what was going on, and as they passed by, mocked the Savior, saying, "If you are the Son of God come down from the cross." The chief priests and scribes smiled as they said: "He saved others; himself he cannot save. If he is the king of Israel let him come down from the cross, and we will believe him. He trusted in God; let his Father save him now, if he is the Son of God."

The soldiers also mocked him, offering him sour wine, and saying: "If you are the king of the Jews, save yourself." One of the thieves at his side repeated what he heard the others say, "If you are the Christ, save yourself and us." The other thief was ashamed of him and told him to stop, saying, "It is right that we should be punished, for we have been wicked men, but this man has done nothing wrong." He then turned to Jesus and said, "Lord, you will remember me when you come into your kingdom?" And Jesus answered. "Today shall thou be with me in Paradise."

The enemies of Jesus were not the only ones who stayed near him; some women drew near the cross, and among them was Mary, his mother. She stood by John, and as Jesus saw them standing together, he said to his mother, "Behold your son;" and to John, "Behold your mother." John knew by this that his Master wanted him to take care of Mary. From that hour he took the Mother of the Christ to his own home, and cared for her.

It was now a little after twelve o'clock, the time when the sun should have been shining more brightly than it had shone all day. But it began to be dark, and for three hours the darkness of night was over the land. The afternoon passed away, and every moment brought greater pain to the Savior. It was dark about him; there was no one to comfort him. It seemed as if even his Father had left him, and he cried, "My God, my God, why hast thou forsaken me?"

Some of the people who stood by, when they heard this cry, said, "He is calling for Elias; let him alone; let us see whether Elias will come to take him down." (One of the words he used was Eloi, which sounded a little like the word Elias.)

A few minutes passed, and Jesus said, "I thirst." Some kind friend dipped a sponge in sour wine and pressed it to his lips. When he had taken it, he cried, "It is finished." Just a moment later he added, "Father, into thy hands I commend my spirit." His sufferings were all over now; his earthly life was ended; his spirit had gone to be with the Father.

Just then there was a great earthquake; the earth shook, great rocks were broken in pieces, a great noise was heard, and the graves were opened. The curtain in the temple, which separated the two rooms, and was never lifted except on the great Day of Atonement, was torn from top to bottom.

When the soldier who was on guard at the cross saw what was done, he said, "Truly this was the Son of God." The people who had come from Jerusalem to see the crucifixion, were afraid, and returned to the city. The friends of Jesus stood afar off, filled with sadness and wonder.

Seven times Jesus had spoken while he was on the cross. These are called now "The Seven Words from the Cross." Notice that there is not one word of anger against those who had made him suffer so, and that three of them were words of kindness. Could we be as loving and kind, if we were being made to suffer so?

There were two men in the Sanhedrin who had tried to save Jesus, for they believed all he said to them; one was Nicodemus, and the other was a rich man by the name of Joseph. Soon after the Savior died, Joseph went to Pilate, and begged that he might have the body. Pilate first called to him the soldier who had guarded the cross, to ask him whether Jesus was surely dead, for sometimes people who were crucified lived and suffered for many days. But the Jews had been very anxious that these bodies should not hang on the cross through that Sabbath, which was especially holy. So the soldiers had broken the legs of the thieves so that they would die more quickly. But they had passed Jesus by, for they saw that he was already dead. The soldier whom Pilate called to him knew that it was really so, for he had himself put a spear through his side. He had done this because, if they had made a mistake, and Jesus was not dead, the soldier's might lose their own lives.

So Pilate gave the body to Joseph. Joseph had a new tomb cut out of the rock, which had never been used. Nicodemus helped him carry the body, and, after wrapping it in pure white linen and some sweet smelling spices, which Nicodemus had brought with him, they lovingly laid it in the tomb, rolled a great stone against the door, and went away.

The women, who had been watching all day, waited till they saw where their Master was laid, and then went to their homes to prepare spices and perfumes. Nothing more could be done until after the Sabbath day. For the disciples were careful to do nothing on the Sabbath day that the Jews could find fault with; and, too, they knew that God had commanded that no work should be done on that day, when it could be helped; but that it should be kept holy to God.

The Sanhedrin were not yet fully satisfied, and went to Pilate, to ask another favor. "Sir, we remember that this deceitful man said, while he was yet alive, 'After three days, I will rise again,'" said these Jews to the Governor. "What we want to ask now is that soldiers shall guard the tomb where he is laid until after the third day, for fear that his disciples should come by night and steal the body away, and then say to the people. 'He is risen from the dead.' That would be worse than anything that has happened yet."

Pilate, who was willing that the tomb should be guarded, said, "You can have watchmen; go and make things as safe as you can." Off they went to the tomb, to see that everything was done right; they left soldiers to guard it, and sealed the stone which was before the door in such a way that it could not be moved without breaking the seal. Anyone who did that would be severely punished by the law.

The Resurrection and Ascension of the Christ

The Resurrection

Very early on the morning of the third day, our Sunday, the women started to the tomb with their spices for the body of their Lord. They did not know that soldiers were keeping watch there, nor that the tomb was sealed. As they walked along they wondered how they could roll away the heavy stone.

Great was their surprise when they reached the tomb, to find that the stone had already been rolled away, and that the tomb was empty. One of the women, named Mary Magdalene, ran back to tell Peter and John about it. "They have taken away our Lord," said she, "and we do not know where they have laid him."

The other two women had gone into the tomb, and as they stood there, wondering what this meant, two men stood by them in shining garments, who said: "Why do you look for the living in the home of the dead? Your Lord is not here, but is risen. Do you not remember what he said to you in Galilee, that the Son of man should be given up to wicked people and be crucified, and the third day should rise again? Go and tell the disciples that their Master will meet them in Galilee."

They did remember these words of Jesus, and now they understood what their Savior had meant by them. They went away quickly to find the eleven disciples, in order to tell them the message which had been given to them.

As soon as Peter and John heard the story of Mary Magdalene, they ran to the tomb. John could run the fastest, and he reached it first. He did not go into the tomb, but as he stooped down and looked in, he saw the clothes that had been wrapped about their Master. When Peter came he went in, and John soon followed him.

Then they saw for themselves that what Mary had told them was true; the clothes were there, but the body of their Lord was not to be seen.

They returned home, but Mary Magdalene, who had followed them back, did not leave the place. As she stooped down to look into the tomb, she saw two angels sitting, one at the head, and the other at the feet, where the body of Jesus had lain.

They asked, "Woman, why do you weep?" She answered, "Because they have taken away my Lord, and I do not know where they have laid him." She turned around, and saw someone else standing behind her, who also asked: "Woman, why do you weep? For whom are you looking?"

Her eyes were filled with tears, and supposing that she was talking to the gardener, she said, "Sir, if you have carried him away from here, tell me where you have laid him, and I will take him away." The voice spoke again, "Mary."

Only one person in the wide world had ever spoken her name as sweetly as that.

Looking up she saw Jesus.

"Master," she cried, and went toward him. "Do not touch me," said he, "I have not yet gone to heaven to live; but I shall go to be with my Father and your Father, with my God and your God. Go to my apostles, and tell them what I have said."

The other women were still on the way to tell the apostles the angel's message when Jesus met them, and said, "All hail." Trembling, they fell down at his feet and worshipped him. Seeing that they were afraid, he said to them: "Tell my brethren to go into Galilee, and there they shall see me. Do not be afraid."

What about the soldiers who were ordered to keep guard over the tomb? As they were watching, they heard a noise, and saw a strange sight. An angel, whose face was like lightning, and whose garments were as white as snow, rolled away the stone and sat upon it. The guards were afraid, and ran to tell the Sanhedrin what had happened.

The Sanhedrin called another meeting in great haste, to decide what they should do about it, and this is what they decided. They gave the soldiers some money, and asked them

The Resurrection

to tell this lie: that, when they were asleep, the disciples came and stole the body.

The soldiers were not willing to say this, for if the Governor heard that they had slept while on duty they might lose their own lives. But the Jews said, "You need not be afraid; we will make it all right with the Governor." So the soldiers took the money, and did as they were taught; and even now many of the Jews believe that they told the truth.

Mary Magdalene went to the disciples, who were very lonely and sad, and told them that their Lord was alive, and that she had seen him. They I could not believe her, nor did they believe the other women who came to them with the same story.

That same day, as two of the disciples were walking toward the village of Emmaus, which was about eight miles from Jerusalem, talking of all those things that had happened, a stranger joined them, and asked them what they were saying that made them look so sad. They told him how their Master, who they thought was to be the king of Israel, had been crucified by the rulers of the Jews. They spoke of the wonderful news that the women had brought to them, that he was again alive. But they showed that they did not yet understand what had happened.

"How hard it is for you to understand all that the prophets said about your king," said the stranger. Then he showed them that what the prophets had said about the king had all come true in the life of Jesus. He talked to them all the way to Emmaus, and they were so delighted to hear him that they asked him not to go farther that night, but to stay with them.

The stranger accepted their invitation, and went into the house. As he sat at supper with them, he took bread and blessed it and then broke it. As he did so they looked more carefully at him than they had before, and they knew that he was not a stranger. They saw that the face was that of one they knew; that it was Jesus, their Lord.

But as soon as they found this out his place at the table was empty; he had suddenly left them.

The two men hurried back to Jerusalem to tell the apostles about it. Their hearts were filled with joy as they told their friends that the Master had walked with them, and had taught them how the sayings of the prophets had come true in his life and death, but that they had not known him until he sat at the table with them, and broke the bread. The apostles said: "We know that he is living, for Peter has seen him."

Just then someone came into the room. They all looked up at once, for they heard a voice say, "Peace be unto you," and as they looked they were afraid. What did they see? Could it be their Master, or was it a spirit?

A spirit could not talk, but they heard a voice saying: "Why are you afraid? Why do you wonder who is with you? Look at my hands and my feet; do you not know whose they are? Take hold of them and make sure; a spirit has not flesh and bones as you see me have."

They were so happy that they could not believe that their Master was really with them until he said, "Have you anything to eat?" They gave him a piece of broiled fish and some honeycomb; and as he ate it he talked with them as he had before his death. "Do you not remember," said he, "that when I was with you I told you that all this must happen? The law of Moses, the prophets, and the Psalms, all say that the Christ must suffer, as I have suffered. As my Father sent me to teach you, so I now send you to teach the world."

Now Thomas was not with the apostles when the Master came. When he joined them again, and they said to him, "We have seen the Lord," he did not believe them. He said: "I will not believe that he is living until I myself can see in his hands the print of the nails, and put my finger into those prints, and my hand on the cut which the spear made in his side."

It was a week later and the disciples were all together, planning what they should do. The doors of the room in which they were sitting were shut. They were always shut in those days, for they did not dare to leave them open, for fear that the Jews who had stopped their Master's work, would try now to hinder them.

As they talked quietly, they heard the words, "Peace be with you," and though the door had not been opened, Jesus stood among them. He went over to Thomas and said, "Reach out your finger and touch my hands; reach out your hand, and put it into my side." Without doing either, Thomas believed and said, "My Lord, and my God." Then said Jesus: "Thomas, because you have seen me, you have believed; happy are those people who have not seen me, and yet have believed!"

The disciples now went to Galilee for a few days, as their Lord had told them. One evening, when seven of them were together, Peter said, "I am going fishing." "We will go with you," said the others, and they went into a boat. But though they were out all night, they caught no fish.

In the morning Jesus came to the shore; but they did not know that it was he. He called to them, "Children, have you caught any fish?" and they answered, "No." Again he called, "Throw your net on the right-hand side of the boat, and you will find some." This they did, and the net was full.

John remembered another time when such a thing as this had happened, and said to Peter, "It is the Lord." Peter thought so too, and, throwing on his coat, he jumped out of the boat and waded as fast as he could to the shore. The other disciples followed him in the boat, dragging their net full of fishes.

As soon as they had come to the land, they saw a wood fire on the beach, and some fish broiling on the coals, and some bread nearby. When Jesus said, "Bring the fish which you have caught," Simon Peter ran to help the others drag the net to land. It was heavy, for there were one hundred and fifty large fishes in it. When they were landed, Jesus said, "Come now and eat breakfast." He broke the bread and passed it to them, then gave them some of the fish.

After they had finished eating. Jesus turned to Peter, and said, "Simon, son of Jonas, do you love me more than the others do?" When Peter answered. "Yes, Lord, you know that I love you," he said, "Feed my lambs." A second time he asked, "Simon, son of Jonas, do you love me more than the others?" Peter gave him the same answer, "Yes, Lord, you know that I love you." Jesus said, "Feed my sheep."

Once more Jesus asked, "Simon, son of Jonas, do you love me?" Peter was grieved that his Master should ask the question for the third time; and he said, "Lord, you know all things; you know that I love you." Once more Jesus said, "Feed my sheep."

The work of the Great Shepherd was done; the sheep must have other leaders now, and that is what the Master wanted Peter to do for the rest of his life. He talked with him more about his work; he told him that it would be hard, and that at last he, too, would suffer a cruel death.

Peter looked round, and, seeing John just behind them, said, "Lord, and what shall this man do?" Jesus did not tell him, but said: "What is that to you? Follow me." And that is what our Master says to us now. He does not want us to look to see if someone else has work to do, and is doing it. He wants us to be sure that we ourselves are doing the work that has been given to us to do; and that we are doing it as nearly right as we can.

Jesus was seen by his apostles again, when, with about five hundred other disciples, they were upon a mountain in Galilee, where their Master had appointed a meeting. It was at this meeting that the great commission was given to the disciples, "Go ye into all the world, and preach the Gospel to every creature."

Jesus may have given this command more than once, and it is certain that the same, in different words, had been given to his followers over and over again. But this time he said it to all his friends, and added other words that have been precious to all his friends ever since that time, "Lo, I am with you alway, even unto the end of the world."

The Ascended Christ

Forty days had now passed since the Christ had risen from the dead, and his disciples were in Jerusalem. He had told them not to go away from that city for a few days, for there the Father would send them the Holy Spirit. The disciples were not yet near enough like their Master to do his work, and could do nothing without the help of this Spirit. Jesus said, "After the Father has given you the Holy Spirit, you shall have power to work and spread my Gospel to every part of the earth."

They were in Jerusalem, waiting till this Spirit should be given to them, when, one day, the Savior came to them, and led them out as far as Bethany. He lifted up his hands in blessing, and while he blessed them he was taken from them and carried up into heaven. A cloud came between him and them. "While they still were looking toward heaven, two men stood by them in white clothing, who said: "Men of Galilee, why do you stand looking up into heaven? This same Jesus, who is taken from you into heaven, shall come again in the same way that you have seen him go into heaven."

The apostles went back to Jerusalem, and there, with the women and the other friends of Jesus, they waited and prayed that the Father would show them what to do. God soon sent the Holy Spirit, and then they went out to teach, though they knew that they must suffer, as did their Lord.

The earthly life of the Christ was ended, but he was not dead. He was living with the Father, and always watching over his disciples, and giving them help and strength as they needed it. Christ was seen by men several times after he ascended into heaven, and we will speak about two of these times.

One of the most active workers against the new religion, was a young Pharisee, named Saul. He was so eager to work that he asked permission to go to other cities than Jerusalem and find and punish any of the followers of Jesus. One day, when he was travelling to Damascus, on this errand, he saw a wonderful sight. A light that was brighter than the sun at noontime shone around him, and he saw a glorious form, and heard a voice, which said, "Saul, why are you persecuting me?" "Who are you?" asked Saul. "I am Jesus whom you are trying to destroy," said the heavenly visitor.

Saul had not wanted to stop the work of the disciples of Jesus because he was a bad man, but because he thought it was right, and this vision of the Master was the means of changing him from a persecutor of the followers of Jesus, to one of the most active and successful of his disciples. For many years Saul, or Paul, as he is usually called, travelled from country to country, telling of the Christ, and proving that he was really the king that the Jews had so long expected.

He always told this story of the time that Jesus came to him on the road to Damascus, when he wished to show why he had become one of his followers, after he had for so long been so active against them. For many years he worked for him, and then at last he gave his life for the Master he had served so well.

One more record there is in the New Testament, of an appearance of the Christ to a disciple. John the youngest of the twelve, who is always called "the beloved disciple," because he was so much loved by his Master, was sent in his old age to a lonely island far away from any of his friends.

While there he had a wonderful vision. First, Jesus, his Lord, came to him, but not in his earthly form. So wonderfully bright and glorious was the Savior, that John "fell at his feet as one dead." But his Master came to him kindly, and spoke to him words, and showed him sights that are too great for us yet to fully understand. John wrote what he heard and saw, and we can read it in the last book of the Bible, "The Revelation."

The Jews as a nation never believed in Jesus, and because they did not believe in him and what he taught, they were terribly punished. Other nations were willing to believe in him, and now he is ruling over almost the whole world, and will reign forever; for the Bible says that at the name of Jesus every knee must bow and every tongue must say that the Christ is Lord.   Are you not glad to have such a king?

51929619R00215